W. H. Davies *The True*

W. H. Davies (1871–1940) w
as the 'tramp-poet' due to l
in Britain and the United States, to considerable literary success.
'Discovered' in part by Edward Thomas, who admired his poetry,
Davies became a prolific memoirist and occasional writer of fiction,
criticism and drama. He is now known almost exclusively for a handful of poems and for his memoir *The Autobiography of a Super-Tramp*;
his other writing has long been out of print. This book collects
generous selections from Davies's prose memoir, poetry, and critical
prose, alongside comprehensive notes. It brings back into print the
work of a remarkable, controversial and unduly neglected author.

Rory Waterman was born in Belfast and grew up mostly in rural
Lincolnshire. He has written two books on twentieth-century poetry
and is a critic for various publications, and his poems have appeared
in the *TLS*, *New Poetries V* (Carcanet, 2011), *Poetry Review, New
Statesman, Guardian, Financial Times, PN Review* and elsewhere. He
teaches English at Nottingham Trent University. *Tonight the Summer's
Over*, his first collection, is a Poetry Book Society Recommendation
and was shortlisted for the Seamus Heaney Prize. He also co-edits
New Walk poetry and arts magazine.

Fyfield*Books* aim to make available some of the great classics of British and European literature in clear, affordable formats, and to restore often neglected writers to their place in literary tradition.

Fyfield*Books* take their name from the Fyfield elm in Matthew Arnold's 'Scholar Gypsy' and 'Thyrsis'. The tree stood not far from the village where the series was originally devised in 1971.

> *Roam on! The light we sought is shining still.*
> *Dost thou ask proof? Our tree yet crowns the hill,*
> *Our Scholar travels yet the loved hill-side*

from 'Thyrsis'

W. H. Davies *The True Traveller: A Reader*

Edited and introduced by Rory Waterman

Fyfield*Books*

CARCANET

First published in Great Britain in 2015
by Carcanet Press Limited
Alliance House, 30 Cross Street,
Manchester, M2 7AQ
www.carcanet.co.uk / info@carcanet.co.uk

The publisher acknowledges financial
assistance from Arts Council England.

A CIP catalogue record for this book is
available from the British Library.
ISBN: 9781784100 872

Contents

Acknowledgements

I am grateful to Professor Nahem Yousaf and Nottingham Trent University for supporting the research that went into this book. I am also grateful to my editors at Carcanet, Luke Allan, Helen Tookey and Michael Schmidt, and the many helpful staff I pestered at the National Library of Wales, in Aberystwyth, and the British Library, in London.

I owe considerable thanks to my wife, Libby Peake, not least for her excellent proofreading and comments. I also owe thanks to many others, for various reasons, including John Clegg, Jess Orozco, Kate Poxton and Adam Charles Tocock.

Introduction

Though he is now principally remembered as the author of the poem 'Leisure' ('What is this life if, full of care...') and the memoir *The Autobiography of a Super-Tramp*, William Henry Davies (1871–1940) was a prolific, engaging and often highly original writer, in many genres. The intention of this book is to bring together a selection of the most intriguing, troubling and enjoyable work of this great literary maverick for a twenty-first-century readership.

Davies's life experiences almost always ostensibly informed his work. Thankfully, then, his life story is a remarkable one – and he made it so. William was born the second of three children in Newport, a large and rapidly-expanding Welsh port on the Severn Estuary, eight miles from the English border. His mother's family were Welsh. His paternal grandparents were English, and his grandfather was a former man of the sea, who had become landlord of the Church House Inn. When Davies was two, his father Francis died and his mother Mary remarried. She remained in Newport, but was forced to leave her first three children to grow up with their father's parents. The two grandparents had very different influences on the young boy: Lydia was a prim and puritanical Baptist, whereas Captain Davies was outwardly gregarious, beer-swilling, and full of stories of the sea. At thirteen, Davies had his first brush with the law when he was caught shoplifting with a group of other boys and received twelve strokes of the birch for his troubles. He left school at fourteen, around the time his grandfather died, and the following year began a five-year apprenticeship to a picture-framer. This came to an end in 1891; Davies moved to London for a few hard months, and soon began working at his new profession in Bristol, where he seems to have spent most of a year living in a terrible slum called the Pity, drinking to excess, and making use of prostitutes. He did not much enjoy the working life.

By this time, his grandmother had also died – and had helped to transform the young man's life. She had invested in property, and her will specified that the rents should be shared between her three grandchildren. This gave Davies a small private income of ten shillings a week: a further temptation not to work. By June of 1893, he had negotiated a fifteen-pound advance and set sail for the USA. He was twenty-two and desperate for adventure.

Davies arrived in New York with his picture-framing tools, but he appears never to have used them, and soon gave them up in lieu of rent. After a short period in New York, he travelled north to

Connecticut, where he asked a man on a town park bench how he might travel to Chicago. This man was Brum, who introduced Davies to the concept of 'beating' one's way: hitching free rides on freight trains by running alongside them as they pull out of stations or goods yards, jumping aboard, and hiding – usually in a goods wagon, but sometimes by taking more precarious but surreptitious locations, such as 'riding the rods' under the car. Brum became Davies's first friend in the USA, travelled with him for several months, and instructed him in the ways of the tramp. The men took some temporary manual jobs, but mainly lived as vagrants, before – at Brum's instigation – beating a journey to Michigan. Here, as the bitter Midwestern winter took hold, they spent long stretches locked happily in the relative warmth of the jailhouse, taking advantage of a legal loophole that allowed corrupt jailers to receive tax money for every prisoner they incarcerated. Davies spent the next summer picking fruit in Michigan, intending to return to Britain with his earnings at the end of the season. However, upon arriving in Chicago he bumped into a tramp called Australian Red and blew his money on debauchery instead.[1] They beat their way to Baltimore, and eventually took work on cattle ships across the Atlantic, first to Liverpool and back, then to Glasgow, and then to London, where he particularly enjoyed the free museums and magnificent parks before returning to America.

His travels between then and 1898 took him across much of the USA. In Chicago, he briefly worked on digging the Chicago Drainage Canal. He sailed south along the Mississippi from St. Louis. He contracted malaria and was treated in a charity hospital in Memphis. At other times he was in Arkansas, Texas, Louisiana – all the while travelling on freight trains and more often than not staying at beggars' camps. In the summer of 1898 he was employed as a fruit picker in Illinois, then travelled to Baltimore, once more intending to work his way back home on a cattle boat. The plan ultimately worked this time: he arrived in Newport later in 1898, where his mother and relatives were somewhat surprised and delighted to discover that he was still alive.

After a brief period of joy at being home, Davies became bored and depressed and started drinking heavily, rapidly eating into his accumulated rentier's income. Within two months he had set off to London with half-hearted plans to open a bookshop, though he had

---

1. Australian Red, Brum: all of the tramps Davies describes are known by nicknames, and we never learn their real names. With Davies himself, it is the other way round, and we have no idea what his fellow tramps called him.

no idea how to go about doing so. Walking through Trafalgar Square in early 1899, he spotted a newspaper report about the Klondike gold rush in north-western Canada. That settled it: within days, he had set sail for Saint John, New Brunswick, from where he travelled to Montreal to see the long winter out before heading across the continent. He was travelling west through Ontario with a tramp called Three-Fingered Jack, whose disability does not need spelling out, when an event occurred that would alter Davies's life dramatically – and lead to one of the most famous chapters of *The Autobiography of a Super-Tramp*. Beating a ride from Renfrew, Ontario, Davies did the honourable thing and let Jack jump aboard first; Jack clambered up the steps but did not move out of the way very quickly, and by the time Davies could jump himself, the train had gathered pace. He slipped, and his right foot was severed beneath a wheel. A three-fingered Jack inadvertently had led to a one-legged William; he spent some time in hospital in Renfrew, where his leg was amputated below the knee, and then he returned to Wales.

Not only did the accident nearly kill Davies and destroy his slim chances of making a fortune in the Klondike, it also took away some of his much-prized physical prowess. Davies's strength of character appears to have been remarkable, however, and he took the incident as a spur. He needed to find another scheme to make money without the grind of a day job, and had always wanted to become a writer. Writing his way to financial comfort may have seemed a quixotic plan even by Davies's standards, but ultimately it worked, and made his name.

The road to success was circuitous, however. Immediately upon his return to Wales, Davies started writing poems and submitting them for publication, but without success. In the late summer of 1899 he moved to London, where his private income just about paid for a cheap life in London doss houses. Existence was hard, but he stayed for several years as his writing life began in earnest. His earliest unpublished works included a blank verse tragedy called *The Robber*, which nobody wanted to publish and which was soon lost to posterity, and a sequence of one hundred sonnets. He decided to print a few of his poems on sheets and hawk them door to door, but found almost nobody willing to part with pennies for his poetry wares – leading him to burn the lot in a fit of resentment and anger.

Nonetheless, he persevered with the grand plan. It is worth remembering that, though his private income may have been tiny, it obviously set him apart from the vast majority of the other tramps he met. Compared to George Orwell, of course, whose time in similar

London establishments a quarter of a century later is recorded in *Down and Out in Paris and London*, Davies certainly lived in genuine destitution – but he nevertheless might have escaped much of that poverty had his literary pipe dream not got the better of him. His dedication to making a literary life for himself is not in any question. In the autumn of 1902, he registered as a hawker in an attempt to save money towards the publication of his first volume of poems, and set off north with a stock of pins and shoelaces, walking arduously on a wooden leg that had been acquired from the Surgical Aid Society.[2] Poor weather ruined his goods, but Davies refused to resort to 'standing pad': purposely capitalising on pathos by begging passively. He headed north through the West Midlands, then over to Newport for Christmas. Early in 1903, he returned to London, to a giant lodging-house called The Farmhouse, from where he sent his manuscript of poems to the printers Watts and Co. The fee required for the printing of 250 copies of his book forced him back to Newport, to negotiate another agreement for a lump sum with the trustee of his grandmother's estate. The agreement he reached was that his income would be accumulated for six months, then at the end of that period double the amount would be added in a loan (and he would forego regular income for another year), giving him the required sum. This meant that he had to leave The Farmhouse and once again take to the road as a beggar in June 1904. At the end of the year he returned to London, the loan came through, and early in 1905 his first collection, *The Soul's Destroyer*, was printed. The title refers to drink, which in the title poem is shown to be deadly. Unfortunately for the author, sales were woeful, and a period of depression and heavy drinking of his own soon followed.

But Davies was nothing if not resourceful and determined. His next ploy was to post copies of the book to eminent literary figures from *Who's Who*, on a sale or return basis – the cost being 2s 6d. George Bernard Shaw received one of these bizarre packages, and sent Davies a pound, also enclosing a list of further names and addresses that might be of use. This put the entrepreneurial author in touch with various influential figures such as the journalist and future poet Edward Thomas. Davies was a bit of a cause célèbre all of a sudden: in July an article, written by Arthur St. John Adcock, appeared

---

2. Davies's first artificial leg had disintegrated beyond use by the beginning of 1902. For someone in his position, getting a replacement at this time meant relying on philanthropy: undergoing the humiliation of sending begging letters to a list of wealthy potential benefactors, the names and addresses of whom were provided by the Surgical Aid Society, until the correct number of 'subscriptions' (fifteen) had been reached.

in the *Daily Mail*, titled 'A Cripple Poet: Realistic and Whimsical Word Pictures, Curious Life History', and many further reviews and articles followed.

Davies was again living at the rather less than bucolic London lodging-house called The Farmhouse, working enthusiastically on his second collection, when Edward Thomas, in the capacity of journalist for the *Daily Chronicle*, called in to see him. Thomas came quickly to admire Davies's poetry and his spirit, and thus began a long friendship that would last until Thomas's death at Arras in 1917. Thomas nurtured and championed Davies's writing, gave him rent-free use of a cottage in rural Kent near to where the Thomas family lived, and arranged for the local wheelwright to make him a new wooden leg, commissioning it as a novelty cricket bat in order to save the future owner's blushes. Thomas also introduced Davies to friends in the London literary scene, and encouraged him to write the first book that would make him a proper income, *The Autobiography of a Super-Tramp*, which related much of his rather fabulous life story. In 1911, Thomas would use what influence he had to help Davies be granted a Civil List pension of £50 per annum (which was later raised to £100, then to £150).

At last, by 1908, Davies was living in comparative comfort, and enjoying the acclaim that being a writer brought him. His books of poems came out on something approaching an annual basis, and in 1912 he had the good fortune to be included in Edward Marsh's hugely successful anthology *Georgian Poetry 1912–13*. His prose works were almost as frequent. These included *Beggars* and *The True Traveller*, further accounts of tramp life, and the semi-biographical and half-baked novel *A Weak Woman*, the hero of which is a glorified Davies: an artist who sails down the Mississippi, contracts malaria, jumps trains, and fights his way out of trouble. *A Poet's Pilgrimage* would appear in 1918, and present as a literary man's journal of a long walk from south Wales, via Newport, and through south-central England.

The autodidact tramp-poet had come a long way and seen a lot of things. However, at times his prose demonstrates a naïve tendency to accept received wisdoms and resort to stereotypes and over-simplifications. In 1915, the Welsh author Caradoc Evans angered many in Wales with a collection of short stories, *My People* (1915), which is harshly critical of the Welsh peasantry, with portrayals of violence, madness and even incest; the title page of Evans's first edition stated that 'the justification for the author's realistic pictures of peasant life, as he knows it, is the obvious sincerity of his aim, which is to portray that he may make ashamed'.[3] Evans's intention was clearly political, for he wanted to shock the Welsh from complacency at their national condition. But just three years later, Davies was noting in passing, and without any apparent motivation other than to foreground his own minor narrative, that 'the poorer classes in Wales have very few interests besides singing, football and fighting'.[4] The Scottish fare little better. In the same book, Davies expresses surprise that an ale which has made him want to laugh was produced in Scotland, 'where there is supposed to be a lack of humour' (p. 92). And the first chapter of *Beggars*, included here, shows Davies turning his bold generalisations on almost every race and nationality he had encountered, and perhaps a few more besides. There seems to be no irony in these wide-eyed comments. Far more shockingly, in the *Autobiography*, Davies describes the mob lynching of a black prisoner in the Deep South of the USA, without stopping to question its circumstances. He *could* be very aware of his environment, a champion of underdogs, a man of acute social conscience; but at other times, he was none of these things, and many of his attitudes are straightforwardly racist.

In January 1914, Davies moved from rural Kent up to London, partly to be among his growing circle of literary friends. He settled in a bedsit on Great Russell Street, and would remain in the capital for eight years. By this time, he appears to have developed a strong sense of his own self-importance, and though he delighted some literary acquaintances, such as Edith Sitwell, others – perhaps unwittingly demonstrating their own class-consciousness – found his combined egotism and lack of sophistication insufferable. Robert Frost, whom Davies visited in Gloucestershire, wrote to a friend in 1914 that Davies's 'is the kind of egotism another man's egotism can't put up with. He was going from here to be with [Joseph] Conrad. He said that would be pleasant because Conrad knew his work *thoroughly*. [...] We asked him if he knew Conrad's work *thoroughly*. Oh no.'[5] Davies's view of himself as one of the country's finest writers was unshakeable, but he was also insecure and fearful of losing his success as quickly as he had eventually found it, which only served to exacerbate his apparent self-regard. It also prompted jealousy of poets more successful than himself, among them Walter de la Mare, John

3. John Harris, 'Introduction', Caradoc Evans, *My People*, ed. John Harris (Bridgend: Seren, 1995), p. 34.

4. *A Poet's Pilgrimage*, p. 71. The chapter containing this quotation, 'Welsh Song and Prize-fighting', is included in the present volume.

5. Quoted in Lawrence Normand, *W. H. Davies* (Bridgend: Seren, 2003), p. 97.

Masefield, Henry Newbolt and W. B. Yeats – and some of this would later come across in his 1924 memoir centred on London literary life, *Later Days*.

Davies's literary response to the Great War was almost to ignore it, though when it took Edward Thomas, by then his closest friend, he wrote a moving poem in commemoration.[6] Certainly, he never fell into any of the exuberant and naïve jingoism that overwhelmed other often younger poets, including his fellow 'Georgian' Rupert Brooke. He did take part in elaborate reading evenings in London, however, which were intended to raise money for the war effort. These cannot have been an unmitigated joy for him: he was alert to the fact that many in fashionable literary London regarded the 'tramp-poet' as a quaint curiosity, which he hated, and he was also naturally shy. By 1921, the year Davies turned fifty, he was tiring of London and its literary bunfights, and keen to find a wife and move to the country. After a few missteps, he eventually met Helen Payne, a woman almost three decades his junior. She quickly became his mistress and housekeeper, and soon his wife, though not until she'd almost died after miscarrying the child of a previous partner, and he'd almost died from venereal disease (also from a previous partner). They moved to East Grinstead, Sussex in 1922, and eventually to Nailsworth, Gloucestershire in 1930, where they would remain. He was back in the countryside, close to Wales without being in it, and within striking distance of his relatives in Newport – all of which suited him.

His poetry had settled into a very familiar pattern, however, and the Georgian poets had by now become unfashionable. Moreover, his later prose works, which he still produced at a fair rate, suffered from a lack of new material or original concerns: his second novel, *Dancing Mad*, is no better than the first, and little more than an overtly fictionalised version of parts of his earlier prose memoirs. But Davies still found himself in demand for articles and other short prose pieces, such as his introduction to an edition of *Moll Flanders*, and was in many ways comfortable and content. This lasted until his last year, in which he suffered a stroke and a series of heart attacks. His quickly declining health, along with the outbreak of the Second World War, depressed him greatly. He died in September 1940 at the age of sixty-nine.

Throughout his hard-won career as a literary man, Davies certainly generated a considerable amount of interest, though it irked him that

---

6. 'Killed in Action', included in the present volume.

this was often more for his prose memoirs than for his poetry: he always saw himself as a poet, and his prose works as secondary. The neologism 'Super-Tramp' served him well, but also came to annoy him. Moreover, it was inaccurate, suggesting a man far more suited to the tramping life than Davies shows himself to be at various points in and beyond the *Autobiography*, such as in the anecdotes recalling Brum's guidance. His second stroke of literary luck was that his initial success as a poet coincided with the rise of the Georgians, and that he fitted their aesthetic so comfortably. But this encouraged others to view him as a simple nature poet, and to dismiss him along with the other Georgians when the movement became unfashionable.[7] He was in some senses a writer of fairly limited range and ability, both in terms of his prose and poetry, but he made the best of what he had, and what he had could be remarkable. Davies's work regularly demonstrates an ear for surprising and apt images, and was unfettered by any concern for literary fashion. His less successful poems suffered from all the banalities and excesses of the worst Georgian poetry, but his best poems are substantial if minor achievements of thought and feeling, often energised by the author's rather unusual perspectives. And beyond his talents as a raconteur, the prose autobiographies provide an exceedingly rare first-hand account of life as a Victorian and Edwardian beggar from one who had lived that life for a number of years. Contemporary stories corroborating Davies's tales of the wiliness of beggars are not uncommon. In the memoir *Goodbye to All That*, Robert Graves, who was born in 1895, recalls the following anecdote from his childhood, at what must have been around the same time Davies was tramping around England after his return from Canada:

> A blind beggar used to sit on the Wimbledon Hill pavement, reading the Bible aloud in Braille; he was not really blind, but could turn up his eyes and keep the pupils concealed for minutes at a time under drooping lids, which were artificially inflamed. We often gave [our pocket money] to him. He died a rich man [...].[8]

This easily could be a character from one of Davies's own memoirs. The immense difference, of course, is that Davies met such

---

7. For example, Laura Riding and Robert Graves referred to his 'simple ruralities' in their *A Survey of Modernist Poetry* (London: Heinemann, 1927), p. 200.

8. Robert Graves, *Goodbye to All That* (1929) (London: Penguin, 1960), p. 13.

figures as an equal rather than a beneficent better. He gets to know them, as one of them, and so we get to know them a little too. That is what fascinated the first readers of Davies's prose works, and that is a large part of why they remain fascinating now.

The stories Davies's prose memoirs recount are frequently insightful, enchanting, enlightening or troubling, then; however, they are also at times quite repetitive. Davies wrote them for money, knew a good thing when he was on to one, and didn't think twice about repeating a story from a previous book or fleshing out a narrative with a few meagre anecdotes, if it suited his imperatives to do so. It is a shame that, with the exception of the *Autobiography*, his books have been out of print for so long; but all of them are too flawed to be considered unmitigated successes from start to finish. The aim of this book is to address both of those matters. I would have liked to include more chapters from the *Autobiography* and more of the poetry, but elected not to on the grounds that readers can find these works elsewhere anyway with relatively little trouble. The focus here is equally on works that are out of print and harder to come by; this book therefore brings together much of Davies's most remarkable writing, including striking excerpts from his memoirs, a selection of his finest poems, and other pieces of criticism, fiction and dramatic writing. Each section begins with a short introduction, giving some context to the work. Those looking for further reading will find a select bibliography at the end.

Though it ends in continued uncertainty, this is an improbable rags-to-more-rags-to-cusp-of-riches tale. Davies describes his six years living as a tramp across North America from 1893 to 1899, the incident in Canada that left him with one leg, his further years as a beggar and struggling would-be writer in England and Wales, and the eventual publication of his poetry.

Davies was encouraged to turn his tramping anecdotes into a book by his friend and sometime mentor Edward Thomas, and was assisted painstakingly in the editing by Thomas and the critic Edward Garnett, after they discovered that Davies's first draft was an unpublishable and lurid account full of sex and booze. Thomas and Garnett encouraged Davies to develop his distinctively straightforward storytelling prose style. Though the book is perhaps best known for its anecdotes of tramping in America, Davies only included his American experiences after the bowdlerisation of his original draft had made it too short. George Bernard Shaw, asked by Thomas to provide a preface, also suggested the title – analogous to that of his play Man and Superman: in a letter to Thomas, dated 7 December 1907, Davies wrote: 'Shaw has sent a postcard suggesting the title "Autobiography of a Super-Tramp", which I have agreed to with pleasure.'[9] Shaw's preface referred to the Autobiography as 'this amazing book' and called its author 'a true poet', before noting that an 'effect of this book on me is to make me realise what a slave of convention I have been all my life'. The book allowed readers to join Shaw in marvelling at the romantic resourcefulness of the 'Super-Tramp' without having to leave their armchairs. Davies came to resent the 'Super-Tramp' label, but it helped to give him the literary lifestyle he'd always wanted.

9. Letter held at the National Library of Wales, MS 23806 D, 33. I am grateful to the National Library of Wales for their permission to quote this excerpt.

Chapter III: Manhood

On arriving at Liverpool,[10] I made the acquaintance of a man who had been in America some years previously, and not having his hopes realised at that time, had returned desperate to England, taken in a fresh cargo of hopes, and was now making a second attempt with as much enthusiasm, if not more, than others in making their first. In him I placed implicit confidence, and received such an extraordinary description of that country, the number of stories of some of its highest buildings which were called skyscrapers;[11] the houses of wood which could be moved from one street to another without in any way interfering with the comfort of the people within, cooking, sweeping and washing going on without hindrance; the loneliness of its prairies and deserts; engineering triumphs over high mountains; and how the glorious South was flushed with roses at a time the North could not save a blade of green from the snow; all this happening under the one wide spreading flag; this made such an impression on me that I at once went to the steerage cabin and wrote a full description of the country, that very first evening aboard; telling of my arrival in America, and the difference between the old and the new world. This letter was given to the steward at Queenstown,[12] and was written to save me the trouble of writing on my arrival, so that I might have more time to enjoy myself. Several years elapsed before it occurred to me how foolish and thoughtless I had been. The

10. In the previous chapters, Davies has outlined his upbringing in Newport, including his propensity for getting into minor trouble, the deaths of his grandparents, and the growing restlessness that encouraged him to pursue his American adventure. This chapter begins with him setting out on that adventure, via the English port city of Liverpool.

11. When Davies sailed for New York in 1893, steel-framed high-rise buildings were being built there and elsewhere in the USA. From 1890 until 1894, the tallest of these was the New York World Building at 99 Park Row, which had twenty floors and stood 309 feet high (actually shorter than Britain's medieval cathedrals at Salisbury, Lincoln and Norwich, and St Paul's in London). The tallest artificial structure in the world, by some distance, was the Eiffel Tower in Paris (completed in 1889), but America was home to the new generation of high-rise, steel-framed buildings. The New York World Building was demolished in 1955, to make way for a car ramp.

12. The official name for the port of Cobh, County Cork, Ireland, from the 1850s until the 1920s.

post mark itself would prove that I had not landed in America, and they would also receive the letter several days before it would be due from those distant shores. I can certainly not boast a large amount of common sense.

It was in the month of June, when we made this voyage, and the great Atlantic was as smooth as an inland river. Everyone sought to escape the thoughts of home, and to do so, we often worked ourselves into a frenzy of singing and dancing. Sometimes our attention would be drawn to an iceberg on the port side, very innocent and beautiful to the eyes of passengers, but feared by mariners, who saw into its depths.[13] And then a ship full sail; or another great Atlantic liner on the starboard bow. There was a total lack of ceremony aboard, strangers familiar with strangers, and the sexes doing each other little kindnesses, who had never met before and probably would never meet again, parting without even enquiring or giving each other a name. As we neared the coast we had a thunderstorm, and I was surprised and somewhat awed at the sound of its peals, and at the slower and larger flashes of lightning. Nature, it seemed, used a freer and more powerful hand in this country of great things than is her wont among our pretty little dales, and our small green hills. I thought the world was coming to an end, and in no way felt reassured when an American, noting my expression, said that it was nothing to what I would see and hear if I remained long in God's own country of free and law abiding citizens.

My impression of Americans from the beginning is of the best, and I have never since had cause to alter my mind. They are a kind, sympathetic race of people and naturally proud of their country. The Irish-American is inclined to be the most bitter, remembering from his youth the complaints of his parents, who were driven through unjust laws from their own beloved land;[14] and such a man is not

---

13. Davies is writing several years before the sinking of RMS *Titanic* in 1912, which took a very similar route after leaving the British Isles.

14. The Penal Laws, established under British rule in Ireland, penalised Irish Catholics and Protestant dissenters. The last of them would not be repealed until the 1920s. They drove many in Ireland to emigrate, some to the USA – where the Irish often also received a stony reception because of their Catholicism. Penal Laws, and the situation whereby Irish peasant farmers typically rented small plots of sub-divided land from absentee Anglo-Irish landlords, had been major contributing factors to widespread Irish dependency on the potato, and thus to the Great Hunger (or Irish Potato Famine) of 1845–52, in which over a million people died. The response of the British government was slow, and Britain offered little in the way of relief. Moreover, throughout the Famine, Ireland continued to export huge quantities of other foodstuffs, leading many to accuse the British government of genocide. After

to be idly aggravated, especially under the consideration that our conscience is not too clean in this respect, and that we are apt to be very slow in making that open confession which is good for the soul. The most pleasing trait in Americans, which cannot for long escape us, is their respect for women and the way in which the latter do their utmost to deserve it. No sight of a woman behind the saloon bar listening to the ribald jests of drunken men, and no woman at the bar's front drinking glass for glass with her associates. However weak in this respect a woman may be in private, she is certainly too strong to make a public exhibition of her weakness. Husband and wife may be unhappy, but you seldom hear of a woman carrying the marks of a man's brutality as witness against him which is common in the police courts of old England. A man in a fit of ungovernable passion may kill his wife; and better so, I should say, than to leave her half killed at the foot of the stairs every Saturday night and holidays for twenty or thirty years, and blacken her eyes before they can recover their natural colour, the brutality that shamed me so much in after years in the slums of London, hearing it so often recorded as a jest.

I was so anxious to see the different states of America that I did not stay long in New York before I succumbed to the persuasion of my Liverpool acquaintance to visit with him some friends in a small town in the state of Connecticut, at which place we soon arrived, with something like ten dollars between us. America, at this time, was suffering from a depression in trade, and people were daily returning to the old country, most of them with the intention of returning again to America at a more favourable time. Not being able to get employment at once, and resolved to be independent of the bounty of strangers, I walked out alone, and sat on a seat in the park, trying to conceive some plans for the future. My box, full of clothes, books, brushes, etc., would amply compensate, I thought, for the week's lodging which I had had. Yes, I would see Chicago: and, suddenly becoming aware of a man occupying the other end of the seat, I enquired of him the way to Chicago, as though the distance was a paltry ten miles, instead of a hundred times greater. This man looked at me in astonishment, and at last asked me if I intended to beat my way. Seeing my lack of understanding, he enquired as to my financial resources. On shaking my head in the negative, implying that I had no money, he said: 'No more have I: and if you are agreeable we will both beat our way to Chicago.'

Britain, America and Australia were the most common destinations for the one million emigrants escaping famine.

This was Brum, a notorious beggar, who made himself at home in all parts of the country, from the Atlantic to the Pacific coast, and from the northern provinces of Canada to the Gulf of Mexico. The easy and sumptuous way of his catering made me indifferent to all manual labour. In that country, where food was to be had for the asking, where it often went begging to be received, and people were not likely to suffer for their generosity, I became, under Brum's tutorage, a lazy wretch with but little inclination for work.

Cockneys[15] make good beggars. They are held in high esteem by the fraternity in America. Their resource, originality and invention, and a never faltering tongue, enable them to often attain their ends where others fail, and they succeed where the natives starve. But my friend Brum held them in great scorn, for their methods were not his methods. Brum was a genuine beggar, who did not make flashes in the dark, having one day plenty and nothing on the next day. What he required he proceeded to beg, every morning making an inventory of his wants. Rather than wash a good handkerchief he would beg an old one that was clean, and he would without compunction discard a good shirt altogether rather than sew a button on – thus keeping up the dignity of his profession to the extreme. He scorned to carry soap, but went to a house like a Christian, and asked to be allowed to wash, with a request for warm water if the morning was cold. Begging was to him a fine art, indeed, and a delight of which he never seemed to tire. I have known him, when surfeited with an abundance of common food, such as steak, chops, etc. – to beg lozenges and sweets, complaining I suppose of throat troubles. Even in a new country like America, there are quite a number of hostile towns, owing to their lying on the main roads between large cities that are not far apart; but Brum never seemed to fail, and would certainly never lower his dignity by complaining of difficulty. In every street, he said, there lived a good Samaritan, and seeing that a good beggar knocks at every door, he must ultimately succeed. She may live in the last house, and therefore the unsuccessful beggar, having no patience and perseverance, fails in his calling. Brum was a slow man in action and went about his business in a dogged way. And that reminds me of how this slowness of action once saved his life. We had built a campfire in the woods, within a mile or more of a small town. Now, it was Brum's habit, before lying down for the night to wind his handkerchief around

15. Londoners; in its most correct usage, specifically working-class Londoners born within earshot of 'Bow Bells', the bells of St Mary-le-Bow church, Cheapside, in the City of London.

his neck, and this he had done. Next morning I was the first to rise, and Brum, deliberately following my example, began in his own easy way to slowly unwind this handkerchief, when to my horror a large tarantula fell from its folds. Now, had Brum been an impulsive man, no doubt the spider would have been squeezed, and would have then fastened on his neck and poisoned his blood mortally.

I was soon initiated into the mysteries of beating my way by train, which is so necessary in parts of that country, seeing the great distances between towns. Sometimes we were fortunate enough to get an empty car; sometimes we had to ride the bumpers; and often, when travelling through a hostile country, we rode on the roof of a car, so as not to give the brakesman an opportunity of striking us off the bumpers unawares. It is nothing unusual in some parts to find a man, always a stranger, lying dead on the track, often cut in many pieces. At the inquest they invariably bring in a verdict of accidental death, but we know different. Therefore we rode the car's top, so as to be at no disadvantage in a struggle. The brakesman, knowing well that our fall would be his own, would not be too eager to commence hostilities. Sometimes we were desperate enough to ride the narrow iron rods, which were under the car, and only a few feet from the track. This required some nerve, for it was not only uncomfortable, but the train, being so near the line, seemed to be running at a reckless and uncontrollable speed, whereas, when riding on the car's top, a much faster train seems to be running much slower and far more smooth and safe. Sometimes we were forced to jump off a moving train at the point of a revolver. At other times the brakesmen were friendly, and even offered assistance in the way of food, drink or tobacco. Again, when no firearm was in evidence, we had to threaten the brakesman with death if he interfered with us. In this way Brum and myself travelled the States of America, sleeping at night by camp fires, and taking temporary possession of empty houses.

One night, when darkness had overtaken us, before we could find a fit and comfortable place for camping, we spied a house, and seeing no light in the window, presumed it to be unoccupied. We knocked at the door, and the hollow sound which followed convinced us that no living person was then on the premises. When we lifted the latch and entered we were surprised to see chairs, a table and various articles of domestic utility scattered in confusion on the floor. In spite of this we proceeded to make ourselves easy for the night, and coming out again began to feel in the darkness for wood. Being successful in our search we returned and made a fire, and there we slept until morning. As usual, I was the first to rise on the following day, and went forth in quest of water to make our breakfast coffee. This I soon found, and was bearing it along, when my attention was drawn to a board nailed to the front of the house. There I saw the letters 'Haunted', painted large, and ragged, as though by a hand that had shaken with fear. If we had seen this board on the night previous, no doubt we would have hurried on in dread of our lives, but as it was, we made our coffee and laughed heartily in the daylight. At this time I took a notion to work for a few days, but Brum showed his grinning face so often that I grew ashamed of him, and discharged myself. He seemed to have taken a strange liking to me, and would not leave me, but swore that not even for my sake would he become a working man.

Chapter XIV: The House-boat

I worked long enough on this canal to save fifty dollars, and then quit, feeling the old restlessness return, which had unsettled me for some time.[16] With this comfortable sum in my possession I kept beating my way west until I arrived at St. Louis, a large city on the Mississippi, having up till now lived frugally, and spent nothing on travelling. This kind of life was often irksome to me, when I have camped all night alone in the woods, beside a fire, when one good sociable companion might have turned the life into an ideal one. Often have I waked in the night, or early morning, to find spaces opposite occupied by one or two strangers, who had seen the fire in the distance, and had been guided to me by its light. One night, in Indiana, when it had rained heavily throughout the day, I had made my fire and camped under a thick leaved tree, where the ground was dryer than in the open. Sometime about midnight, I felt myself roughly shaken, at the same time a sudden shower fell that pinned me breathless to the earth. I looked here and there, but could see no one. Then I left the shelter of the tree and saw to my surprise that the night was fine, and that the stars were thick and shining. As I replenished the fire with wood, of which I always gathered in an abundance before darkness came, it puzzled me much to account for this. Although I thought the shaking must have been a dream, my wet clothes were a sufficient proof of the rain's reality. Every man I met on the following day enquired where I had lodged during the earthquake shock on the previous night, and that question explained everything. The earth had shaken me, and the leaves of the tree, which had been gathering all day the rain drops, had in one moment relinquished them all upon my sleeping form.

On reaching St. Louis I still had something like forty dollars, and

---

16. In Chapters IV to XIII, Davies describes, among other things: other temporary tramp companions such as Australian Red and New Haven Baldy; the life of a tramp; and several forays into the world of itinerant work, including a summer picking fruit in Michigan with intentions to return to England on his savings (which come to nothing because he drinks them away), working cattle boats between Britain and Baltimore, and labouring on a canal in Chicago, almost certainly the 28-mile-long Chicago Drainage Canal (now the Chicago Sanitary and Ship Canal), which was completed in 1900.

being tired of my own thoughts, which continually upbraided me for wasted time, resolved to seek some congenial fellowship, so that in listening to other men's thoughts I might be rendered deaf to my own. I had bought a daily paper, and had gone to the levee, so that I might spend a few hours out of the sun, reading, and watching the traffic on the river. Seeing before me a large pile of lumber, I hastened towards it, that I might enjoy its shady side. When I arrived I saw that the place was already occupied by two strangers, one being a man of middle age, and the other a youth of gentle manly appearance. Seating myself, I began to read, but soon had my attention drawn to their conversation. The young fellow, wanting to go home, and being in no great hurry, proposed buying a house-boat and floating leisurely down the Mississippi to New Orleans,[17] from which place he would then take train to southern Texas, where his home was. 'We will go ashore', he said, 'and see the different towns, and take in fresh provisions as they are needed.' The elder of the two, who had a strong Scotch accent, allowed a little enthusiasm to ooze out of his dry temperament, and agreed without much comment. 'Excuse me, gentlemen', I said, ' I could not help but hear your conversation and, if you have no objection, would like to share expenses and enjoy your company on such a trip.' The Texan, being young and impetuous, without the least suspicion of strangers, jumped to his feet, exulting at the social project. Scotty, more calm, but with a shrewd eye to the financial side of the question, said that he thought the trip would certainly be enjoyed better by three, and that the expense would not be near so great per head. We had no difficulty in purchasing a house-boat. Hundreds of these are moored to the banks, lived in by fishermen and their wives, and others in various ways employed on the river. But, of course, the one we required was to be much smaller than these. We found one, at last, rather battered, and ill-conditioned, for which we were asked eleven dollars. Scotty, to our unfeigned disgust, acted the Jew in this matter of trade, and had succeeded in beating the price down to nine dollars and a half when we to his annoyance offered to pay that sum without more ado. But Scotty, although mean in these business matters, was strictly honest and just in paying an equal share; for, after I had paid the odd half a dollar, he did not forget that amount when we came to stocking the boat with provisions. We lost no time in getting these, and then went ashore for the evening's enjoyment and the night's sleep, intending to start early the next morning. And with these prospects before us, a very pleasant

---

17. A distance, by river, of about a thousand miles.

evening we had.

At nine o'clock the following morning, we weighed anchor – our anchor being a large stone – and drifted into the current, the young Texan using an oar as a tiller. And what a strange voyage we had, fraught with more danger than many would dream. This Mississippi river often had only a few yards for navigation purposes, even when the distance from bank to bank was between two and three miles. Sometimes we were in the middle of this broad river, and yet were in extreme danger of foundering, for we could touch the bottom with a short stick. Yes, we were in danger of foundering, and yet our ship drew less than six inches of water! Trees, whose branches were firmly embedded in the mud, had their roots bobbing up and down, bobbing up unawares, and we were often in danger of being impaled on one of these ere we could steer clear of it. Sometimes we would see villages and small towns that in the remote past had been built flush on the banks of this river: now they were lying quiet and neglected a mile or more away, owing to this river's determination to take his own course. Hundreds of lives had been sacrificed, dying of swamp fever, in building levees and high banks to prevent this, and millions of dollars utilised for the same purpose – but the Father of Waters has hitherto had his own will, and can be expected to be seen at any place, and at any time.

Towards evening we would put ashore on a sand bar, making a fire of driftwood, of which there was an abundance. Here we cooked supper, slept and enjoyed breakfast the next morning. There was no other water to be had than that of the river, which the natives of the south claim to be healthy. We had no objection to using it for cooking and washing, but it was certainly too thick for drinking cold – or rather lukewarm, for it was never cold in the summer months. We would fill a large can and let the water settle for twenty or thirty minutes, and, after taking great care in drinking, a sediment of mud would be left at the bottom a quarter or three-eighths of an inch deep.

We put ashore at one place where a number of negroes and white men had assembled in expectation of work, when man again proposed putting forth his puny strength against the Mississippi, where we decided to wait a day or two and take our chance of being employed. Unfortunately the ill feeling which invariably exists between these two colours, came to a climax on the first day of our arrival. The negroes, insulting and arrogant, through their superiority of numbers, became at last unbearable. On which the white men, having that truer courage that scorned to count their own strength, assembled together, and after a few moments' consultation, resolved to take advantage of the first provocation. This came sooner than was expected. A negro, affecting to be intoxicated, staggered against a white man, and was promptly knocked down for his trouble. The negroes, whose favourite weapon is the razor, produced these useful blades from different parts of concealment, stood irresolute, waiting for a leader, and then came forward in a body, led by a big swaggerer in bare feet, whose apparel consisted of a red shirt and a pair of patched trousers held up by a single brace. These white men, who were so far outnumbered, said little, but the negroes were loud in their abuse. This soon led to blows and in the ensuing fight, knives, razors and fists were freely used. Only one shot was fired, and that one told. When the negroes, whose courage had faded at such a determined resistance, were in full flight, the tall swaggerer was left behind with a bullet in his heart. Several men were wounded, with gashes on necks, arms, and different parts of the body. Small fights continued throughout the day, but it was left for the night to produce a deed of foul murder. A white man was found next morning with his body covered with blood from thirty-nine wounds. Half a dozen razors must have set to work on him in the dark. The razor is a sly, ugly-looking weapon, but is far less dangerous than a knife, a poker, or even a short heavy piece of wood; and as it cannot pierce to the heart or brain, that is why this man took so long in the killing. This deed roused the sheriff and his marshal, and they followed the black murderers to the adjoining state, but returned next day without them.

We embarked again, but owing to the young Texan being taken sick with malarial fever, resolved to put ashore for medicine at the first large town. This malarial fever is very prevalent in these parts, especially this state of Arkansas, which is three parts a swamp. He suffered so much that we decided to call on the first house-boat seen, and ask assistance of the fishermen, and soon we had an opportunity of doing so. Seeing a large house-boat moored at the mouth of a small creek we put the tiller – which as I have said, was an oar – to its proper work, and sculled towards the shore. We ran to land within ten yards of the other boat, and the fisherman, who had seen us coming, stood waiting on the sands to know our wants. He was a typical swamp man, with a dark sickly complexion, thin-faced and dry-skinned and, though he was nearly six feet in height, his weight, I believe, could not have exceeded one hundred and twenty pounds. His left cheek was considerably swollen, which I thought must be due to neuralgia until the swelling began to disappear from that side; and, after witnessing for a few seconds a frightful, even painful contortion of the face, I saw the right cheek come into possession of the same beautiful round curve, leaving the left cheek as its fellow had been. It was now apparent that the one object of this man's life was to chew tobacco. To him we related our troubles, asking his advice, and for a little temporary assistance, for which he would be paid. Up to the present time he had not opened his lips, except a right or left corner to squirt tobacco juice, sending an equal share to the north and south. 'I guess there's some quinine in the shanty boat', he said, after a long silence, 'which I reckon will relieve him considerably, but he ought ter go home ter th' women folk, that's straight.' He led the way to his boat, and we followed. We soon had the young Texan in comfort, and Scotty and myself returned to transfer some provisions to the fisherman's house-boat, for the evening's use. While doing so, we decided to sell our own boat, at any price, when we would walk to the nearest rail road, and send the young fellow home; after which we would seek some employment and settle down. We cooked supper, and then slept in the open air, beside a large fire, leaving our sick friend comfortable in the boat.

The next morning we offered our house-boat for sale for six dollars, with all its belongings. The fisherman explained to us that he not only had no money, but rarely had use for it. Everything he needed he paid for in fish, and often went months at a time without a glimpse of money of any description. To my surprise the one thing that did seem to claim his attention, for which he could not help but display some greed, was the large stone which we had brought with us from St. Louis, and which we had used for an anchor. This stone certainly had no vein of gold or silver in it, it was not granite or marble, and could boast of no beauty, being a very ordinary looking stone indeed, but it seemed to have a strange fascination for this man. The fisherman had no money, and had nothing to barter which might be of use to us, so we made him a present of the whole lot, and left him sitting on the stone, watching our departure. 'He seemed very eager to possess that stone', I remarked to Scotty, as we followed a trail through a thicket, so that we might reach the high-road. 'Yes; said Scotty, 'for in this part of the country, where there is little but sand, wood and mud, a stone, a piece of iron, or any small thing of weight, can be put to many uses.'

After reaching the road we had twenty miles to walk to reach the nearest railway station, at which place we arrived late that night, the young Texan being then weak and exhausted. A train was leaving at midnight for New Orleans, and, after seeing him safely aboard we sat in the station till day-break. Early the next morning we were examining the town, waiting for business to start, so that we might enquire as to its prospects for work. This seemed to be good, there being a large stave factory which employed a number of men. We succeeded in our quest, starting to work that morning, and at dinner time received a note of introduction to an hotel. That evening we associated with our fellow workmen, and, in the course of conversation, we discovered that there was no particular time to receive wages, there being no regular pay day. Sometimes wages ran on for a month, six weeks, two months, etc. 'Of course', he explained to us, 'anything you require you can easily get an order for on the stores.' We worked two weeks at this factory, when I was taken ill myself with malaria, and not being able to eat, soon became too weak for work. In this condition I went to the office for my money, but could not get it, and saw that nothing else could be done than to get an order on the stores, and take my wages out in clothes, shoes, etc. Scotty was scared at this, and quitted work at once to demand his wages in cash, and there I left him, waiting for a settlement. I intended going to Memphis, the nearest large town, and placing myself in its hospital, whilst Scotty was going to New Orleans, where I promised to meet him in a month, providing I was sufficiently recovered to do so.

I don't know what possessed me to walk out of this town, instead of taking a train, but this I did, to my regret. For I became too weak to move, and, coming to a large swamp, I left the railroad and crawled into it, and for three days and the same number of nights, lay there without energy to continue my journey. Wild hungry hogs were there, who approached dangerously near, but ran snorting away when my body moved. A score or more of buzzards had perched waiting on the branches above me, and I knew that the place was teeming with snakes. I suffered from a terrible thirst, and drank of the swamp-pools, stagnant water that was full of germs, and had the colours of the rainbow, one dose of which would have poisoned some men to death. When the chill was upon me, I crawled into the hot sun, and lay there shivering with the cold; and when the hot fever possessed me, I crawled back into the shade. Not a morsel to eat for four days, and very little for several days previous. I could see the trains pass this way and that, but had not the strength to call. Most of the trains whistled, and I knew that they stopped either for water or coal within a mile of where I lay. Knowing this to be the case, and certain that it would be death to remain longer in this deadly swamp, I managed to reach the railroad track, and succeeded in reaching the next station, where most of these trains stopped. The distance had been less than a mile, but it had taken me two hours to accomplish. I then paid my way from this station, being in a hurry to reach Memphis, thinking my life was at its close. When I reached that town I took a conveyance from the station to the hospital. At that place my condition was considered to be very serious, but the doctor always bore me in mind, for we were both of the same nationality,[18] and to that, I believe, I owe my speedy recovery.

18. It is unclear whether he means the doctor was Welsh or British.

from Chapter XV: A Lynching

Upon leaving the hospital, I remained several days in Memphis, spending most of my hours enjoying the shade and sunshine of a small park, which is pleasantly situated in the main portion of that town. One morning, while doing this, I was accosted by one whom I soon recognised as a fellow-worker of mine in the stave factory. From him I learnt that the firm had smashed, no pay day had come, and the stores had all absolutely refused to honour the firm's orders; while some men had left the town disgusted, and others were patiently waiting a settlement that would never come. This man was going north, so I left him at Memphis, intending to beat my way to New Orleans, and from that town to the state of Texas.

These states of Tennessee, Arkansas, Mississippi and Louisiana, are the homes of the negroes of old. It is a strange contrast to see the old negroes, who in their young days were slaves, reverently raising their hats to any seedy looking white man whom they meet, calling him such titles as captain, major, colonel and even general – and the half defiant gloom of the free, young generations, who are still in some respects slaves to the white men. These negroes lived in small wooden shanties, and rarely received money for their labour. They worked for the planter at so much a day. This gentleman kept on the plantation a large general store, and supplied their wants at such an exorbitant price that the negroes were seldom out of debt, when the busy season commenced. In the cities, silk would be far cheaper than the common flimsy muslin which poor black Dinah so much coveted from her master's store. I have heard many an old negro say that he was far worse off as a freeman than as a slave.

The prisons in the north were like hotels, but here in the south went to the extreme of cruelty. In some places a man would be tried and perhaps fined ten dollars and costs. A citizen, having need of a cheap labourer, would pay this fine, take possession of the prisoner, and make him work out his fine on the farm. This citizen would buy the prisoner cheap overalls, dungarees, shirts, shoes, etc., for a few dollars, and charge the prisoner four times their amount. The prisoner was not free to refuse these, and being forced to work out their price, was kept in this way twice the number of his days. I was very much afraid of all this, although a wandering white man was not in nearly so much danger as a negro.

Some days after leaving Memphis, I arrived at a small town, where I was surprised to see an unusual amount of bustle, the surrounding country for miles having sent in all its able bodied men. Every man was armed with a gun, and they stood in small groups talking outside the various stores. It seemed as though there had been rumours of an invasion, and that these men were organising to defend their homes and country, but I had not the least idea of what had really happened. The small groups now began to join together into larger ones, and the larger groups joined until they became one large body of men. This one body then shouldered guns and moved quickly along the main street, the men's faces being drawn and pale. I followed on, perhaps the one unarmed man among them, curious to know the meaning of it all. They came at last to a halt, and, to see the reason for this, I stepped across the way, and saw that they had halted before a large building, which, by its barred windows, I had no difficulty in recognising as the jail. One man had curled around his shoulders a long rope, and this man with two others knocked loudly with the butt ends of their guns on the prison door. Almost in an instant the door was flung wide open, and the sheriff stood in the open way to know their wants. The men must have demanded the prison keys, for I saw the sheriff at once produce them, which he handed to these men without the least show of resistance. This man with the rope and several others then entered the jail, and the silent crowd without cast their eyes in that direction. Up to the present time I had not heard a distinct voice, nothing but the buzz of low whispering. But suddenly from the jail's interior there came a loud shriek and a voice crying for mercy. Men now appeared in the open doorway, dragging after them a negro at the end of a rope. This unfortunate wretch was possessed of a terror that is seldom seen in a human being. He fell on his knees to pray, but was jerked to his feet ere he could murmur the first words, O Lord. He staggered to and fro and sideways, at the same time howling and jabbering, foaming at the mouth, and showing the horrible white of his eyes. I can well understand a man screaming, trembling and crying for mercy, when actually enduring bodily pain, but that one should show such a terror at the thought of it, filled me more with disgust than pity. That this prisoner should have been so brutal and unfeeling in inflicting pain on another, and should now show so much cowardice in anticipation of receiving punishment in- adequate to his offence, dried in me the milk of human kindness, and banished my first thoughts, which had been to escape this horrible scene without witnessing its end. For it was now I remembered reading of this man's offence, and it was of the most brutal kind, being much like the work of a wild beast.[19] They now marched him from the jail, their strong arms supporting his terror stricken limbs, but no man reviled him with his tongue, and I saw no cowardly hand strike him. Soon they came to a group of trees on the outskirts of the town, and, choosing the largest of these, they threw the rope's end over its strongest branch, the prisoner at the same time crying for mercy, and trying to throw his body full on the ground. When this was done a dozen hands caught the rope's end, made one quick jerk, and the prisoner's body was struggling in the air. Then all these men shouldered their guns, fired one volley, and in a second the body was hanging lifeless with a hundred shots. In five minutes after this, nothing but the corpse remained to tell of what had occurred, the men having quietly scattered towards their homes.

A few days after this, I was in New Orleans.

[…]

I soon left New Orleans, being possessed with a restless spirit, and, after visiting Galveston, Boston, and many more towns of less importance, I made my way through the heart of Texas to the town of Paris, which lies on the borders of the Indian territory. It was in a saloon in the main street of this town that I had my attention drawn to a glass case, wherein was seen hanging a cord, at the end of which was something that looked very much like a walnut. On looking closer, I saw a small heap of dust at the bottom. Seeing that this case contained no stuffed animal, nor any model of ingenious mechanism I began to read the printed matter, curious for an explanation. This small thing dangling at the end of the cord purported to be the heart of a negro, whom the people had sometime previously burned at the stake. He had suffered a terrible death: so had his little victim, a mere child of a few years, who had been found in the woods torn limb from limb. This negro had been arrested by the sheriff, and sentenced to a short term adequate to his offence. After he had been released, he had taken his revenge on the sheriff's child, bearing her off when on her way to school. The sheriff's wife, being the child's mother, had with

---

19. The reader hardly needs informing that these may have been trumped-up charges in the racist environment of the Deep South in the 1890s, and Davies's credulity is perhaps surprising, considering his general support for the marginalised. One wonders what, if any, editorial input was made on this report by Thomas, Garnett and Shaw. I have found nothing to indicate strong unease at anything Davies writes here.

her own hand applied the torch to this monster, and if her hand had failed, any woman in this land of many millions would have willingly done her this service.

I left Paris that night, catching a fast cattle train, and arrived the following morning at Fort Smith, Arkansas. Bill Cook, the train and bank robber, and his gang, were being tried this morning, and a special train was now waiting to convey them to the penitentiary.[20] I saw this notorious freebooter, when he was brought to the station – a young man between twenty and thirty years, receiving a sentence of forty years' imprisonment. One of his gang, Cherokee Bill a desperado of nineteen years, was indicted for murder, and remained in Fort Smith to be hanged. The train steamed out with its many deputies to guard a few prisoners – few, but proved to be very dangerous.

20. Bill Cook (1873–1900), leader of the Cook Gang, was found guilty of bank robbery in February 1895, and transported to the federal prison in Albany, New York, where he later died of consumption.

Chapter XIX: A Voice in the Dark

At this place I remained several weeks,[21] watching the smiling Spring, which had already taken possession of the air and made the skies blue – unloosing the icy fingers of Winter, which still held the earth down under a thick cover of snow. What a glorious time of the year is this! With the warm sun travelling through serene skies, the air clear and fresh above you, which instils new blood in the body, making one defiantly tramp the earth, kicking the snows aside in the scorn of action. The cheeks glow with health, the lips smile, and there is no careworn face seen, save they come out of the house of sickness or death. And that lean spectre, called Hunger, has never been known to appear in these parts. If it was for one moment supposed that such a spectre possessed a house in this country, kind hearts would at once storm the place with such an abundance of good things that the spectre's victim would need to exert great care and power of will, if he would not succumb to an overloaded stomach. This spectre is often seen in the overcrowded cities of Europe, and one of its favourite haunts is the Thames Embankment, in front of the fine hotels where ambassadors and millionaires dine sumptuously. Where they sit or stand at their windows watching the many lights of the city, and to see the moon dipping her silver pitcher in the dark river, and they swear, by Jove! it is worth seeing. But they cannot see this spectre of Hunger, moving slowly, and sometimes painfully, from shadow to shadow, shivering and anxious for the sun, for they have no other fire to sit before, to make their dreams of the past pleasant.

I remained three weeks in this inexpensive hotel, and decided to travel on the following Monday, although the snow was still deep in Montreal, and would be yet deeper in the country. I had a small room for sleeping purposes, at a cost of fifteen cents per night. There were several others of the same kind, each divided one from the

---

21. In Chapters XVI to XVIII, Davies describes his sudden desire to return home to Newport after five years in America, his return, and the reaction of his family, who had assumed him dead. Soon he becomes bored, and moves to London, where he learns about the Klondike Gold Rush. This prompts him to travel to Liverpool, and take passage to Canada. He arrives at the end of winter 1899, and settles briefly in a Montreal lodging-house.

other by a thin wooden partition, which was high enough for privacy, but did not prevent curious lodgers from standing tip toe on their beds, and peering into another's room. Going to bed early on Sunday night, previous to continuing my journey on the following day, I was somewhat startled on entering my room, to hear a gentle rap on the partition which divided my room from the next. 'Hello!' I cried, 'what do you want?' The man's wants, it seemed, were private, for he seemed frightened into silence at this loud tone of demand, which would most certainly draw the attention of others. At last he cleared his throat by a forced fit of coughing, and then whispered, in a low distinct voice – 'I want a match, if you can oblige me with one.' Of course, smoking was not allowed in the bedrooms, but in this respect we were nearly all breakers of the law. Taking a few matches from my pocket, I threw them over the partition, and heard him feeling in the semi-darkness, after hearing the sound of them falling. Then he gently struck one, and, by its light, gathered in the others. In a moment or two he addressed me in his natural voice, and, to my surprise, it sounded familiar, and filled me with curiosity to see this man's face. I encouraged him to talk – which he seemed determined to do – thinking a word might reveal him to me, and the circumstances under which we had met.

His voice in the dark puzzled me, and I could not for my life locate it. A hundred scenes passed through my memory, some of them containing a number of characters. In my fancy I made them all speak to me, before dismissing them again to the dim regions from which they had been summoned, but not one of their voices corresponded with this voice heard in the dark. Above this voice I placed thin and thick moustaches, black, grey, brown, red, and white; under this voice I put heavy and light beards of various hues, and still, out of all my material, failed to make a familiar face. Still sending Memory forth in quest of the owner of this voice, and she, poor thing! bringing forward smiling men and stern men, thin men and fat men, short men and tall men, tame men and wild men, hairy men and bald men, dark men and fair men – until she become so confused as to bring back the same people the second time; still sending her forth on this vain quest, I fell asleep.

It was a dreamless sleep; no sound broke its stillness, and no face looked into its depths; and, when I awoke the next morning, this voice seemed to be already in possession of my thoughts. I lay awake for about ten minutes, and was just on the point of rising, thinking the man had left his chamber, when I heard a stir coming from that direction. He was now dressing. Following his example, but with more haste, so as to be the first ready, I waited the unbolting of his door, so that I might meet this man face to face. I unbolted my own door, and opened it when I was but half dressed, but there was no necessity for doing this, for my arms were in the sleeves of my coat when his bolt was slipped back and we simultaneously appeared, at the same time wishing each other good morning. I recognized this man without difficulty, but apparently had the advantage of him. To make no mistake, I looked at his right hand, and saw the two fingers missing, knowing him for a certainty to be Three Fingered Jack, who had been a cattleman from Montreal, whom I had met in Glasgow when I had gone there from Baltimore, three years previous to this. On that occasion I had been in this man's company for only half an hour, and since that time had heard thousands of voices, but was still positive that I had heard this voice before.

We stood side by side washing, and preparing for breakfast, and, although I remained a stranger to him, as far as former acquaintance was concerned, I mentioned to him in confidence that I was going west that very morning, after breakfast. 'So was I', he said, 'as far as Winnipeg, but thought to wait until some of this snow cleared. Anyhow, as a day or two makes little difference, we will, if you are agreeable, start together this morning. I know the country well', he continued, 'between Montreal and Winnipeg, having travelled it a number of times, and, I promise you, nothing shall be wanting on the way.'

This man had lost his two fingers at work in the cotton mills, some ten years before, and ever since then had been living in idleness, with the exception of two or three trips he had made as a cattleman. Certainly he lived well on the kindness of these people, as any able bodied man might do in this country, without being in any way afflicted. Though he was going to Winnipeg, he was in no hurry, had no object in view, and had not the least idea of where that town would lead him, and he soon tired of one place.

Three Fingered Jack was a slow traveller for, as he with some emotion said – it broke his heart to hurry and pass through good towns whose inhabitants were all the happier for being called on by needy men. This slow travelling suited me for the time being, for we were having another fall of snow, and I half regretted having left Montreal, although, day after day I was certainly getting a little nearer to the gold of Klondyke. But I determined to shake off this slow companion on the first approach of fine weather.

We loafed all day in the different railway stations, in each of which was kept a warm comfortable room for the convenience of passengers. Although we were passengers of another sort, and stole rides on the trains without a fraction of payment to the company, we boldly made ourselves at home in these places, being mistaken for respectable travellers, who were enjoying the comforts for which we paid. Sometimes a station master would look hard on us, suspecting us for what we were, but he was very diffident about risking a question, however much he was displeased at seeing us in comfortable possession of the seats nearest to the stoves. Towards evening we made application for lodgings at the local jail, at which place we would be accommodated until the following morning. I was now without money, with the exception of that which was concealed and reserved for the most hazardous part of the journey, which would be its western end. Now, in all these jails we were searched and examined before being admitted for a night's shelter, but often in a very indifferent manner. One night we arrived at a small town where a double hanging was to take place in the yard of the jail early the next morning. A woman, it seems, had called on her lover to assist in the murder of her husband, which had been brutally done with an axe, for which crime both had been pronounced guilty and condemned to die. Thousands of people had flocked in from the neighbouring country, which in this province of Ontario was thickly settled, and a large number of plain clothes detectives had been dispatched from the cities, there being supposed some attempt might be made at rescue, owing to one of the condemned being a woman. We arrived at this town early in the afternoon, and were surprised at the unusual bustle and the many groups of people assembled in the main thoroughfares. Thinking the town contained, or expected, some attraction in the way of a circus or menagerie, we expressed little curiosity, but returned at once to the railway station, intending to possess its most comfortable seats against all comers, until the approach of darkness, when we would then make application at the jail for our night's accommodation. When this time came, we marched straight to the jail, and boldly hammered its door for admittance. It was at once answered by a police officer, to whom we explained our wants, and he, without much ado, invited us indoors. Expecting the usual questions, and being prepared with the usual answers – expecting the usual indifferent search, and having pipe, tobacco and matches artfully concealed in our stockings – we were somewhat taken by surprise to find a large number of officers, who all seemed to show an uncommon interest in our appearance. The Officer, who was examining us previous to making us comfortable for the night, had finished this part of the business to his own satisfaction, when one of these detectives stepped forward, and said

– 'We cannot admit strangers to the jail on the present occasion, so that you had better make them out an order for the hotel.' This order was then given to us, and we immediately left the jail; and it was then, curious to know the reason for this action, that we soon made ourselves acquainted with the true facts of the case. When we arrived at the hotel, we were informed that every bed had been taken since morning, and that, as it was, a number of men would be compelled to sit all night dozing in their chairs, and it was with this information that we returned to the jail. For the second time we were admitted, and were advised to walk to the next town. This, Three Fingered Jack absolutely refused to do, saying that his feet were too blistered and sore to carry him another hundred yards. All these detectives then got together, and, after a rather lengthy consultation, one of them came forward and, after plying us with a number of questions, proceeded to examine our clothes, and that so thoroughly that I feared for the result. At the beginning of the search, I gave him my razor, a small penknife, my pocket-handkerchief and a comb, but he was not satis-fied until his hands were down in my stockings, and bringing up first my pipe, then my tobacco, and lastly the matches. What worried me most was the belt next to my body, which contained my money. I had not much fear of Three Fingered Jack, when confronting each other openly, though he was a tall active man, but had he known of these dollars, I had not dared in his presence to have closed my eyes, believ-ing that he would have battered out my brains with a stone, wooden stake or iron bar, so that he might possess himself of this amount. This detective certainly discovered the belt, and felt it carefully, but the money being in paper, and no coin or hard substance being therein, he apparently was none the wiser for its contents. At last this severe examination was at an end, and we were both led through an iron corridor and placed in a cell, the door of which was carefully locked. I don't believe we slept one moment during that night but what we were overlooked by a pair, or several pairs, of shrewd eyes. They could not believe but that we were other to what we pretended and had come there with designs to thwart the ends of justice. Next morning our things were returned to us, and we were turned adrift at a cold hour that was far earlier than on ordinary occasions.

The snow was still deep and the mornings and evenings cold when, a week after this, we reached Ottawa. This slow travelling was not at all to my liking, and I often persuaded my companion to make more haste towards Winnipeg. This he agreed to do; so the next morning we jumped a freight train, determined to hold it for the whole day. Unfortunately it was simply a local train, and being very slow, having to stop on the way at every insignificant little station, we left it, at a town called Renfrew, intending that night to beat a fast overland passenger train which would convey us four or five hundred miles before daybreak.

With this object we sat in the station's waiting room until evening, and then, some twenty minutes before the train became due, we slipped out unobserved and took possession of an empty car, stationary some distance away, from which place we would see the train coming, and yet be unseen from the station's platform. This train would soon arrive, for passengers were already pacing the platform, the luggage was placed in readiness, and a number of curious people, having nothing else to do, had assembled here to see the coming and going of the train. At last we heard its whistle, and, looking out, we saw the head light in the distance, drawing nearer and nearer. It steamed into the station without making much noise, for the rails were slippery, there still being much ice and snow on the track. 'Come', I said to Jack, 'there is no time to lose', and we quickly jumped out of the empty car.

This fast passenger train carried a blind baggage car, which means that the end nearest to the engine was blind in having no door. Our object was to suddenly appear from a hiding place, darkness being favourable, and leap on the step of this car, and from that place to the platform; this being done when the train was in motion, knowing that the conductor, who was always on the watch for such doings, rarely stopped the train to put men off, even when sure of their presence. If he saw us before the train started, he would certainly take means to prevent us from riding. When we had once taken possession of this car, no man could approach us until we reached the next stopping place, which would probably be fifty miles, or much more. At that place we would dismount, conceal ourselves, and, when it was again in motion, make another leap for our former place. Of course, the engineer and fireman could reach us, but these men were always indifferent, and never interfered, their business being ahead instead of behind the engine.

The train whistled almost before we were ready, and pulled slowly out of the station. I allowed my companion the advantage of being the first to jump, owing to his maimed hand. The train was now going faster and faster, and we were forced to keep pace with it. Making a leap he caught the handle bar and sprang lightly on the step, after which my hand quickly took possession of this bar, and I ran with the train, prepared to follow his example. To my surprise, instead of at once taking his place on the platform, my companion stood thoughtlessly irresolute on the step, leaving me no room to make the attempt. But I still held to the bar, though the train was now going so fast that I found great difficulty in keeping step with it. I shouted to him to clear the step. This he proceeded to do, very deliberately, I thought. Taking a firmer grip on the bar, I jumped, but it was too late, for the train was now going at a rapid rate. My foot came short of the step, and I fell, and, still clinging to the handle bar, was dragged several yards before I relinquished my hold. And there I lay for several minutes, feeling a little shaken, whilst the train passed swiftly on into the darkness.

Even then I did not know what had happened, for I attempted to stand, but found that something had happened to prevent me from doing this. Sitting down in an upright position, I then began to examine myself, and now found that the right foot was severed from the ankle. This discovery did not shock me so much as the thoughts which quickly followed. For, as I could feel no pain, I did not know but what my body was in several parts and I was not satisfied until I had examined every portion of it. Seeing a man crossing the track, I shouted to him for assistance. He looked in one direction and another, not seeing me in the darkness, and was going his way when I shouted again. This time he looked full my way, but instead of coming nearer, he made one bound in the air, nearly fell, scrambled to his feet, and was off like the shot from a gun. This man was sought after for several weeks, by people curious to know who he was, but was never found, and no man came forward to say – 'I am he.' Having failed to find this man, people at last began to think I was under a ghostly impression. Probably that was the other man's impression, for who ever saw Pity make the same speed as Fear?

Another man, after this, approached, who was a workman on the line, and at the sound of my voice he seemed to understand at once what had occurred. Coming forward quickly, he looked me over, went away, and in a minute or two returned with the assistance of several others to convey me to the station. A number of people were still there; so that when I was placed in the waiting room to bide the arrival of a doctor, I could see no other way of keeping a calm face before such a number of eyes than by taking out my pipe and smoking, an action which, I am told, caused much sensation in the local press.[22]

22. The *Renfrew Mercury*, 24 March 1899: 'he lay in the snow for some time, but finally his cries attracted Mr Jas. Galvin, who went to investigate, and soon had the victim of the accident in the station. Here he displayed wonderful nerve [...]. Drs.

Chapter XX: Hospitality

I bore this accident with an outward fortitude that was far from the true state of my feelings. The doctor, seeing the even development of my body, asked me if I was an athlete. Although I could scarcely claim to be one, I had been able, without any training, and at any time, to jump over a height of five feet; had also been a swimmer, and, when occasion offered, had donned the gloves. Thinking of my present helplessness caused me many a bitter moment, but I managed to impress all comers with a false indifference.

What a kind-hearted race of people are these Canadians! Here was I, an entire stranger among them, and yet every hour people were making enquiries, and interesting themselves on my behalf, bringing and sending books, grapes, bananas, and other delicacies for a sick man. When a second operation was deemed necessary, the leg to be amputated at the knee, the whole town was concerned, and the doctors had to give strict injunctions not to admit such a number of kind-hearted visitors. At this time I was so weak of body, that it was thought hopeless to expect recovery from this second operation. This was soon made apparent to me by the doctor's question, as to whether I had any message to send to my people, hinting that there was a slight possibility of dying under the chloroform. A minister of the gospel was also there, and his sympathetic face certainly made the dying seem probable. Now, I have heard a great deal of dying men having a foresight of things to be, but, I confess, that I was never more calm in all my life than at this moment when death seemed so certain. I did not for one instant believe or expect that these eyes would again open to the light, after I had been in this low vital condition, deadened and darkened for over two hours, whilst my body was being cut and sawn like so much wood or stone. And yet I felt no

---

Connolly and Murphy were summoned and bandaged the foot at the station, preparatory to having the man removed to the hospital. While the bandaging was in progress, Davies took out his pipe and had a smoke. [...] Dr Connolly said that it was easy to understand how Britishers won victories, if they were made of such stuff as he was'. Quoted in Richard J. Stonesifer, *W. H. Davies: A Critical Biography* (London: Cape, 1963), p. 40. Renfrew Victoria Hospital had opened in the spring of 1898, a year before the accident.

terror of death. I had been taken in a sleigh from the station to the hospital, over a mile or more of snow; and the one thought that worried me most, when I was supposed to be face to face with death, was whether the town lay north, south, east or west from the hospital, and this, I believe, was the last question I asked. After hearing an answer, I drew in the chloroform in long breaths, thinking to assist the doctors in their work. In spite of this, I have a faint recollection of struggling with all my might against its effects, previous to losing consciousness; but I was greatly surprised on being afterwards told that I had, when in that condition, used more foul language in ten minutes' delirium than had probably been used in twenty four hours by the whole population of Canada. It was explained to me that such language was not unusual in cases of this kind, which consoled me not a little, but I could not help wondering if the matron had been present, and if she had confided in her daughter. The latter was a young girl of sixteen years, or thereabouts, and was so womanly and considerate that her mother could very well leave her in charge of the patients for the whole day, although this had not been necessary during my stay.

For three days after this operation I hovered between life and death, any breath expected to be my last. But in seven or eight days my vitality, which must be considered wonderful, returned in a small way, and I was then considered to be well out of danger. It was at this time that the kindness of these people touched me to the heart. The hospital was situated at the end of a long road, and all people, after they had passed the last house, which was some distance away, were then known to be visitors to the matron or one of her patients. On the verandah outside sat the matron's dog, and, long before people were close at hand, he barked, and so prepared us for their coming. When it was known that I was convalescent, this dog was kept so busy barking that his sharp clear voice became hoarse with the exertion. They came single, they came in twos and threes; old people, young people and children; until it became necessary to give them a more formal reception, limiting each person or couple, as it might be, to a few minutes' conversation. On hearing that I was fond of reading, books were at once brought by their owners, or sent by others; some of which I had not the courage to read nor the heart to return; judging them wrongly perhaps by their titles of this character: *Freddie's Friend*, *Little Billie's Button*, and *Sally's Sacrifice*. With such good attendance within, and so much kindness from without, what wonder that I was now fit to return to England, five weeks after the accident, after having undergone two serious operations! My new friends in that distant land would persuade me to remain, assuring me of a comfortable living, but I decided to return to England as soon as possible, little knowing what my experience would be in the years following.

When the morning came for my departure, the matron, in a motherly way, put her two hands on my shoulders and kissed me, her eyes being full of tears. This, coming from a person whose business was to show no emotion, doing which would make her unfit for her position, made me forget the short laugh and the cold hand shake for which my mind had prepared itself, and I felt my voice gone, and my throat in the clutches of something new to my experience. I left without having the voice to say goodbye. On my way I had to wish goodbye to everyone I met, and when, at last, this ordeal was over, and I was in the train on my way back to Montreal, I felt that I was not yet strong enough to travel; my courage forsook me, and I sat pale and despondent, for I never expected to meet these people again, and they were true friends.

Soon I reached Montreal. Only two months had elapsed, and what a difference now! Two months ago, and it was winter, snow on the earth, and the air was cold; but I was then full limbed, full of vitality and good spirits, for summer like prospects golden and glorious possessed me night and day. It was summer now, the earth was dry and green, and the air warm, but winter was within me; for I felt crushed and staggered on crutches to the danger of myself and the people on my way. I soon got over this unpleasant feeling, roused by the merry-makers aboard ship, the loudest and most persistent, strange to say, being a one legged man, who defied all Neptune's attempts to make him walk unsteady. Seeing this man so merry, I knew that my sensitiveness would soon wear off; and, seeing him so active was a great encouragement. I was soon home again, having been away less than four months; but all the wildness had been taken out of me, and my adventures after this were not of my own seeking, but the result of circumstances.

Chapter XXI: London

Sitting at home, thinking of future employment, manual labour being now out of the question, it was then for the first time that I expressed gratitude for my old grandmother's legacy, which on my homecoming from the States had been reduced from ten shillings to eight shillings per week.[23] In the past it had been sniffed at and scorned, being called several ill-natured names, such as 'a week's tobacco', 'a day's grub,' or 'an evening's booze without cigars'. I had been very bitter, on the reading of her will, that the property had not come into my hands, to sell or retain, spend or save; but a little common sense now told me that if such had been the case I would, at the present time, have been without either property or income, and had been so less than twelve months after her death. The old lady, no doubt, had noted my wildness, and to save me the temptation to squander my brother's share, who was incapable of taking charge of his own affairs, and whose share I must have ill managed, after the passing of my own she had wisely left this property to remain in the hands of a trustee, which now turned out as lucky for myself as for my brother.

I was now more content with my lot, determined that as my body had failed, my brains should now have the chance they had longed for, when the spirit had been bullied into submission by the body's activity.

It was now the middle of Summer, and daily I sat dreaming, reading, and occasionally writing in a leafy bower in the garden. I could now dispense with crutches, having just received from London an artificial limb, and on this was practising, taking short walks at night, with a success that was gratifying. A far different Klondyke had opened up before my eyes, which corresponded with the dreams of my youth. I pictured myself returning home, not with gold nuggets from the far West, but with literary fame, wrested from no less a place than the mighty London. This secret was never divulged to my people, and, in the after years, this reticence saved them from many a

---

23. This small legacy had been left to Davies after his grandmother's death, and had helped to fund his adventures. The full sum of rents was split between Davies and his two siblings, and this was Davies's share. See 'Introduction'.

pang of disappointment, and freed me from many an awkward question. Determined to lose no time in the conquest of that city, which I expected would be surrendered to me some time within twelve months, I began, without wasting more time in dreams, to make preparations for this journey. Alas! how many greater men failed in a lifetime at this attempt, although they now stand triumphant in death, holding in their spiritual hands the freedom and keys of the whole world's cities!

With a cotton shirt, a pair of stockings and a handkerchief in a brown paper parcel, and the sum of two pounds in my pocket, after the expense of train fare, I started for London, filled to the brim with the aforesaid designs. My failure in the States, and again in Canada, had made me a little more chary with my confidence, but I was not in the least the less optimistic. My first dreams were, and are, my best. I scorn clothes and jewellery; I would rather take a free country walk, leaving the roads for the less trodden paths of the hills and the lanes, than ride in a yacht or a coach; I would rather see the moon in the ruins than the gas light of an assembly room; gluttony I despise, and drink is seldom taken except at the invitation of other eyes: then what, in the name of everything we know, would be to me the silver and gold of all Alaska!

I arrived in London early the following morning and at once made my way towards Lambeth. Early that night, being tired with the exertion of an unusually long day, I went seeking for lodgings in Blackfriars Road,[24] and, seeing several signs that claimed to accommodate working men with good clean beds at six pence per night, entered one of these establishments, paid the amount demanded, and was then ushered into a long kitchen, preferring to sit and smoke for an hour before retiring for the night. Some thirty or forty men were in this kitchen, but the British Workman had either not yet arrived, was out drinking his pint, or had gone early to bed. This was not by any means my first experience in England of lodging houses, for I had been forced to live in similar places on my visits in cattle ships from America; but I certainly did not like the look of this place, where no sign of authority was to be seen, and which seemed to be entirely left to the control of these noisy men. Some of these lodgers had been old soldiers, had just received their pensions – the accumulation of three months. A number of them were bringing in cans of

---

24. Lambeth is a part of south-central London immediately south of the River Thames. Blackfriars Road runs south from Blackfriars Bridge for ¾ mile, roughly between Lambeth (to the west) and Southwark (to the east).

beer, and the kitchen was in an uproar. Many of them were too drunk to perform this task, but were sufficiently sober to sit awake and give money and orders to others, and there was no lack of willing hands to bring them what they required. I left the kitchen at once, determined to seek another place, without troubling the landlady to refund my money. As I left the kitchen, two drunken men began to fight; others interfered, and this fight threatened to become an all round affair. When I had reached the top of the stairs, feeling my way in the dark, I found the landlady standing at the office door. Seeing me, as I was about to pass her, she said, in a voice which was the worse for drink – 'So you want to go to bed? Here, Jim, show this gentleman to his bed.' Jim obeyed, a small, pale-faced child, whom I mechanically followed up two flights of stairs, which were better lighted than those leading to the kitchen, which was in the basement of the house. He then showed me into a room where there were a number of beds, and, pointing to one, said – 'You are number forty-five', and then he left the room. Many of the beds already contained sleepers. I sat down on the edge of mine, wondering if there would be any disturbance in the night, whether any of these men would take a fancy to my clothes, or in the dark were likely to rummage their contents. The man in the next bed coughed, and then, turning towards me, said gently – 'The beds are good, I admit, but that is about all you can say of this house.' Second voice, not far away: 'You've come to a good house, you have, and yer don't know it.' First voice: 'If I hadn't been drunk last night and got chucked out of Rowton's, I wouldn't, on any account, be here.' A third voice, distant, but loud and angry: 'Give over, will yer: when are you coves going to sleep? I ain't done any labour for three weeks, and now as I've got a chance at four in the mornin', blow me if I ain't robbed of my slumber. Take care I don't set about yer at once, yer blooming lot of bleeders. If I come arter yer body, yer'll know it, and no mistake about it, either.' No more was said after this. I at once made up my mind to try Rowton House on the following day. That they had refused this man a bed owing to his being drunk, and, more than likely, quarrelsome in drink, was a strong recommendation to me after my experience here, where it would be impossible to either read, write or think, or to even partake of my meals in comfort.

The following morning, after having had breakfast at an eating house, I enquired for Rowton House, and when the first person I addressed asked which one I wanted, I answered him – 'the nearest one'. This proved to be in Newington Butts[25] and, after receiving instructions, I proceeded accordingly, and was soon standing outside that place, where I was to remain for two years, without in the least impressing London. To my surprise, I found this house to be a fine large block of red buildings, with an imposing front, and a fine entrance, polished and clean; and, facing its many front windows, was an old church tower and clock, set in an old leafy churchyard that had stones for the dead and a number of wooden seats for the living.

On making an application for a bed, I learnt that this could not be granted until nine o'clock in the evening, but was courteously allowed the privilege of remaining indoors until that time. This place surprised me by its accommodation of dining rooms, library, sitting rooms, baths, lavatories, etc., all being kept clean and in thorough good order by a large staff of men, its charge being sixpence per night.

On making my way into the library, and seeing two large cases of books, one containing fiction, and the other being enriched by the poets, historians, essayists, with biography and miscellaneous literature, and hearing how quiet this room was, in spite of the presence of over a hundred men, I at once made up my mind to pay a week's lodgings down, indifferent whether the sleeping accommodation was good or bad. This I did at nine o'clock, after which I sat sometimes reading the paper, and again watching the faces of this mixed assembly. Some of them were of refined appearance, with their silk hats, their frock coats, cuffs and collars, and spoke in voices subdued and gentle. Some of them were of such a prosperous appearance that no doubt I had already passed them in the street, thinking they were either merchants or managers of great concerns; and, more likely than not, the paper boys had followed on their heels, and the cab men had persistently hailed them.

If I wanted to devote my time to study, living on eight shillings per week, this was apparently a suitable place for my purpose. Being my own barber, doing my own plain cooking, and living abstemiously, renouncing drink and the pleasures of theatres, and other indoor entertainments, and retaining tobacco as my sole luxury — I saw no reason why this could not be done, at the same time making up my mind that it had to be done.

I had been here little more than a week, when I set to work in earnest, and the result of two months' diligence was a tragedy, written

25. About half a mile south of the end of Blackfriars Road, and now in the London Borough of Southwark.

in blank verse, and which I called *The Robber*. Never dreaming but what it would at once meet with success, owing to its being full of action – a very difficult thing to marry to verse, but which I thought was successfully accomplished – I was somewhat taken aback to have it returned to me on the third day, with the manager's regret. Now it seemed that the Rowton House had a bad name, owing to the great number of criminals that were continually in the Police Court s giving that address. Some of these lodgers, for that very reason, had their correspondence addressed to various small shops, where they were customers for tobacco, papers, and groceries.

On having this tragedy returned, I, thinking of this, came to the conclusion that no respectable person would be likely to consider or respect any work, or application for the same, that emanated from a house of this name. I spoke to a gentleman with whom I had become acquainted, on this difficult subject, and he agreed with me, saying that such were the true facts of the case. 'But', said he, after a thoughtful pause, 'as your means are so limited, and the shopkeepers charge one penny for every letter they receive on a customer's behalf, would it not be as well to still have your correspondence addressed here, but in another way, of which you probably have not heard? Give your address as number one Churchyard Row, and, although people will not recognise this house under that name, yet the post office authorities will know it for its proper address.' This I did, without further question, and *The Robber* was despatched on a second journey. Fourteen days after my robber returned to number one Churchyard Row. Bothering my head to account for this, I came to the conclusion that my tragedy had not been read farther than the front page, and that a tragedy that was born and bred in such a place as Churchyard Row – the address being so appropriate to the nature of the work – was enough to make any man, who had the least sense of humour, condemn it with a laugh. My conceit, at this time, was foolish in the extreme, and yet I was near my thirtieth year.

The next work was a very long poem, in which the beasts of the field, the birds of the air, and even the fishes of the sea, met in a forest glade to impeach man for his cruelty to them, and went on to describe their journey at midnight to the nearest town, and the vengeance they then took on the sleeping inhabitants. My confidence in this work being accepted could not have been altogether whole-hearted, for the following reason: I made two copies of this poem, and posted them simultaneously to different publishers. I felt quite satisfied that one of these would be accepted, but when a whole week had passed on, and I had received no communication from either publisher, I was then horrified to think that they both were giving the poem such a consideration that there was a probability that both of them would accept it, and that both publishers would call on me to make terms, perhaps at the very same hour. This thought so preyed on my mind that I did not feel at all easy until I had one of the copies returned; but it was a great disappointment to receive the second copy on the following day.

Thinking that short poems would stand a better prospect of being accepted, I set to work on a hundred sonnets, writing five, and sometimes six a day, but when this number had been accomplished and submitted, this work met with the same failure.

After this I wrote another tragedy, a comedy, a volume of humorous essays, and hundreds, I believe, of short poems. I was always writing at this time, either beginning or finishing a work, but, strange to say, none of this work was being sent out, but was safely treasured, under the impression that it would some day find its market.

After having had twelve months' practice, in the last months of which no attempt had been made at publication, I decided to make one more effort, this time with a small volume of short poems. This was immediately sent to a well known publisher, who in a few days returned answer, offering to publish at the author's expense, the sum needed being twenty five pounds. This success completely turned my head. With all my heart I believed that there would not be the least difficulty in procuring money for such a grand purpose, and at once wrote to several well known philanthropists, writing six letters. Two of them never murmured, and the other four set their secretaries to snap me up in a few words. Exasperated at this I wrote to several others, all my trouble being to no purpose.

Now, when I first entered this lodging house, I had something like thirty shillings to the good, being ahead of my income, and up to the present had no reason for spending this amount. Could I put this to some use? – My mind had several plans, and one in particular seemed good and feasible. I would write three or four short poems on a page, get them printed, and sell them from door to door. Two thousand of these sheets, sold at threepence per copy, would be twenty five pounds, and, no doubt, I could sell quite a hundred of these copies a day, providing I went from house to house, from street to street, from early morning till late at night. With this object I lost no time in seeing a job printer, and was told that thirty five shillings would be needed to defray expenses. This large amount disappointed me not a little, but I paid a deposit and went back to the house, where I lived and nearly starved in saving four shillings that were short, which was done in two weeks out of the sixteen shillings that were to maintain me in food and lodgings for fourteen days. At last, after great privation and sacrifice, it was done, and I received from the printer two thousand and some odd copies. Early the next morning I was to be seen in the suburbs of London, with my hands and pockets full of these copies, going from door to door. I mentioned to the inhabitants that I had had an offer from a publisher, and that he could not undertake to publish my work under twenty five pounds. All these people did was to stare, none of them seeming to understand, and no one seemed inclined to ask questions. I had, I believe, visited the doors of some thirty houses or more, and had not sold one copy. Most of these people were poor, and some had become sufficiently interested to enquire the price of my copies, seeming inclined and willing to trade with me in a small way, but none of them seemed to be anxious to give threepence for a sheet of paper which they did not understand. At last I chanced upon a house that was much larger than the others, at which place a servant answered the door. I lost no time in relating to her the true facts of the case, and she was standing there silent and puzzled as to my meaning, when her mistress called to her from the top of the stairs – 'Mary, who's there?' On which the maiden gave answer in a halting voice – 'Some man selling some paper.' At this there was a pause, and then the same voice said, from the direction of the stairs – 'Give him this penny, and tell him to go away', and, almost instantly, that copper coin fell at the bottom of the stairs, and came rolling rapidly towards us, as though aware of its mission. The girl handed me this penny, which I took mechanically, at the same time persisting in her taking a copy to her mistress. That lady, hearing our further conversation, and perhaps, guessing its import, cried again, this time in a warning voice – 'Mary, mind you don't take anything from him.' This crushed the last hope, for I began to think that if this lady, who might be a woman of some cultivation and rich, could only see and read what had been done, she might have at once, in her deep interest, merged the whole twenty five pounds, at the same time befriending me for life. Alas! I have been unfortunate all my life in believing that there were a great number of rich people who were only too eager to come forward and help talent in distress.

I was so disgusted at receiving this single penny, and being so dismissed, that I at once put the sheets back in my pockets and returned to the city. How long would it take to get twenty five pounds, at this rate? What am I talking about! Money was lost, not even this single copper was a gain; for this penny-a-day experience had cost me three pennies in tram fare, without mention of a more expensive breakfast than I usually had.

When I got back to the house I started, with the fury of a mad man, to burn the copies, and did not rest until they were all destroyed, taking care not to save one copy that would at any time in the future remind me of my folly.

It was at this time that I came under the influence of Flanagan. That gentleman, seeing me often writing and apparently in deep thought, at once gave me credit for more wisdom than I possessed. He was a very illiterate man, having no knowledge of grammar, punctuation or spelling. The upshot of this acquaintance was that he informed me in confidence that he was the lawful heir to nearly half the county of Mayo, in Ireland; on which estate was a house like the King's palace. In exchange for this confidence I told him that I was the author of a book of verse, which could not be published except the author defrayed expenses. On which Flanagan expressed much sympathy — more especially when I read him aloud a few lines expressing my disapproval of landowners and rich tyrants — and promised sincerely to relieve me of all difficulty providing, of course, that he made good his claims to the estate. Flanagan then proposed that I should put some of his arguments in grammatical form, which he would immediately forward to the proper authorities. This I began to do at once, and some of Flanagan's arguments were so strong that I am surprised at the present day at being a free man. I told one eminent statesman that he should retire and give place to a more honest man, and another that though he was born in Ireland and bore the name of an Irish man, yet he was a traitor, for his heart had ever been in England. Despite these powerful letters, the County Mayo never to my knowledge changed hands, and I was disappointed in my expectations, and Flanagan grieved daily. At that time, I must confess, I thoroughly believed Flanagan, perhaps through being blinded by my own ambitions as an author.

Even at the present time, though I have cut down the estate considerably, from half a county to half an acre, and have taken out quite a number of windows from the estate's residence — after doing this, I still believe that poor Flanagan was robbed of a cottage and garden by an avaricious landlord.

This was at the time of the Boer War and Flanagan's long dark beard and slouched hat gave him the exact appearance of one of those despised people. Therefore we seldom took a walk together but what we were stoned by boys in the street, and even grown up people passed insulting remarks. In fact everywhere we went we were regarded with suspicion. Our clothes not being of the best, drew the attention of attendants at museums and art galleries, and we, being swarthy and alien in appearance, never paused near a palace but what sentry and police watched our every movement. One morning we were passing through Whitehall, what time a regiment of soldiers were being drilled and inspected by a gentleman in a silk hat. Now Flanagan was a man of great courage and never thought it necessary to whisper. Therefore a vein of savage satire broke in Flanagan's heart when he beheld a man in a silk hat inspecting a troop of soldiers. 'See!' he cried, 'there's a sight for the Boers.' A number of bystanders resented this remark, and there were loud murmurs of disapproval on which Flanagan asked the following question: 'Will the best man in the crowd step forward?' But no man seemed inclined to attempt Flanagan's chastisement, without being assisted. Although I did not entirely approve of him on this occasion, still, seeing that the words could not be recalled, I was quite prepared to be carried with him half dead on a stretcher to the nearest hospital; for I liked the man, and he certainly seemed to like me, since he always took his walks alone when I did not accompany him.[26]

---

26. In the rest of *The Autobiography of a Super-Tramp* (which ends with Chapter XXXIV), Davies describes tramping, mainly around central England, and continued attempts to get his poetry published. This culminates in the eventual publication of his first collection, *The Soul's Destroyer* (1905), and his decision – after this book seemed to have gone almost completely unnoticed – to send copies to eminent persons. This is summarised in my 'Introduction'.

Davies sought to capitalise on the success of The Autobiography of a Super-Tramp *by writing further volumes that are concerned one way or another with his life as a tramp.* Beggars, *the first follow-up, also concentrates on the author's experiences as a tramp in America and England, but takes the form of a compendium of essays. The success of the* Autobiography *meant that Davies had no need to tell his own story this time around; as a result,* Beggars *lacks the narrative thread that made its predecessor so popular, and is instead a series of independent anecdotes and societal observations. The truth of them is typically impossible to vouch for, of course. Some of the anecdotes are repeated by the author in other volumes.* Beggars *was Book of the Week in* Country Life *magazine.*

Chapter 1: The Nationalities as Beggars

There is no question but that the American beggar is the finest in his country; but in that land of many nationalities he has a number of old-country beggars to contend with. Perhaps it would interest – it certainly should – a number of people to know how well or ill their own nation is represented by beggars in that most important country; whether England, Ireland, Scotland, Germany, and other countries have cause to be proud or ashamed of their representatives. Both France and Italy have much cause to complain, for you may often travel many miles and not be approached by a French or Italian beggar. If you meet an Italian, you can safely despise him as a working man with hard-earned money in his pocket, though he may be stealing rides like a beggar, and making coffee with real beggars at their camps.

With regard to Germany, she can place in the field a very large army of second-rate beggars; but it is seldom that you meet a German beggar whose ambition raises him above that. Other nationalities, who go to private houses and beg ready-cooked meals, despise the German beggar for his low taste in being satisfied with no more than common dry food. All beggars make coffee at camp-fires, but it is only the German that takes the trouble to carry on his travels his own tin can; for every town has near it a beggars' camp, and cans are always to be found. The German's method is to beg the baker for bread, the butcher for sausage, and the grocer for coffee. When he is successful, he repairs to the camp, and makes what he calls 'an excellent meal' on these dry Materials; whereas other beggars have either had a good hot meal at a private house, or have begged a number of paper parcels, in which is buttered bread, and there is cake, and one parcel may have fish as a change from the meat in another, and there is often an apple, orange, or banana for dessert. The German does not aspire to these luxuries, and is well satisfied to get the plain diet of his native land – without taking advantage of the offers of a richer country – and to do no work for it. He is not a true beggar either, for he is always ready to do odd jobs, such as fruit or hop picking and potato digging, but is not eager for steady work.

Few people would think the Scotsman makes an excellent beggar, seeing that his manner is so undemonstrative. Although he is seldom heard to raise his voice above one distinct pitch, or to indulge in loud laughter, or to show emotion of any kind, yet, for all this, he is an excellent beggar. There is quite a large clan of Scotties among American beggars. He is a good beggar for the simple reason that he is a good talker. Almost every Scotch beggar I met in the States of America was inclined to be talkative, and yet they all managed to conceal their private affairs. Although a Scotsman would be one of the last men to go hungry in a civilized land, yet he must be objected to as a true beggar in that he is avaricious for money, and would immediately take advantage of remunerative employment.

Alas for the poor Irishman! for he is the most timid beggar of all. Though he is so independent in throwing up a job, he is always glad, when his money is gone, to seek another. How the poor fellow does suffer hunger when seeking work, not having the courage to beg; and how independent and forgetful he is when his appetite is satisfied. Even the German, who as a beggar is despised by American, English, and Scotch beggars, stands head and shoulders above poor Pat. I am sorry to say so, but the truth of the matter is that Pat receives charity from other beggars – English, Scotch, and such American beggars as are proud of their Irish extraction. If these men do not feed him, they often show him a good house where he only has to show his face and be fed.

I remember a very mean trick being served on two Irishmen, Pat and Tim. The guilty one was a Cockney, and he was lucky to escape with his life. Seeing at the camp two hungry and helpless Irishmen, he promised to show them a good house, at which no beggars, however often they came, were refused food. The elated pair accompanied 'Cockney' for this interesting purpose, and were soon shown a very large house, at which, the Cockney said, 'he had been treated with as much consideration as though he were the Pope of Rome'. He then left them to make their own arrangements, and, after much indecision, it was arranged that Pat should go first, and, on his return, his companion Tim should try his luck. Pat, with every confidence, approached the big house and rang the bell; but the door was almost immediately opened, as though the inmate had been lying in wait. The Irishman had scarcely opened his mouth when the man that answered the door shouted, 'What, you big, able-bodied rascal? I'll give you something to eat', and rushed at the poor Irishman with a thick walking-stick. This was very serious, for Pat also saw the grinning face of a stalwart nigger behind his master, and the Irishman thought the best thing he could do was to leave in a hurry without more words, which he did.

It quite upset Pat to think that he had been induced to go first, so he made up his mind that Tim should share his misfortune. Therefore, when he returned and Tim asked, 'What luck, Pat?' Pat rubbed his body, saying, 'Begorra, there was more mate than five min could ate'. On hearing this good news Tim braced himself and, after a long pause, walked with reckless determination towards the house. But Tim had no time to ring, for the door was suddenly flung open, and, before he could utter one word, a white man and a nigger began to attack him with sticks. Tim did not wait to argue or fight, but took to his heels at once. 'This is a noice thrick, an' the both from Kilkenny', said he to Pat. 'Spake out', said Pat innocently, although he had seen the whole transaction; 'shure, we are frinds, and frinds should share and share aloike'. I am very pleased to say that the two Irishmen had their reward when they returned, for three good American beggars had thoroughly worked the town, and had in their possession enough food for ten men – but the Cockney never returned to the camp. It was certainly a cruel joke to play on two hungry men, innocent and unsuspecting.

The English easily come next to Americans as beggars, especially when England is represented by the Cockney. He will often attain his ends after failing in a cross-examination and discovered in a lie; for his witty excuses and peculiar manner of expression are not to be resisted by Americans. Even the Irish-Americans, who are so bitter against Englishmen, make an exception of a Cockney, because of his witty talk and his disinclination to be serious. This impudence and command of speech have become proverbial among American beggars, and he is so much liked that I have seen men, who were about to leave a town, remain at a camp for two or three days longer, so as to enjoy the anecdotes and queer sayings of a Cockney that has just arrived. The Cockney – and he alone – is admired by those extraordinary beggars who are born Americans, and who are conceited enough to think that they could by their energies live well as beggars in the poorest slums in the cities of Europe. Aye, even the beggars of the Western States, who, owing to the great distances between towns, must never be without a dollar or two in their pockets – even these energetic beggars have great respect for a Cockney, though they scorn the petty food-begging operations of others.

I never in all my acquaintance with 'Brum'[27] saw him look so

27. 'Brum – of America – the greatest beggar I have ever met' (Chapter XXXV, *Beggars*, p. 270). As described in Chapter III of the *Autobiography*, included in the present volume, Brum is the first tramp Davies records meeting in America. He inducted

alarmed as when he entered a camp and saw a man making coffee, and near him was a pile consisting of a number of parcels of food. This man, who was a Cockney, confessed that he had just begged the town – and we soon had cause to know it, for I had great difficulty in getting one little sandwich, and though Brum brought to the camp enough for two, he must have had a great struggle, for he was away much longer than usual. That he had struggled hard was apparent from his behaviour, for in spite of the Cockney's friendly advances, Brum would hardly give him a civil word. Yes, there was not the least doubt but what Brum was jealous. Although we three remained in the camp together for two days, I could not help but notice that Brum would never allow the Cockney to get the start on him, but every time we went begging he quickly followed the other. And what do you think this Cockney had the impudence to say to Brum? 'Old man', said he, 'I'll see if I can beg you a pair of trousers'. When he heard this Brum almost foamed at the mouth, for he prided himself on being one of the best beggars in America, whether it was in getting money, food, or clothes.

I know very little about the Welsh as beggars, as I have only met about half a dozen in America, and they were so timid that Wales had as little cause to be proud of them as Ireland of hers. I don't think Welshmen take kindly to begging, for, according to my later experience at home, half the beggars in Wales are Englishmen, though many of them can explain themselves in Welsh, having been in the country a considerable time. They certainly have good cause to remain there, for Wales runs America a good second in her generosity to beggars; as also does Ireland, but she is less able to give.

No doubt Russia, Spain, Greece, Japan, and other countries have their beggars by thousands at home, but they are ill represented in America. England has only Germany to fear, who has six beggars to England's one; but they have little energy and are badly trained, and one Cockney is equal to ten.

Davies into the life of the road. The name 'Brum' presumably appears in quotation marks here to indicate that it is a nickname. Tramps' nicknames tended to relate either to physical or personal characteristics or geographical origins, and previously it has sometimes been suggested or assumed this man was originally from Birmingham, England, where the locals are colloquially known as Brummies. One of Davies's biographers refers to him as 'Brum from Birmingham' (see Barbara Hooper, *Time to Stand and Stare: A Life of W. H. Davies* (London: Peter Owen, 2004), p. 39), but there is no solid evidence of this whatsoever, and in fact it is highly probable that he was American. Davies gives the nicknames for most of the tramps he discusses, but never discloses his own.

from **Chapter IV : Dilemmas of Travellers**

However careful a tramp may be to avoid places where there is abundant work, he cannot always succeed. It was in a small town in Texas that I had such a narrow escape of losing the delightful companionship of Brum. I had gone to a sawmill boarding-house in expectation of getting a good free dinner, having taken the precaution to wait until all the men had returned to work, so that I would then see no other than the lady of the house, and she, of course, would know little about work at the mill. When I knocked, the lady answered the door, and after hearing my story invited me indoors. She was a fine, motherly-looking woman, stout – the very kind of creature in whom Brum had so much confidence, that she herself lived well, and would sympathize with others that could not do the same. But who should I see when I got inside but the manager or owner of the mill, who, for some reason, had not yet returned to business. As a general rule a woman is trustful, and will believe almost anything; but I was now unexpectedly confronted by a hard business man, who would probably ask a number of awkward questions of trades that maybe he knew something about. While I was having dinner, these questions were put to me and apparently answered to his satisfaction. 'Now', said he, when I was preparing to leave, 'I can find yon work at the mill, and you can start at once. I am not reckoned to be a bad master; the wages will certainly not be bad for a beginner, and you will never, I am sure, have cause to complain of this boarding-house. Your face appears to be open and honest, and you have a straightforward look that I like'. The last remark made my face as red as a beetroot with guilt, which he, no doubt, took to be a pleasant sign of modesty. This was a most awkward position, and I began to explain myself. 'Sir', said I, 'I am a tailor by trade, and am now on my way to Houston, where I am sure of getting work. I earn three, four, and sometimes five dollars a day at my trade, and am the main support of a family of little sisters and brothers. So you see how others must suffer if I accept work in a mill at a dollar and a quarter a day. Not of myself I think, but others.' The man seemed to be quite satisfied with this explanation, and said, 'At any rate, you shall have a little job and earn a dollar to help you on the way'. Then turning to the landlady, he asked the following

Beggars

question, which almost froze the marrow in my bones: 'Where is that dark pair of trousers that were split?' As the reader will guess, I was no tailor, and could do no more than sew a button on a pair of trousers. So what a sigh of relief I gave when the kind-hearted woman said that she had given them away some time before. The man was now thoughtful, and I was very much afraid that he was trying to bring to mind other wearing apparel that would need repair. Being afraid of this, I rose, and hastily thanking them for my good dinner, walked towards the door. He followed me, being on his way to the mill, and before I left him he placed in my hand a silver half-dollar, wishing me good-bye and good luck.

Brum was very pleased to see me coming, as he had begun to have fears that I had been arrested, or had been offered work and accepted it. Brum was very particular as to what kind of companions he made, and if he lost me he might have travelled alone for a considerable time.

Some time after this Brum and I were very awkwardly placed when a party of boys determined, in pity for our idleness, to find us work. These boys were squirrel-shooting in the woods, and seeing our camp-fire at once came forward and began a sociable conversation. All the boys were armed with guns, and that is the reason why boys in that part of the world are not in much fear of tramps, in fact the fear is more likely to be on the tramps' side. Now it happened that some railroad work was being done close to our camp, and the work was in the hands of Italians. The boys, having probably heard their elders speak ill of such people, determined that we two idle Americans – judging by our language – should be installed in the place of the Italians, and the latter driven out of that part of the country. 'Come!' they said to Brum and me, 'we will soon find you work'. This was very awkward indeed, and poor old Brum began to totter in the camp and groan. 'What's the matter?' asked one of the kind-hearted lads. 'Boys', said Brum slowly, and with great difficulty, 'I am a very sick man. I am now making my way to Houston as fast as I can, to get hospital treatment'. 'Yes', I said firmly, and with quick apprehension. 'Yes, and it shall never be said that I deserted a sick companion'. 'Good luck to you', said one of the lads, after which they soon left.

There was no other course now than to leave this place at once, for if we stayed any longer we were certain to see one of these lads again, seeing that there were so many of them and that the town was very small.

In spite of this disinclination to work, there are times when a tramp feels inclined to break the monotony by doing a little light labour. With such a noble resolve Brum and I left Houston to pick strawberries on our way to Galveston.[28] On reaching the land of strawberries, we immediately made enquiries as to the prospect of work, and were recommended to a large farm which was under the control of a syndicate of Chinamen. On approaching the boss Chinaman and explaining our wish, we were at once engaged. At this farm each Chinaman seemed to be allotted one task. One was to be seen with a large watering-can watering the plants from morning till night, in sunshine or rain.

The next morning we started to pick after having received our instructions from the boss China man, namely, 'To pickee clean, and leave a little stem so as people can catchee hold of the bellies'. Alas! The difficulty was to find the berries, and we were to be paid according to our picking; the water-carrier was far too industrious, for his watering beneath a hot sun was certainly bad for the plants; it did not require a farmer to know that. Needless to say, we remonstrated in a very short time and demanded our wages, in spite of the boss Chinaman coming forward with three berries on the palm of his right hand, and crying exultingly, 'Lookee at the big bellies I pickee!'

We received our money, which amounted to very little, less than half a dollar between us, and left. It is surprising the number of jobs that I have left with very low wages to come, just enough to buy a bag of peanuts or the price of a shave. [...]

---

28. A port city located predominantly on a barrier island on the Texan Gulf Coast, about fifty miles south-east of Houston. It is now on the fringes of the greater Houston metropolitan area, but was an entirely separate conurbation in the late eighteenth century. In 1900, not long after Davies was there and nine years before the publication of *Beggars*, it would suffer one of the deadliest hurricanes in US history, which killed between 6,000 and 8,000 people.

Chapter X: The Happy Life

It is certainly a mystery how man got into this tangle, having to conform to the rules of civilization – up in the morning at a certain hour, and to bed at a certain time at night, with certain limited intervals for meals; in fact a very slave to these conditions, and so often without power of being otherwise.[29] If he breaks his fetters by indulging in more sleep, or prolonging his meals, he will starve, for nuts are not now free for the picking, and fruits are not now the free gift of Nature; for she herself is made the servant of landlords who are tyrannical over their rights. It is only the small boys who occasionally defy such laws by robbing an orchard and putting to shame their big, cowardly fathers.

When I consider what pleasure it gives me to lie abed in the mornings at my own sweet will, I cannot help but feel pity for the great majority who must needs rise to answer the demands of civilization. Of course, I could not myself be so independent if I were not contented with very little, and did not prefer freedom to fine clothes and furniture and the luxuries of food.

We know very well that the one happy hour in the week for a man of business is when he wakes on a Sabbath morn, or a holiday, at his usual time to rise, and finds, O joy! that he is privileged to lie in bed, a free and a happy man.

What a strange contrast there is between the man who lives in a small house with just enough means, and no more, to keep him in idle content, and the man who, to keep up a position, has a large house with several servants, and worries himself night and day in business to keep things standing! What a wise man is the former, and what a poor fool is the latter! Position! What is it? It is to be pestered by invitations to other people's houses, and to be worried again in returning those invitations. How foolish is that business man, that he does not sell out and retire to a small country cottage, with his little income of a pound or twenty-five shillings a week, where he

---

29. This chapter expresses some of the rudimentary philosophical ideas that would also be the basis of 'Leisure' (1911). Now Davies's best known poem, it is included in the relevant section of this book.

could eat, sleep, and read in peace, and walk abroad admiring Nature. Thousands of business men could do this, and would, if they were wise enough to see what an empty thing position is.

There are not many men in this world who appreciate more than I do that precious gift called sleep. When I wake in the morning and look at my watch, it may be seven o'clock. Then I question myself – 'Shall I get up? If I do, what for? No, gentle Sleep, one more hour with thee.' Then I sleep again and wake the second time, and ask this question again – 'Shall I get up?' What with yawning and stretching it usually takes a quarter of an hour to answer, which makes the time quarter past eight. Then I say to myself, 'I will count fifty before I get up'. This I begin to do, very slowly; but when I have done I usually make the fifty a hundred. This dallying with time is very pleasant. Sometimes I return to bed after I have got up, and have even undressed for that purpose. To make a candid confession, I have – not often – got up, dressed, and then returned to bed with my clothes on, so as to enjoy another nap and be at no pains to dress again.

I remember making one trip on a cattle-boat, and on the return voyage to Baltimore there was no work to be done, we cattlemen being then counted as passengers.[30] The nearest approach to work of any kind was that two men were commissioned each day to fetch food from the galley and to sweep the forecastle – the latter duty not to be strictly enforced. Now, it happened that there were fifteen cattlemen, so that one man would be exempt from even such petty duties as these. We therefore cast lots, and the laziest man was fortunate to win. It was Baldy, who, on hearing the decision, crept back into his bunk and remained there for the rest of the voyage. When the meals came, he sat up and requested some kind hand to pass him his food, and, after returning the empty dishes to the same kind hand, settled down for another sleep. One night the ship, being light, rolled so much that we were all thrown out of our bunks, all except Baldy. That same night we rushed on deck, cattlemen, sailors, and firemen, for the coal-bunkers had been broken in by the waves, and coal filled the galley, and the cattle-pens were smashed and taken to sea, and crash followed crash until we thought our end had come – and yet Baldy, whatever his feelings were, never left his bunk.

When we arrived at Baltimore we were all, as usual, without money. On Baldy being roused and told we were about to go ashore,

---

30. During his time in America, Davies undertook such work on several ships between Baltimore, Maryland, and various ports in Britain, such as Liverpool and Glasgow.

Beggars

he began slowly to rise, but it was only after making several attempts that he succeeded in standing on his feet. My heart went out in pity for the poor fellow, for it was as much as three of us could do to get him up the forecastle steps. It was with great difficulty that he passed the doctor, for that gentleman happened to see him totter, and he had an idea that Baldy and, in fact, all the crew should be quarantined; but on receiving an explanation that Baldy's legs were weak through inactivity, he allowed us to go ashore. The distance to the cattlemen's office was over a mile, and poor Baldy could not possibly walk that distance, and, as I have said, we were all without money. But as luck would have it, a gentle man saw Baldy's condition and gave him five cents to pay car fare, so we helped the poor fellow into the car, which would take him right to the door of the office.

Honestly, if I had not been cursed with ambition to excel in literature, I would have remained a beggar to the end of my days; to winter in such towns as Baltimore, and spend my summer months in travelling through the green country, with short stops here and there in cities and large towns.

What a life it is! To study faces and the strange humours of different people. Yes, when I was about to call at a house for my dinner, the Baltimore Kid suddenly clutched my shoulders, and said impressively: 'Whatever you do, do not address that woman as Lady, but call her Madam, or Mrs'. Just to humour the Kid, for I thought such advice was ridiculous, I addressed the lady as Madam, and explained my needs. She motioned me to a small, wooden outhouse, which I entered, and seeing a chair and a table, sat down. In about two minutes the lady reappeared, carrying a hot dinner, for which I stood, as became a gentleman, and thanked her, saying: 'I thank you, Madam', but was almost on the point of saying 'lady'. After having had dinner, I went to the back door and knocked, to thank her for her kindness. 'You are quite welcome', she said; 'the only people I refuse are those who say "lady", for I have cause to believe that such people are professional beggars'. You see, by this instance, how one little word can assist or spoil a man in his profession.

The Baltimore Kid was one of the keenest beggars in America. The sight or sound of money put the very devil in him. If he heard coins rattling in the pockets of a passer-by, he would follow that person side by side, up one street and down another, until he had succeeded in talking the man out of a coin. If he saw a lady open her purse, he was at once at her side, and explaining his position. He boasted that he had begged the President, when the latter was visiting his paternal home. The Kid had intended to beg the house for clothes, but, seeing the President alone in the garden, quickly altered his mind. He claimed to have then talked the gentleman out of a five-dollar bill. Whether this story was true or not, I cannot say, but I am certain of one thing – that it was only the want of opportunity that would keep it from being attempted. The pomp and splendour of Solomon's throne would not have daunted the Baltimore Kid, if he saw the way clear of stern guards and meddlesome attendants. Many of the great capitalists of America, and many Europeans of title, had succumbed to the Kid's voice. Yes, he has often related to me how easy he found the Grand Duke of Gorgonzola, and how long it took to convince Tomkins the millionaire butcher.

Chapter XXVIII: Navvies and Frauds

Navvies[31] in common lodging-houses receive much contempt from pedlars,[32] grinders,[33] and true beggars.[34] They are always washing clothes and making shackles (soup) on Sunday, owing to their perspiration and dry food during the week; and while they are going about these long tasks, others cannot find accommodation. They always manage to get the use of the whole fire – centre, sides, and front – just before public-houses open; after which they booze until closing time, and then return to fill every utensil in the kitchen – basins, teacups, and saucers – with their greasy shackles. Although generous to one another, they would not let the smell of their shackles reach true beggars, if it could be prevented; and yet, when a navvy is reduced to the price of his bed only, he hints at his wants in a common lodging-house kitchen, expecting assistance from beggars, instead of making his wants known outside.

The navvy is more often than not a very timid beggar, and, when he can, lives upon stolen apples, turnips, blackberries, etc.; aye, and the picked-up bread that true beggars have cast away. In spite of this, I have seen an exceptional navvy that had the impudence to stand pad in a crowded market-place; which means that he would stand in the street gutter with a few laces or pins in his hand, a thing that only afflicted ones are expected to do. He does this on the night that follows pay-day, and it must be confessed that he meets with some reward. Sometimes a servant girl gives him a penny through admiration of his stalwart form; sometimes an old lady gives him a penny because his

---

31. Short for navigators, and applied to labourers on major civil engineering projects such as railways, roads and canals. Navvies might move from one job to another and experience periods of unemployment as a result.

32. Hawkers, selling usually inexpensive and easily transported goods such as shoe-laces and needles. To work legally, they needed a certificate. Davies presents pedlars as tramps, essentially using their trade as an excuse to beg. He had been one in England and Wales, as he waited for funds to cover the printing of his first poetry book to accrue from his grandmother's legacy.

33. Organ-grinders: street musicians of a kind, whose instruments play automatically when they turn a handle.

34. The implication being that pedlars and organ-grinders are essentially beggars too, though they nominally have a trade.

nose is like her son's; and, seeing that on this particular night everybody is happy with money in their pockets, it is not to be surprised at that a number of stray coppers find their way into his pocket. In this instance, charity is certainly not misplaced, for this man would rather work than beg. If he was engaged to be at your house to do a job on the following day, you could have little doubt but what he would appear. Only one thing would prevent him, and that is the arrival at the lodging-house of moneyed navvies that have just finished a job. In that case he would not need the little work offered to him, and it would be the best policy not to absent himself from his new friends – not even for a few minutes, for, when men are drinking, they are apt to change suddenly. As long as he is face to face with them, all goes well, but he no sooner turns his back than a word of suspicion is dropped, and he returns to find that his former friends are – if not drunk – cold and reserved; and if they are drunk he will find them not only ready to quarrel, but to murder.

The navvy is a real working-man, but he has to travel for work from place to place, and his jobs are very often short through no fault of his own. Being a rough, uncouth, and ill-mannered man, fond of drink and freedom to chew and smoke tobacco, to spit, and use strong language, he has no other option than to live in a common lodging-house, even though he is earning as much money as a good mechanic.

Now, although a navvy spends the best part of his life among beggars in common lodging-houses, it is surprising how simple and innocent he is as to beggars' tricks and dodges. If he saw a man in a fit in the street, the navy would be one of the last to suspect that man of being a fraud. If he saw a man making feeble attempts to climb a bridge's wall or railings, and drop into the river, the navvy would be the last to have suspicion that that man was doing so to introduce himself to one who would listen to his pitiful story, and help him with a shilling or more. And the navvy would never suspect the child that pretends to lose money and begins to cry in a loud voice. And yet this navvy spends his life in a lodging-house, where these cunning mortals live.

These tricks are not so common as people suppose; they are in fact very rare. Many an honest man has fits, the rivers give up a number of suicides, and with regard to the child losing money – was there ever a child that did not?

Beggars have various ways by which they can get shillings instead of pennies. When a beggar in a lodging-house kitchen produced a massive ring for the inspection of his fellow lodgers, it was eagerly commented on as 'a good one'; by which they meant to say that it was a good imitation, for they all knew that it was a dummy. But a navvy saw that it was marked so many carats, felt that it was heavy, saw that it was of good colour, and exclaimed, to the derision of the lodgers assembled: 'It's real gold! Did you pick it up?' 'Will you give me sixpence for it?' asked the other. The navvy did not answer, for this question seemed to enlighten him.

The ring dodge is a paying concern, for the sale of one ring often means dinner, drinks, supper, bed, and breakfast. The ring is, to all appearance, valuable; according to its colour, finish, weight, and – the best sign of all – its mark of carats. All that is to be done is to invite inspection, and if you are suspected of being a thief who is afraid to enter a pawnshop, so much the better, for you are almost certain to find an avaricious victim. Very few men can resist giving a couple of shillings for an article which they feel satisfied can be again easily disposed of at a good profit. I have often been invited as a would-be purchaser to examine a ring in the hand of a seedy-looking man, and, if he persists, I simply say, 'I live in a dosshouse', and he does not waste any more time on me.

Then there is the razor-man, with his very cheap razors, which look so very good. It is generally in public-houses where the razor-man succeeds. Producing a fine-looking razor, he invites inspection, and when it meets with approval he offers it for sale. If he cannot get more than three times its worth, he is in bad luck indeed.

Then there is the man who carries a few cheap spectacles, which never cost him more than twopence-halfpenny a pair. At night this man finds victims in public-houses, and by day the ladies must suffer. Sometimes he carries a few laces, pins, and needles, etc., so as to get a few coppers at places where spectacles would not be needed. When an elderly lady answers the door, he, after a while, introduces the spectacles, taking them from his inside pocket. It is more than probable that she uses glasses to read and sew, even if she is not wearing them then.

In a case of this kind women, also men, are very curious, and they cannot resist the temptation to try the glasses, even though they are well suited with what they possess. Moreover, it is well to have several pairs of glasses, in case of accidents.

Now, sometimes a very common pair of glasses will suit better than costly ones for which the eyes were tested; even as a brass watch may keep better time than a gold one, or a pair of ready-made boots fit better than a pair made to order. If the old lady is satisfied that she can see as well as with her own, the glasses at once assume value, and this is known to the pedlar, for he never mentions a word about price until he hears her verdict. First she tries one pair, and then another, until she confesses that one pair in particular suits her eyes. On hearing this the man gives his price, which is according to what he thinks the woman can afford. If she can afford to make a purchase, she does, and tells him that she can see better with his eighteen-penny glasses than with a pair for which her eyes were tested, and which cost her seven shillings and sixpence, or more. And these spectacles cost the pedlar two shillings and sixpence per dozen.

A little originality converts a common beggar into a great one. When I was in the Welsh hills, where common lodging-houses were scarce, I found a house to my liking, and, seeing that there were a number of good-sized towns near, within three or four miles, determined to make it my quarters for a month or more, and thoroughly work the country around. I was selling laces at the time, and on my visit to one of the towns, I had remarkably good luck. Seeing a long street, I called at every house and received in all one shilling and twopence for my trouble, with the sale of four pairs of laces, which cost me less than twopence. I mentioned this to a fellow-lodger, who had been staying at the house for several days. When at his request I described the position of the street, he said, with a quiet smile: 'I got eight shillings and sixpence out of that street'. 'What were you selling?' I asked, thinking he must be in a large way of business, and wondering why he lived at a common lodging-house. 'Nothing', he answered, to my amazement; 'it was all profit'. This made me curious, for I knew that he, being a man apparently unafflicted and in good health, could not be very successful as a plain beggar. Before we went to bed this man gave me a letter to read, and in this letter it said that he was one of the strikers at M—, and that he had a wife and four children to maintain, and ended with a polite and dignified request for assistance. With this letter he did his business, simply handing it to whoever answered the door, with the request that they would take it in and read it. His time was night, when the whole family were at home, probably two or three working sons and the father; and when he could go from door to door without attracting notice.

Who could insult this man with a common penny? No doubt two or three people that had given me pennies refused this more ambitious man; but others, who thought a penny quite enough for me, gave him sixpence or a shilling. The letter – what originality! It did not give a servant chance to dismiss him, for she had no suspicion of his wants; and it did not give one of the family power to speak for all. And yet, in spite of knowing these tricks, I still continued the far less profitable traffic in laces.

Beggars

Chapter XXXII: Lady Tramps

Almost all tramps who travel alone object to women in a common lodging-house. Even the landlord of such a place soon learns from experience that women take out in accommodation the worth of their money, for they make the place too much of a home. If they are bad wives they are continually squabbling with their husbands, or scolding their children; if they are good wives they are always cooking, or covering the limited number of seats and tables with sewing material, or surrounding the fire with newly washed clothes; and the poor bachelor, who is more indifferent to cleanliness, and often prefers a slice of bacon quickly done to the labour of cooking vegetable meals – this poor bachelor complains not only that he cannot get near the fire, but that there is not enough room on the tables to lay his food, which is not often the truth.

As for the landlords, they are becoming more bitter every day, and these unfortunate women now find it so difficult to get lodgings, that they dare not visit any town haphazard, but must make enquiries of their fellow travellers as to accommodation for women. Often they hear, to their disappointment, of houses that formerly lodged women being changed into houses for men only. And if these women have children, matters are still worse, for they are objected to on that account. It is therefore not the least wonder that when a man, his wife, and two or more children, succeed in being lodged, they are loth to leave that town until they have tapped it thoroughly – north, south, east, and west, house and shop; and sometimes they remain so long in that one town – perhaps three months or more – that their faces become known, and they are not supposed to belong to a tribe of wanderers. It is in the summer months, when the nights are warm, and they are independent of lodging-houses, that they prove themselves to be true travellers.

Perhaps it is because women are so much better beggars than men that they are disliked both by bachelor beggars and lodging-house keepers. The former know well that if a woman once starts in a street, she will carry all before her – money, clothes, and food; and the landlords know that a woman is so successful that she is soon back again in the lodging-house; in fact she is often there twenty-three hours out of the twenty-four. Whereas the man, however good a beggar he may be, is absent several hours in a day, for he not only takes much longer than a woman to earn a living, but he is fond of standing at street corners, and sometimes he visits a library. The woman is instinctively inclined to make the place a home, but the man more often uses it simply as a place wherein to eat and sleep.

The woman, whether she has little ones or not, is always believed when she claims to have a family, and she receives wearing apparel for them, and food. The former she sells cheaply to the poor but more respectable class of people that live in the locality of cheap lodging-houses. But the man can never do business with children in the spirit; he needs them in the flesh at his side, or he is not believed to be a father.

After a woman has been on the road a little time and become familiar with lodging-houses and begging, she finds little difficulty in maintaining a husband that will neither work, beg, nor steal – especially if she has a child for the poor fellow to look after; to wheel in a box, when he must take great care to stop in front of the house where his wife is. The most hard-hearted cannot withhold their charity, for the child's sake. As soon as the man hears the front door open, he must become very interested in his offspring, and move in a circle round the box, trying to make the child more comfortable. His solicitude is almost certain of reward, for the lady of the house cannot fail to see this, and her tender heart overflows in pity for the whole family. 'Whatever his faults are', thinks she, 'he undoubtedly has a father's feeling for the poor child'. Of course the father is as fond of his child as any other father would be, and he would do anything in reason for it – anything, except work.

Another objection lodging-house keepers have to women lodgers is that when they begin a quarrel they are so long in bringing it to an end, especially if under the influence of drink. Whereas in the case of men it is often a short violent tussle of two or three minutes – fifteen minutes would be unusual for two untrained men – and that is the end of it, for neither one has a wish to renew hostilities. It is all over before a constable can be found, much less dragged unwillingly to the battle ground.

'Yes', I heard one lady lodger say to a landlord, who had threatened to eject her for speaking her mind – 'Yes', said she, 'and if I had Liverpool Nora and Brummagem Sal at my side, instead of this' – pointing to her husband – 'we would soon see who's who in a very short time'.[35] Some time after I had the pleasure of meeting Liverpool Nora, and my opinion is that if Brummagem Sal was as high-spirited and brawny as that lady, well, it would be folly to aggravate them singly, much less the twain.

There is one man who favours the presence of women, and that is the true working-man, who is travelling for work, and after paying his last few coppers for a bed, sits hungry in the lodging-house kitchen, for he is a poor beggar indeed. As a rule the men are indifferent, but these women always guess his secret and pity him. They watch, and if they see no sign of food cooked, or to be cooked, it is not long before he is asked to have a basin of broth or stew, and, if he accepts, the other women – being now correct in their surmises – supply him with bread. In fact, after this initial movement, he is certain of a full stomach as long as he remains at that particular house. Many a poor fellow would have gone supperless to bed, and begun another weary day's march without breakfast, were it not for some thoughtful and unselfish beggar woman in a lodging-house kitchen.

Now, as I have said, five women under the influence of drink are less likely to go quietly to bed than twenty or thirty men in the same condition, and that is the landlord's one just objection to female lodgers. With regard to his other objections they are of little account; for, though these women are in the kitchen almost the whole day, continually using the cooking utensils and the fire, do they not wash the former and keep the latter's hearth clean? If he had all male lodgers he would have to keep a man or woman to do these things, or either he or his wife be kept busy; for no lodger, whether it be man, woman, or child, can be expected to do these things themselves, after paying for accommodation. The truth of the matter is that these landlords are like a good many others – they want both rent and possession; and it is the limited number of these places – especially for families – that makes these men so independent.

Sometimes, where the accommodation is outrageously bad, the woman lodger stores her resentment until it serves her purpose, and, the morning she is going away, she will often make an hour's delay to tell the landlord her opinion of his place, and he never likes to hear the truth; whereas men come and go, and are not so particular.

On one occasion I had the pleasure of hearing Irish Molly speak

---

35. Brummagem Sal is presumably from Birmingham: Brummagem, now a local name for the city, was until the early twentieth century a largely interchangeable alternative. It gives rise to the colloquial term for the city, 'Brum', and for a local and his or her accent, 'Brummie'.

her mind to a landlord who begrudged coke for the kitchen fire, making it necessary for lodgers to bring in pieces of wood, picked up in the streets. Molly, her husband, and two children, had been here for two weeks, and, having thoroughly begged the town and its surrounding districts, were to seek fresh quarters on the morrow. But Molly swore the night before that she would not leave until she told the landlord what she thought of him. At nine o'clock on the following morning, they were ready to leave, and in spite of the husband's hurry to be off, Molly would not budge until she saw the lodging-house keeper. At last that gentleman entered the kitchen, and Molly at once rose to her feet, and set on him like a fury. For a moment the man was astonished, and tried to pacify her, but failing to do so, he hurriedly left the kitchen, and took refuge in his private room. Irish Molly at once followed and, standing outside, emphasized her words with her fists on the door. For ten minutes she hammered and abused; and the men and women in the kitchen encouraged her with their laughter. 'I shall send for a constable', shouted the landlord from behind the door. 'Send for fifty', cried Molly. 'I shall have you locked up', he shouted. 'Come out, and be knocked down', cried she.

Now it happened that Molly's husband and two children had stood waiting at the front door all this time. More than once he had asked her impatiently if she was coming, and at last, receiving no answer, went away with the children. Love in Molly's bosom was stronger than revenge, for she at once prepared to follow them. But, wishing to give the lodging-house keeper a new specimen of her powers, she sang him one verse of a ditty, beginning, 'O, I am waiting for you, love'. After which she danced the chorus down the wooden passage, arriving at the front door just in time to give it the final high kick.

Chapter XXXVII: The Sport of Fame

People have professed themselves amazed at my past life, and perhaps I can amaze them a little more by relating what great sport I and Fame have had; how she coaxed me into making several attempts to enrich the English language – some people think the attempts successful – and how she served me afterwards.[36] Other people can be amazed at my past life, but my turn to be amazed comes now. The world has had its revenge for the few years I made it keep me as an idler.

In fact I have found Fame to be the most amusing companion I have ever had. She has placed me in such a position that I am now regarded as a liar, a miser, and a woman-hater. I am considered to be a liar by those who have read so much about my work, and who at last begin to doubt when I say that Fame in England does not pay so good as begging in America, and that a very small income of my own supports me. They cannot believe this to be possible after reading such noble accounts of my work – therefore I am a liar.

Again, I am regarded in the neighbourhood as a miser and a woman-hater because I do my own cooking, washing, and housework, when there are plenty of women around that would be glad of such work. Of course, these things are not done thoroughly and well, or I would have very little time to make attempts to enrich the English language. The truth of the matter is that they are so ill done, that I have had to write and stop several people from coming to interview me, because of spiders that often rope me to the ceiling, Jacky Longlegs that dance on my head, and – fleas. I am quite used to these things now, and take little notice of them, regarding them indeed as peculiar to the house of Fame.

Again, see what fun there must be when a man, grown famous, receives scores of letters, most of which address him as 'Esquire' – 'Esquire', mark you, and living in a three-shilling-a-week cottage! How his Majesty's proud servant in uniform must be amused at this,

---

36. This is the only chapter in *Beggars* to deviate entirely from the book's eponymous subject – ostensibly, at least. It is perhaps a plea for financial support from wealthy admirers, and hence a sort of beg of a different and subtle kind.

knowing that a man who lives in a cottage no larger than his cannot be of much consequence. He knows full well that innocent people far away mistake such a man for a fine gentleman, and he is apt to laugh at times, and in his serious moods to pity him. He has seen inside the cottage of this man, called 'Esquire', and he saw nothing but bare walls and a few common things on the floor. If the poor man of genius said that he had enough praise to paper his walls, he would be laughed at for taking more pride in that than in a nice, comfortable home; and the idiot deserves to be laughed at, and to hang his head for shame.

Nothing worse could befall a living writer than to be compared to the mighty dead. It is most certainly a great compliment, and a great help to a man's spirit, but the consequence is apt to be fatal to his flesh. The mistake is that people are likely to think of him as one dead, and, of course, dead men need no food, clothing, or rent. Being regarded as one dead, he is naturally not thought of when there is anything given away; and the vast multitudes of powerful English people who are so eager to reward struggling genius – foreign or native – must, in consequence, overlook a man so highly rated.

All this is quite natural, but it is very amusing. It is very amusing to receive by post a request for one's autograph when one is in the act of washing a dirty pair of stockings, and lucky to have them to wash.

In spite of leading a lonely life, I do not often talk or laugh aloud, but I did on this occasion. It was that merry kind of laugh a man makes when he has just had a letter to say that he is ruined and a beggar, and while he is in the act ·of reading it his wife comes into the room and says, 'George, I want ten pounds for a new dress'. He has read the letter, and he has heard his wife's words, and he shrieks with merry laughter – as I did.

I know well that a man of genius has shivered on a winter's night, in a bed with insufficient clothing, in spite of using all his wearing apparel, after having received that day a noble tribute from the press, in which a well-known critic said he was unrivalled by his contemporaries. That he lay all night shivering with the cold, and expected to be poor Cock Robin before morning.[37]

True, a man's first book of poetry may run into a second edition, but people should not write and congratulate him on his success before they know what that means. He may have received a cheque that never mentioned pounds, only shillings and pennies, and perhaps

---

37. i.e. dead – though in the song 'Cock Robin' (Roud 494) he had apparently been murdered with a bow and arrow.

Beggars

far more pennies than shillings. Of course, these are the impish tricks of Fame, and people can hardly be blamed.

But the innocence of this world has often annoyed and surprised me. A man, who knew my circumstances thoroughly, was so little astonished to know how I could buy provisions, coal, oil, wood, clothes, boots, etc. etc. etc., and to also answer a kind world's forced correspondence – he, I say, was so little amazed to know how all these things could be done on a paltry few shillings a week, that he suggested it would save me much time and trouble to hire a woman once a week to clean the place; and that it would only cost two or three shillings; I did not answer him, for I was very much afraid of having one of those merry laughing fits that have come on me so often since I have been the companion of Fame.

I shall never forget the day when I was compared to the great Daniel Defoe. At that time I could not spare money for a pair of stockings, so I tore an old shirt in strips and wound them round my feet, as tramps often do. Several times I noticed that people glanced down at the feet of the second Daniel Defoe, but I could not think how they could possibly know of my self-made stockings. In fact Fame was having such sport with me on this occasion that I had forgotten all about them. The name of Daniel Defoe had had a wonderful effect on me; it had put fire under my feet, and a steel rod in my back.

While I was marching along in this stiff frame of pride, a little girl came running forward, and said, 'Please, sir, you've dropped something'. Looking on the ground I saw, to my amazement, that one of the toe-rags, which had unwound itself, was lying in sight, but still attached to my boot.

But what amused me more was to think that it had been trailing on the ground for a considerable time, and that I had passed several ladies; and one of them I was beginning to be interested in, for she had often looked at me as if she knew I was famous. This is only one of the many funny little things that have happened since I have been compared in England to the mighty dead, and you can imagine my laughter.

The following day a great literary paper praised my work, and said that it deserved its success, and that no man would envy such a writer a four storey mansion in the West End. Alas! a few days after this I received a letter to congratulate me on my success, which made special mention of my four-storey mansion; whereas at the same time I was living in a small cottage with no more furniture than a little boy could lift, and a friend[38] was paying my rent.

Of course, we know very well that nothing can be done for genius. Unfortunately, Nature does not mark him at birth, or we could soon put an end to him; and not only save the State worry, but, better still, save him from the cruel sport of Fame. If we give him twenty pounds, what will he do with it? Will he open a fish shop or buy a milk round? Not he; he has not the sense to do anything of the kind. The idiot will buy books, and idle his time away at writing, and his twenty pounds is soon gone, and the money is wasted. 'But if he enriches the English language?' one suggests. Ha! ha! tell that nonsense to an Organized Charity, and hear their opinion. No, he had his chance to open a fish shop and make a living, but he sat down and idled his time away at writing.

For all that we cannot allow this poor wretch to suffer; but what, in the name of goodness, can we do? I suggest this: no sooner is a man acclaimed as a genius, and compared to the mightiest dead, than the State should at once supply him with a distinguishing uniform; so that he would not only be sure of clothes, but would also be able to command the respect of strangers, however humble his circumstances are. Not only that, but the vast multitudes of powerful English people who are so eager to reward genius would then have an opportunity to recognize him in the street, and assist him with cheques, banknotes, etc.; which the man of genius – poet, painter, musician, no matter what – could take with dignity, as his due, and not be expected to demean himself by a great show of thanks. All he would then have to do would be to walk abroad, and give his address to such rich people as accosted him, so that they could send to his house food ready cooked, clean bed-clothes, money for rent, and other things.

---

38. Edward Thomas, principally. See 'Introduction'.

Beggars

Chapter XXXVIII: Beggars in the Making

I often feel upset to think that these articles on begging may rob honest men of charity; that people will become under the impression that beggars are born instead of made; aye, even born full-fledged, without having had childhood or youth.[39] I would not like people to think that every man that knocks at their door is a professional tramp; or every voice they hear singing in the street is that of an impostor. It must be confessed that the latter is very probably one, seeing that a man either has to be on the road a long time before he takes courage to sing in public, or must be under the influence of drink. I have seen in provincial towns as many as four men singing together. In a case of this kind, they are almost sure to be real out-of-works, and the reason they sing instead of beg houses is that they cannot all four go to one house, and individually they lack courage; but they can sing all together, each one getting courage from the presence of his companions.

People never give it a thought how difficult it is for a stranger to get work, even where there is work in abundance. In new countries[40] things are different; a man is hired at once, without a question of name and address. But in our old countries masters will not hire strange tramps, until they are at the last extremity. I have seen, this last summer, almost within a stone's throw of me, a farmer let his hay be spoilt by the rain, through having insufficient labour, and refusing to employ one or two of the many poor fellows that came looking for work. He, and the few men he had, worked day and night, rather than he would hire a stranger. No doubt he expected Providence to withhold the rain for his sake, and she, kind soul, gave him more than two weeks' happy sunshine, quite sufficient if he had not been too greedy to do as much work as possible himself, and pay away little to others. So the rain came, and he suffered in consequence. If people knew the number of men of this kind there are in the land, they would not be so hasty in telling tramps that the farmers are busy with their harvest,

39. This is the final chapter in *Beggars*, which explains the concluding tone Davies adopts here.

40. i.e. the New World: countries such as the US and Canada, where Davies had had so much experience.

and are in sad need of men.

Although I have met several men and women that could claim to being born beggars, having been born of beggars on the road, yet for all that, people must not think that this is quite common. One time I met one of these in Bedfordshire,[41] and he recommended me to a good row of houses, which he advised me to call at that evening. What this man did not know about begging was not much. After doing business in several streets, and finding trade very quiet indeed, I made up my mind to call at that row of small cottages on my way back to the lodging-house. It was then almost dark, being winter, and I could not well make out my surroundings. However, I went the whole length of the row, and was only refused at one cottage. Two of them gave pennies, one gave a halfpenny, one gave three farthings, and two gave food. This was certainly not bad, in so short a time, and from such humble dwellings, and considering the ill-luck I had had at rows and rows of fine villas. That night, when I was in the lodging-house kitchen, my born beggar asked me if I had called at the cottages, and, if so, how they had treated me. 'Splendid', I answered, with a smile of gratitude, for it is not often that a beggar will give information of this kind to a stranger. 'The almshouses are always good', he said, in a whisper. 'Almshouses!' I ejaculated, with astonishment, and a good deal of annoyance. 'Yes; you will always find them good', he continued, with the utmost unconcern, and beginning to whistle a popular tune. This man was a born beggar, without the least shame.

But men of this kind are rare, and people must not forget that the man who stands before them has gone through the various stages – from a respectable working man with a home, to a man without employment, who is looking for work; one that must either beg or starve, who has wandered from his native town, where his friends are, to places where cruel Rumour has said abundant work is to be had. For three or four months he is an honest seeker of work, but after that despair makes him indifferent. He gets disappointed so many times, running here and there, at the recommendation of people that would do him a kindness, and others that tell him lies to get rid of him – he gets disappointed so often that in a short while he will not go out of his way at all, although he says that he will do so. He soon begins to see that there is not very great difficulty in getting enough to eat and a few coppers for his lodging, and, of course, the consequence is that he soon becomes contented with a beggar's lot. It will not be long after this change of feeling that he will be heard to say in a

---

41. A small, landlocked county in south-central England.

lodging-house kitchen, while he is drinking hot tea and eating fresh toast – 'Who's looking for work, eh? Not me!' But people must remember that this man may come to beg them when he is in the first stage, and desirous of work, and is therefore a well-deserving man.[42]

The fact of the matter is that no outsider can tell a beggar from an honest seeker of work. A woman gives a man charity because he talks nice and approaches her in a respectable manner; and she believes him at once when he says that he has only been out of work six weeks. The dear lady cannot see that he has not a thing on his body that was bought by himself. His boots are two sizes too large, and have turned up at the toes; his coat is too short, and his waistcoat is too long; his trousers were made for a fat man, not to mention a shirt that either cannot be buttoned at the collar, or could be buttoned around two necks like his. Even if the lady or gentleman noted these things, they could not read any tales in them, and it would never occur to them to try to do so. Now, seeing that this man is so ill-fitted, it plainly shows that all his things are begged; and seeing that clothes last a man a considerable time, and that this beggar has nothing of his own, is sufficient proof that he must have been on the road six months at the least.

Of course, there have been cases of men starting on the road with good clothes and boots, which they had to sell almost at once for food and lodging at a second-hand shop. The dealer that buys must give these men substitutes to cover their nakedness, and these old things would be hardly likely to fit well. This would account for the strange appearance of a few men, but very few; for when men start on the road they are so full of confidence in getting work soon that they do not dress in clothes good enough to sell, but leave them at home, or in their lodgings, to be sent for when they are settled.

One way to tell a beggar who has been on the road a long time is to employ the slang of the road, which few people can do. When a beggar came to my door the other day, he first asked for a drink of water. I gave him this, and had a penny ready in my hand to give him when he returned the glass. I may as well say here that I never refuse these men a penny, poor as I am, and whatever he is to my judgment. If I think he is a working man, he gets the penny out of pity and sympathy; and, if I judge him to be a real beggar, I give it to him out of admiration. However, this man drank the water and then – not to my surprise – asked for a mouthful of something to eat. With a smile

---

42. Davies discusses this process in greater depth in his article 'How it Feels to be Out of Work', included in this book.

I gave him the penny and prepared to shut the door. But this man was a true beggar, for getting a penny so easy, without having to talk for it, emboldened him; so he began in a ready voice to lament his old clothes, and to ask me if I could assist him with others. 'Look here', I said, with deliberation, and looking him straight in the face – 'Look here, matey; if I could patter[43] as good as you I'd go on the toe-be[44] to-morrow'. For a moment he seemed taken by surprise, and then he drew his hand down over his face, in an attempt to wipe out a smile; but it was of no use, for the next moment he stood grinning from ear to ear.

'I see you know the biz, gov'nor', he said, going away; but you know very well that sixteen farthings for the feather[45] takes some getting'.

---

43. Talk.
44. On the road.
45. A bed, in a lodging-house.

The True Traveller *covers much of the same ground as* The Autobiography of a Super-Tramp, *though with greater emphasis on Davies's wanderings in England, and there is some continuity of narrative between chapters (unlike in* Beggars). *The book is often far less guarded than either of the earlier volumes, perhaps including some of the tales of encounters with prostitutes that Thomas and Garnett had successfully encouraged Davies to leave out of his first prose book. Davies clearly sympathised with prostitutes (whom he variously refers to here as 'courtesans' and 'women of fashion'), and he tended to enjoy their company in more ways than one. Moreover, as Lawrence Normand points out, 'The book implies that the true traveller is not simply one who begs for a living, but one who lives a sexually free and unencumbered life.'[46] Normand goes on to claim that 'this broader image of freedom does not exclude women too from being true travellers', which is perhaps to overlook the fact that prostitutes are not necessarily in charge of their own lifestyle – are not necessarily 'sexually free' in the slightest, but might indeed be the exact opposite. Davies, however, is alert to this – albeit from the perspective of a man who is occasionally keen to pay for their services.*

---

46. Lawrence Normand, *W. H. Davies* (Bridgend: Seren, 2003), p. 90.

Chapter IV : The Woman in the Woods

Some time after leaving Chicago, I had a very strange meeting with a woman in the woods of Illinois, which ended much more pleasantly than it began. I had no money to pay my fare as a passenger, so I had jumped on a fast cattle train that was going west, with the intention of stealing a ride for a hundred miles or more. But unfortunately one of the brakesmen discovered me, after I had travelled about fifty miles, and told me that I would have to get off at the next stop. I was quite satisfied to do this, after having ridden so far, and told him I would. Of course I expected the first stop would be at a town, where I could wait for another train on which to try my fortune for the second time. But when the train began to stop and I could see no sign of any house, I began to get alarmed. At last, the train, which was now going very slow, left the main track and went on to a side one, where it came to a stop. I got off at once and began to look around, and then saw that I was in the wilderness, with no idea of the distance to the next town. The next minute a fast passenger train came along, and it was to let that train pass which had caused the cattle train to go on a side track. As soon as the passenger train had passed the cattle train began to move, and it was not long before I was left there alone, amazed and looking after it. This was very annoying, for a dozen trains might pass and not one of them have to take the side track, so that I would have to walk to the next town, which was likely to be from six to ten miles away. While I was thinking of these things, I caught sight of a boy some distance away, who was coming down the railway truck in my direction. As soon as I saw this boy I slid down on a sleeper at the side of the track and waited his approach, thinking he would be able to I give me all the information I needed. He had something in his hand, which I at first thought was a stick, but when he drew nearer I could see that it was a gun. No doubt he was going squirrel shooting, as boys do in that country, and was now making his way to the woods which were near me.

It was a considerable time before this boy reached my side, for he seemed to have his attention often drawn to sounds around him. However, at last he came, and I at once asked him how far it was to the next town. 'It is only about half a mile from here', he answered.

'Is it a large town?' I asked. 'Oh yes', he answered without hesitation. Of course I knew that it was hardly likely that this boy had ever been very far away, and would therefore have little idea of a large town, so I asked him about how many houses were there. 'More than twenty altogether', he said in a proud voice. I now knew that it was only a small village. However, what I wanted to know was whether any trains stopped there, so I asked him that question. 'Yes', he said, 'there is a coal-shute there, and a water-tank too'. When I heard this I was quite satisfied, for I knew that trains would stop there for either coal or water, and that it would be no difficult matter to catch a train there at almost any time. So I thanked the lad for his information, and he went his way.

At this spot, where I was now sitting, the railway track had been cut through a wood. Seeing this, I thought it a fine opportunity to retire out of sight for a few hours and sleep. I happened to have enough provisions on me for a couple of meals, and as I had had little steep the night before, I made up my mind to take things easy for a few hours. It was now about noon, and time for dinner. I knew that there would be a tramps' camp somewhere near, seeing that trains came to a stop not far away. So I began to walk up the track towards the town, looking for a path into the woods. It was not long before I saw one and determined to follow it. I entered the woods, and in a little while came to a small open space, where I saw several tin cans in which tramps had made coffee. But I did not know whether they had carried the water all the way from the village, or whether there was a spring in the woods. However, I soon saw another path leading out of the camp, and guessed right that it led to a spring. So I filled one of the cans with water and returned to the camp, where I at once lit a fire and prepared for dinner, after having which I intended to take a few hours' sleep.

It suddenly occurred to me that this would be a good opportunity to wash my shirt, which could be drying while I slept. The air was warm enough for that, even if I had no fire. So I stripped there and then, and in a pool made by the spring washed my shirt and socks, and soon had them stretched on sticks stuck in the earth within a few feet of the fire. After doing this I made my coffee, had dinner, and lay down to sleep. I made a pillow of my coat, and my arms were bare to the shoulder. However, that did not matter, for I was not likely to be disturbed by any other than a fellow-tramp. Even tramps had not been there lately, which I could tell by certain signs.

But I could not sleep after all, and was soon sat up in front of the fire, smoking my pipe and thinking of old acquaintances. I must have sat there for over two hours in that way, until about three o'clock, and was getting restless to be either on my travels or visited by human company. However, I did not want to leave my camp-fire and the water-spring until I had had the last meal of the day, which would be about six o'clock, so I lay down to make another attempt to sleep. Whether I should have succeeded or not I cannot tell. All I know is that I suddenly heard dried twigs breaking under someone's feet, so I sat up at once, prepared to greet whoever should come. Of course I did not expect any other than a squirrel-hunting boy, or a beggar that knew the camp, or was looking for one, as I had done. The sound of an axe carries a long way in the quiet woods, and as I had not heard that sound, I knew that there was no woodman within a mile or more from where I was. I was in hopes it was another tramp, for I was in need of a companion, not having had one for several days. The last companion I had had was a Scotchman called Sandy, who had been arrested in Chicago. He had started an argument on religion with an Irishman. It was late at night, and the three of us were standing on a street corner. The argument had continued for more than an hour when a policeman came forward and told us to go home. The Irishman wished us all good night and went his way, and Sandy and I started off in another direction. However, Sandy took a foolish notion to argue with the policeman, and turned back for that purpose. But the latter did not want to argue, and told Sandy to be gone. Sandy then wanted to know if we were not in a land of free thought and speech. The policeman could make no other answer to this question than by taking Sandy by the collar and making a prisoner of him. And that was the last I saw or heard of my friend Sandy.

As I have said, when I heard this sound I sat up ready to greet the new-comer, who I felt certain would be a fellow-tramp. But when I could see the new-comer through the trees, I saw, to my horror, that it was not a man, but a woman! I at once made a grab for my coat, in haste to cover my nakedness. Unfortunately I had turned the sleeves inside out, so as to save the cloth when I lay on it, for the coat happened to be a good one. The consequence of this was that the woman walked into the camp before I could get it on, and while I was still nervously fumbling with it. 'Don't be alarmed, my good fellow', she cried, laughing with amusement: 'don't be alarmed, for I am only come to gather a few sticks. But, seeing you here alone, I will now sit down and have a chat with you'. Saying this she sat down at the other side of the fire, with her two hands in her lap. I began to get more nervous than ever now, for I saw that she was quite indifferent to arranging her dress, and sat there showing her two legs with the utmost unconcern. I could not help noticing that, although her clothes were of little account, yet, for all that, her boots were tight and good, and she had on a fine pair of stockings, which fitted tight, and were worked in colours. I could also see that she was a fine stout woman of about thirty-five, and one that appeared accustomed to good living. Of course it did not surprise me in the least that such a woman had come to gather a few sticks. She had come not so much on account of economy, but because she had nothing else to do. But what alarmed me was to see her unconcern at the position in which she sat. It suddenly occurred to me that she must be crazy, and that someone would soon come looking for her. This was a terrible thought, for I knew that men in that country never went looking for lost people without first arming themselves with guns. And I was very much afraid that, when I was found in this woman's company, they would shoot me without waiting for an explanation. They would think that I had met her wandering on the iron track and then decoyed her into the woods. Again, even if they were willing to hear me, there was no accounting for what a crazy woman might say. When I thought of this I got up at once and took hold of my shirt, which had been hanging there dry for a long time. Of course I could not put it on while she was there, so I threw it over my shoulder, with the intention of carrying it a little way until I had a chance to dress. The woman understood my last thoughts and intentions, for she began to laugh, and then said, 'Don't be afraid of me, for I am not afraid of you. Have you just come from Chicago?' 'Yes', I answered, lighting my pipe at the fire, for I had no intention of staying any longer, in spite of her cheerful assurance. She was silent for a moment or two, and I was just on the point of saying good-bye, when she said in a clear, distinct voice, 'Do you know where Carrie Watson's house is?' When I heard this question I was astonished and too interested to leave until she had told me more. However, in spite of my burning interest, I was very careful to show none, and answered quietly, 'Yes, I know where Carrie Watson's house is'. 'If you do', she said, with a laugh, 'we can get on very well together, for I lived in that house for over six months. Come and sit at my side as close as you like.' This was a bold invitation indeed, and I felt somewhat confused in accepting it.

The woman she had named, Carrie Watson, was a well-known courtesan,[47] who kept a house in South Clark Street, Chicago. It was a fashionable house, with a large number of women there, and it

---

47. Prostitute.

was not unusual to see a carriage waiting near. It was so well known that it was not necessary for its courtesans to stand in the doorway or look through its windows to attract notice, as they had to do in other houses of that class. It was a quiet looking building, and no stranger would dream of the life inside, where a score of beautiful women were willing to sell their love to any strange man that had enough money. It was a very respectable sporting house,[48] where a man was as safe from being robbed as at his own home. For that reason there were no disturbances there, and the police were never brought to its doors through a man's complaints. In that house the liquor could be drunk without fear of its being drugged, and the women trusted more to the generosity of their visitors than to their own greedy tongues. Knowing this, men who visited the house often would not keep away if they had not so much to spend as when they were there before.

When I heard this woman in the woods say that she had lived in Carrie Watson's house for over six months, I looked at her with a great deal of interest. I knew that a woman would have to be attractive indeed to hold a place in a fashionable sporting house of that kind. She would not only be chosen for beauty, but for her charm and manners as well. Thinking of this I looked at my fair companion with more interest, and I could then see that she was a fine-looking woman indeed. If she had been dressed in good clothes, she would have looked far different from the common village woman that had come to gather sticks. She was a fine, magnificent looking creature, I could see that now.

I sat down at her side, with the intention of letting her have her own way, and to take no liberty of my own accord. However, there was no necessity for me to make the least advance, for I was no sooner within her reach than her arms were around me, and I was kissed and hugged until I could not help returning her passion. 'I am not particular about gathering sticks to-day', she said at last; 'to-morrow will do for that'.

After a time I asked my strange companion to tell me something of her life, for I was wondering how an attractive woman that had led a gay life in a large city could be now settled in a small village which no doubt was quiet and dull. She only took a few minutes to tell her story, which was quite simple and clear. She was born in the village where she now lived, which was about half a mile away, and where she lived until her twenty-fifth year. Then she married a

---

48. Brothel.

poor man of the neighbourhood, but was sorry for it soon after. They had only been married twelve months when they began to quarrel seriously, and she threatened to leave him. However, they managed to live for three years in that way until one night he struck her. There were no children to grieve over, so she left the house the next morning and went to Chicago. As soon as she arrived there she went to a music-hall. While she was there she got into conversation with a woman she sat next to, and told her her history. This city woman had a good look at the fine-looking countrywoman at her side, and then made an offer to introduce her to a sporting house, which the countrywoman, having had several drinks, accepted with thanks. So they both left the music-hall together, and it was not long before the both of them were in Carrie Watson's house, where the city woman was a courtesan. This countrywoman stayed there over six months, and then, being tired of a fast life, and having saved a little money, returned to her husband. He was very glad to see her again, so she settled down with him to a quiet life, without letting him know the life she had led while she was away from him.

When she had finished her story it must have been about five o'clock, and I told her that however much I enjoyed her company, she must leave, or someone would come looking for her. So she left, saying she would like to meet me again some day in the future.

It was a most extraordinary thing to meet a woman of that kind in the woods, far from any large town, and I often think of it now, for this woman was so loving that, although I was a complete stranger, she could not help making herself a sweet nuisance, and I was very sorry to see her go.

For over three weeks after this I worked on a fruit farm, and finished the job with fifty-three dollars in my pocket. With this sum I made my way towards St. Louis, determined to have a few days' pleasure. I was well accustomed to beating my way on the trains, so that it cost me nothing to reach St. Louis, although that town was two hundred miles from where I had worked. I reached it in a couple of days, having spent only a dollar on the way, which was for food. I knew St. Louis fairly well, having been there several times before, and had no need to question strangers as to where to get what I wanted. The Levee, which was down at the waterside, being the Mississippi embankment, would be a fine place to see life and spend money. It was a free and easy place, where the police allowed more liberty than in any other part of the city. Street fights were common.

At this time I was very careful of myself, only drinking enough to keep myself cheerful and to see the inside life of the different saloons.

Some of the drinking-houses had white men and others had black, for no landlord could cater for both, seeing that his customers would not mix. It was a southern town, and the colour line was never allowed to go slack.[49]

As I was walking along a woman came to the door of a house and, seeing me passing close, asked 'Have you come to have your fortune told?' 'I have', was my answer, wanting a new experience. How much do you charge?' 'Only half a dollar', she said. This was not much, and I was always a fool with money, so I followed her into the house. When we were inside a room, she motioned to a seat, and I sat down. As soon as I was seated she brought another chair und sat close to me. She was a fine-looking woman, with large dark eyes and small white teeth. Her skin was dark, and I judged her to be either Spanish or Italian. However, she spoke good English, and appeared to have no difficulty in finding words to express her thoughts. I could not help being affected at being so near a beautiful woman as that, in spite of her cold ease.

I was surprised more than once at the truth of her words. For it was not long before she had taken my hand and begun commenting on its lines. After that she told my fortune by the cards, telling me, before they were cut, to wish for something. Now, what could I wish for? Here was a fine, beautiful woman sitting near me, with no one else in the house, that I knew of. I must confess that I stood in some awe of her, and yet l had the courage to make a certain wish.

After the cards had been spread she began to tell me something of my future, which could be believed or not, but not contradicted. However, she told me one thing that surprised me very much, which was that I would return to my own country and make a name for myself. If she had predicted wealth, as all fortune-tellers do, I would not have been surprised. This woman seemed to know that even that very day I had been indulging in ambitious dreams, in which common money played no part. After telling me this she rose, and I judged the interview to be over. I felt quite satisfied, especially as she had touched a part of my future that tallied with my ambition.

I had forgotten all about my wish, but before I had gone three steps it suddenly occurred to me. So I turned around and faced her again, where she stood standing in the middle of the room. 'What

---

49. Explicit racial segregation was widespread in America during Davies's time there, but especially so in the South, where the racial segregation laws known as Jim Crow laws would not be technically abolished until the 1960s. St. Louis is in Missouri, which had been one of the 'border states' during the American Civil War of 1861–5: slave states that did not declare secession from the Union.

about my wish?' I asked, laughing and turning red. I was in great confusion now, for I did not want her to know my wish unless she was a woman to gratify it. And yet, for all that, it was necessary that she should know it, if I was to be gratified, for I dare not mention it openly. So I thought there would be no harm in risking that question, and asked the second time, seeing that she was slow to answer 'What about my wish?' 'Oh, your wish', she said, looking at me sternly; 'how dare you mention it, you wicked man! This is how I answer it'. The next instant she had a dagger pointed at my heart. When I saw this I was filled with confusion. However, in spite of the drawn dagger and the sparkling of her white teeth, she did not look evil in any way. In fact, I thought there was a good-natured smile in her eyes. I came to the conclusion that she forgave my wish because it flattered her fine beauty, but that she was not the kind of woman to gratify it. That she knew what I had wished I had not the least doubt. She had told me other things so remarkable, that I believe she could feel my thoughts without looking into my face.

'I am very sorry to be so wicked', I said, as I was leaving; 'but with such a woman so near him a man could not possibly have any other wish.' When she heard this she replaced the dagger in her bosom, smiled and bowed, and then said 'Good-bye'. 'Goodbye', I answered, and left the house, disappointed that she had been too virtuous to gratify my wish, and pleased to think that she had not put so great a price on her virtue as to think I was a monster of sin, instead of a man of ordinary passion. She had proved that she was a broad-minded woman that understood and could forgive the desires of the flesh. I don't suppose I had been the first by a good number of men that had been tempted by her beauty, and the privacy around, to make a dangerous wish. However, she would have far more women than men as customers, for, it must be remembered, I did not go there of my own accord.

Chapter VII: A Night Out

After this trip to Scotland, I returned to America on the same boat,[50] the trip having lasted thirty days in all. For several years I wandered North, South, East, and West, during which time I made a few trips with cattle to Liverpool and London. But after this strange life had been going on for over five years, I suddenly made up my mind to return to my native land for good. What brought this determination to a head was the knowledge of having a sum of money saved – over a hundred pounds – resulting from a small income that I had let stand. So one morning I set sail from Baltimore and landed in Liverpool on the twelfth day. On the afternoon of that day I took train for South Wales. However, being young and hardy, I found it impossible to settle after so much travel abroad. So I soon grew tired of my native town, and made up my mind to leave it before my money was gone. There was still a considerable sum left, over sixty pounds, when I took train for London, arriving in that city some time about midnight.

Now while I was standing on a corner, leaning against a lamp-post and resting, I felt a touch on my shoulder, and turned to see who it was. To my surprise I saw a fine tall girl, richly dressed, standing there and holding out her right hand to give me something. Wondering what she meant, my own hand went forth mechanically, and the next instant two pennies were in it and the girl was going away at a great pace. However, I had seen in that short time that her face was painted, and I knew what kind of girl she was to be out alone at that hour. Of course, she had taken me for a poor homeless wretch that had to walk about all night and was penniless. No doubt my appearance had deceived her, for she could not see my white collar owing to my coat being turned up high; and she could not tell the quality of my cloth owing to the bad light. I began to go after her, but she appeared to be in a great hurry to get somewhere, and I did not like to shout, so I let her go her way. In a few moments after I saw a poor ragged woman sitting in a doorway, and I gave her the twopence, which I had kept

---

50. In the previous chapter, Davies mentions being in Glasgow, one of the British ports he visited when he took work as a cattleman on boats between America and Britain.

in my hand for that purpose.

In about an hour after this, I happened to be passing one of those coffee-stands that open at night, when another woman, not nearly so well dressed as the other, came up to me and said, 'Get yourself a cup of coffee', and slipped a penny into my hand. 'No', I answered at once, giving her the penny back 'no, you shall not pay for me, but I will pay for you'. She seemed greatly surprised at this, and said, 'I thought you had no home and were out for the night'. I made no answer to this, but invited her to follow me to the stand, which she did. While we were standing there drinking our coffee, she was very curious to know something of my affairs, for she had taken me to be homeless and poor. However, I did not satisfy her curiosity, but merely paid for a cup of coffee and a cake. After doing this, and drinking a cup of coffee myself, I gave her sixpence, for she looked so wretchedly poor. I told her then that I had but little money, but could afford that amount for her very kind intention. After I had left her I could think of nothing else but these two women, and wondering at their extraordinary sympathy for the poor. Of course, if they had seen a white collar and a fashionable tie they would not have made such a mistake, and would have approached me with a different purpose. Since these two incidents I have never been able to be other than patient with women of that kind, even when I have heard their loud mouthed abuse in public-houses.

Since those days my knowledge of life has increased, and I know well that whatever may be said of a woman of that kind, it must be confessed that her sympathy for the poor and the afflicted is most extraordinary. She is not blind or deaf to distress, in spite of the wild, careless frivolity with which she tries to attract strange men and keep them as long as they have money to spend, and perhaps rob them. No matter how well dressed she is, she never shrinks from dirt and rags, and she never ridicules the odd and the afflicted, as so many respectable women do. If a poor man with a double nose passes by, or with his two eyes looking at each other instead of straight on – he will set all the respectable shop girls tittering. But there is one who sees nothing to laugh at, and that is the woman who is an unfortunate. What draws her attention is his rags, his tired limp, and his troubled looks; and if she has a few pennies in her pocket, she will give him one. From the point of view of those poor homeless wretches in London, it is a pity that there are not more women of her class. The Salvation Army will shelter him for twopence, but who gives him the twopence? Other charitable institutions will give him bread and soup for a penny, but who gives him the penny? For it must be remembered that these very poor people are not beggars, and whatever they get is unsolicited. Then who is their support? The woman whose eyes never fail to see someone more unfortunate than herself, who cannot keep a penny in her pocket when she sees others in want.

How these women help one another is wonderful. The sacrifices they make look foolish in the eyes of respectability. These are the women whose hearts shed tears of blood when their eyes show no water and their lips utter no sympathy. Those ragged, wretched-looking old women whom we see so often in the streets of London, know very well who to appeal to. Not to the respectable lady, but to the girl who is so easily known by her roving glances. And many a homeless man knows that he is more likely to receive unsolicited charity at night, when only a few rakes and fast women are in the street, than by day, when it holds hundreds of respectable people. These are strange words, but the truth is in them, as I know well from my own experience of poverty.

As I was going along I saw a man coming towards me laughing, with a woman at his heels, who was scolding him. When they reached my side the man stopped and said to the woman, in a warning voice, 'I am going down this street, and if you dare to follow me it will he the worse for you'. Saying this he left Oxford Street and went down a dark narrow street adjoining it. 'I will follow you', screamed the woman. Then she turned to me, and said, 'What do you think of this man; he has been with me and now refuses to pay the shilling he promised'. 'Oh, he'll pay you all right', I answered, thinking the man was teasing her. For I could never think there was a man in the whole world that would be base enough to take advantage of a woman of that kind. This was that very low class of unfortunates who had no homes and were nearly always out in the streets, night and day. But I was deceived in this, for the man turned and threatened to strike her. Then he altered his mind, for she shrank back. He then started down the street, as he had said he would. 'Let us try him again', I said to the woman, beginning to follow after him. When the man turned and saw the both of us close behind him, he stood with his back to a wall, not knowing what to do. 'Why don't you pay this poor woman!' I asked. 'Surely you will?' 'Yes', screamed the woman in a voice so loud that I was afraid the police would hear her. 'Yes, you pay me before you go'. 'Go away, you', the stranger growled in a threatening voice, and made another motion to strike her.

I did not know what to do under these circumstances. First I thought to give the woman a shilling out of my own pocket, and persuade her to trouble about him no more. But after that I began to think it was a shame that a mean, unprincipled fellow like that should be allowed to have his own way. Of course, I dared not get mixed up in a fight and be arrested, for, as I have said, I had a considerable sum on me, and it would not be a very noble case to appear in. It suddenly occurred to me to risk the consequence of one attempt. As I have said, the man was standing with his back to a wall, so with one bound I sprang forward and with my open hand pushed his head back with all my force. There was a dull thud and then a groan, and the next moment the man fell to the hard pavement, where he lay without making another move. The woman no sooner saw the success of this than she was on her knees at his side, with her hands in his pockets. 'Come away', I said, 'or the police will he here'. While I was saying this she not only had the man's money in her hand, but his watch and chain also.

It was only a few steps to the corner and, when we reached it, I left her at once. As we parted I saw a policeman in the distance, and he was looking our way. But it was too late for him to know our business now, however much he might be interested. As a rule policemen have much sympathy for a girl of this kind. If she is not too bold, and is not drunk enough to make a nuisance of herself, very few policemen will interfere with her. Of course there is an occasional policeman of a different character, who will even suspect and arrest a respectable woman, when she stops a strange man to ask him a simple question – but such a policeman is one in a hundred. There have been a great number of poor men and women who have been assisted by police-men. Many a policeman, whose wages are less than thirty shillings a week, has given a poor man or woman as much as sixpence to get a bed with. The heart is big, indeed, when it does that.

There is a certain class of men that always take a delight in an-noying these unfortunate girls, talking to them and wasting their time, and having no intention of going with them. Some of these are drunken married men. But the very worst men are those – like the one I have mentioned – who go with these women and then refuse to pay for their enjoyment: or having paid for it, rob them of the money they have given. Such a man is the meanest and most despicable scoundrel in the world, and should never escape heavy punishment. He knows very well that he has nothing to fear from the law, and the only thing he has to put up with is the woman's tongue, which amuses the coward. And when her voice becomes too loud for his amusement, he takes to his heels.

Chapter XXI: Mad Kitty

When I had been at this lodging-house, which I found to be clean and comfortable,[51] about a week, I made up my mind to have a night out. I always like to see the night-side of London, once now and then, providing I am rich enough to rest on the following day and recover some of my lost sleep. With this intention I made my way towards the West, and found myself in Westminster Bridge Road early in the evening.

As soon as it became dark I could see that the courtesans were not only increasing in number, but were also becoming bolder, and I knew that their hour had come. In less than ten minutes, when I stood on a street corner, I had been passed and spoken to by several. At last one came boldly up to me and asked if I would go home with her for a short time. After I had told her no, she went away at once. I did not like the look of her much, for she did not appear to be very attractive. She was the very kind of girl that I would suspect of keeping a lazy man whom she foolishly loved or feared. These kind of girls can always he recognized, for they do not dress so smart nor look so cheerful as other girls that are free. A well-dressed courtesan never has a lazy, drunken scoundrel to live on her immorality, or she would have no money to spend on good clothes. And even if a rich admirer occasionally bought her clothes as an extra kindness, the man she keeps would soon have them in a pawnshop. I made no mistake in my opinion of this girl, for as soon as she had left me, I saw a common-looking fellow standing on the opposite corner, and he was watching her wherever she went. And when I saw her cross the road and speak to him, and then leave him to accost another man who took no heed of her, and then return to the corner loafer again – when I saw these things I knew for certain that I had judged right. After that I saw her speak to him several times, but he still remained standing where he was, watching her while she tried to stop other men. How I hated a lazy scoundrel of that kind! There should be no

---

51. The previous chapter ends with Davies recalling his arrival at a lodging-house in Whitechapel, London, which he immediately decides is agreeable because it is quiet and the first lodgers he encounters take no notice of him.

mercy for him when he is tried for beating a girl he is not married to, and who keeps him by her immorality. The unfortunate part of it is that a man of this kind is a thorough bully and threatens to murder a girl if she leaves him, which she often feels inclined to do. She could do much better alone, for she could dress better and attract rich men, and have good rooms to take them to. Whereas, having a drunken, lazy bully to keep, she cannot dress well, and must live in the commonest rooms in the slums. However, when a courtesan has no man to keep her poor, she has another enemy to take advantage of her. This is her landlady, who knows the great difficulty these girls have in getting rooms. So this landlady not only charges a girl for one bed-sitting room almost as much as will pay the rent of the whole house, but also expects the poor girl to pay for drinks and take her to a place of amusement. I was with a girl one night who only had one room, which was below the level of the street, and not very well furnished; this girl told me that her expenses ran to twenty-five shillings a week, for one room, the commonest board, washing, and attendance. And if she did not attend on herself and often do her own cooking, she would have often gone out hungry and returned to an unmade bed. The landlady was too proud to wait on a girl of that kind, but she demanded such money all the same. What could the girl do? It is so difficult for a courtesan to get rooms in a superior-looking street. And when she once succeeds she will put up with anything, and pay all she can, rather than explain to other landladies what she wants the rooms for, and the kind of living she makes. No wonder there are so many girls of this kind that will rob a man, when they are robbed so much themselves.

It was about twenty minutes past eleven, and I was standing at a bar, smoking my pipe, when all at once the barman – a serious-looking man who had not spoken one word all the time I was there – cried in a cheerful voice, 'Hullo, Kitty!' 'Hullo!', answered a girl's voice, in the same cheerful manner, and beginning to laugh. 'A glass of stout, Kitty?' asked the barman, beginning to draw it at once, as though he knew what her answer would be. 'Of course', answered the girl called Kitty, placing her money on the bar. I turned my head slowly, so as not to appear rude, to see what kind of girl stood at my side. 'Good evening', she said, laughing, as soon as our eyes had met. 'Good evening', I answered in her own pleasant way, for it was impossible to treat so friendly a girl in any other manner. When the barman heard this greeting he moved some distance off and did not speak again. He knew that she had business to do, and did not want to spoil it by idle talk, although he seemed disappointed in not being able to crack a few jokes with her. One look was quite enough, for I felt attracted to her at once, and asked if she would have another drink, which she did.

After she had had this drink she, of course, asked me if I would go home with her. 'Not to-night', I answered, 'for I have very little money'. Hearing this she laughed cheerfully and said, 'Never mind, perhaps we shall meet again'. In a few moments after this she left, waving her hand to the barman, who was standing some distance away. As soon as she was gone the barman came forward and said, 'Do you know Mad Kitty?' 'No', I answered, 'this is the first time I have met her'. 'She's an extraordinary girl', said the barman; 'I shall never forget the first time that I met her. I was not a barman here then, although it was in this house that I met her. In fact, I was standing there, where you are now, and the same thing happened to me as have happened to you, except that I went home with her and you have not.' 'Will you have a drink?' I asked, being interested in Mad Kitty, and wishing to know more about her. 'Thank you', he answered, and drew himself a glass of beer, which I paid for. There happened to be very few customers there at the time, and there was another barman standing idle, so that I knew my barman would have time to tell a story. 'What do you mean', I asked, 'by saying she's an extraordinary girl? Did she rob you, or get you into trouble of some kind?' 'Oh. No', he answered, 'she is quite honest, and you never need to be afraid of going home with Mad Kitty. As I have said. I met her in this bar and, after having a drink or two, we left the house together, just after midnight.' Saying this he took another drink of his beer, and then, leaning his two arms on the Bar, he prepared to tell the full story, which he begun without loss of time.

'As we walked along this girl Kitty was continually laughing, al-though her words were mostly serious. She seemed to be a wild, erratic creature that would be capable of any kind of mischief at an impulse. "I have never seen you before", she said, looking at me with her face shining with pleasure. "No", I answered, "neither have I seen you before". "You will always know where to find me now" she continued, "for I go into that house, where you met me, every night at about the same time. If you do not see me there, ask the barman if Mad Kitty has been in, and he will tell you. They all call me Mad Kitty." Saying this she began to laugh heartily. For a moment or two I thought that the girl was really mad, and was almost afraid to go home with her. But in a little while I came to the conclusion that she was only childishly wild and full of life. In spite of that, I began to wonder whether a girl like that would he safe; for those very merry

The True Traveller

girls are often apt to change suddenly, without sufficient cause. And when they do, they make so much noise over nothing that the whole neighbourhood must hear them. However, I thought I would risk it, so I walked quietly at her side, while she continued to talk and laugh.

'In about ten minutes we came to a side street, down which she turned, and I followed. It was not a very respectable-looking street, but I was not surprised at that. For Mad Kitty was not so well dressed that she could live in a finer neighbourhood, although she was far from being an untidy sloven. What had attracted me was her high spirits, and not her clothes. So that I was not much surprised to see that she lived in a mean, narrow street. For one thing I felt quite safe in her company wherever she might lead me. She had a reputation in the neighbourhood, as I could tell by the way in which the barman had greeted her. Moreover, she had told me almost at once that she was called Mad Kitty, and that she was to be found or sought in that one particular public-house. If she had intended to rob me, or get me robbed, or lead me into trouble of some kind, she would not have been so foolish as to tell me these things, I felt sure of that.

'When we got some distance down the street she stopped in front of a house, took a key out of her pocket and opened the door. "Don't make more noise than you can help", she whispered, as I followed her in. However, there was no light in the passage and, be as careful as I could, it was impossible for me to walk a strange place in the dark without stumbling now and then. In fact, when I was climbing the stairs, which had no carpet at all, I kicked it several times and made quite a noise. Each time I did so Kitty came to a halt and whispered "Sh!" I was somewhat nervous at this, for I was under the impression that her landlady, and others in the house, knew what kind of girl she was, and would expect to hear a little noise when she brought a stranger home at night. And, seeing that she was as careful as this, it entered my mind that they did not know what was going on. However, that fear soon vanished, for I knew that she could not keep her life a secret long, seeing that a man must be either seen or heard the next morning, when he leaves the house. And yet why was this wild, erratic, dare-devil girl so particular not to make the least sound? At last, after much care, we reached the top of the stairs and she opened a door that led into a room. It was dark in there too, so I stood waiting until she made a light. This was done almost immediately, and I then walked in, shut the door after me, and sat down.

'As soon as I was seated she came close to me and, placing her finger on her lips, whispered, "Don't speak very loud, for there is a boy lying dead in the next room". When I heard this I was startled, as you may well believe. I looked at her face, which for one moment had a very serious expression; and I was startled to see the difference in her, for she now looked like a woman of middle age. When she smiled she did not appear to be much over twenty, but when she had this serious look she appeared to be over forty. I had never before seen a smile make so much difference in a face. When she looked serious I could see that her face was full of lines, but when she smiled it was as smooth as a baby's. It was very fortunate for her that she was always smiling, for she would not be able to attract many men with her serious look. Judging these two expressions – how young she looked when she smiled, and how old she looked when she did not – I halted half-way and came to the conclusion that she was about thirty years of age. She told me, later in the night, that she was twenty-seven, which I had no doubt was right. However, this serious expression, which had surprised me by the difference it made in her, only lasted an instant, and I never saw it again.

"'I am rather surprised", I said, after a while, "that you have been allowed to bring a strange man home with you when there is a dead child in the house". "That cannot be helped", she answered in a low voice. "We must all live. My landlady is very poor, and must pay her rent to-morrow, and I must pay her my rent too. Business must go on, for we have to pay our way, whatever happens." I was sorry now that I had met her and accompanied her home, but it was too late to make other plans.

'When we settled for the night she began to tell me, as quietly as she could, what had happened, which I was surprised to hear. "It all happened because he was jealous that I took more notice of a baby than of him", she whispered, with a soft laugh. "He was only seven years old", she continued, "and was my landlady's youngest son. I was very fond of him and, to tease him, I used to make much of a baby belonging to another lodger that lives in the top room. When he saw this he used to get furious and said he would kill himself. 'Are you jealous', I used to ask him, 'because I am making much of the baby?' 'Yes', he said, 'I am, and I will kill myself'. After saying that he picked up a knife, which we had to wrench out of his hand. Then he got a rope and said he would hang himself, but his mother took it from him. But he still kept on saying that he would kill himself, and his mother had to put everything she thought would do him harm out of his way. But yesterday he found a bottle with poison in it, which he drank. When he began to feel pain he told his mother what he had done. She called me at once and said, 'Kitty, he has poisoned himself, run and fetch a doctor'. Before I went, I said to him. 'Were you jealous because I made much of the baby?' 'Yes', he said, 'and I have poisoned myself'. That was the last time I heard his voice, for when I came back with a doctor – I could not find one for a very long time – he was dead in his mother's arms."

'I was surprised in more ways than one when I heard this strange story. I could not help noticing, by the tone of her voice, that this simple, childlike, and mad-brained young woman took some pride that a life had been sacrificed for love of her – even though it was only a little boy of seven years of age. For she said again, after a pause, "He was jealous because I made more of the baby than of him, and when I asked him point-blank, he said, 'Yes, I will kill myself'".

'After saying this she was silent, but I thought I would ask her a question before she went to sleep. "Where did he get his knowledge from?" I asked. "Surely a child of that age would not be able to read papers and books and understand them". "Oh, that is easily explained", she answered. "You see, his mother used to take him to picture shows, where he would see such things done. He got his knowledge of stabbing, hanging, and taking poison in those places of amusement. He very often used to threaten to stab his mother, and one day he took a rope and hung the cat until it was almost dead."

'I said no more after this, but I could not sleep for thinking of the strange things I had heard. I knew that these courtesans were very fond of children and made every effort to win their love. That is the reason why they are never scorned by respectable mothers who are very poor. A respectable mother, who is very poor, is not ashamed to be seen out with one of these courtesans, for she knows that cakes or sweets, aye, sometimes clothes or boots, will be bought for the children, which she cannot afford to pay for herself. A courtesan will be her most faithful and practical friend, if she will allow it. While I was thinking of this, I heard Mad Kitty say distinctly in her sleep "Jealous because I made much of the baby. Poor little devil!" That was my experience with Mad Kitty the first time I met her.'

While the barman was relating this strange experience, he had to leave me several times, owing to customers coming in. In spite of that, I followed his continuations without much trouble. After he had done I paid for another drink for him and then left the house.

Chapter XXIII: The End

I ought not to finish these adventures without mentioning one strange girl that I met one day near the 'Elephant and Castle' public-house.[52] She was such an exception that I don't believe there was another courtesan like her in all London, big as that city is. I happened to be standing at a corner, when I had my attention drawn to a fine tall girl dressed in black, who was standing like a statue on the opposite side of the road. For a moment or two I thought she was a respectable girl waiting for a bus to take her home, or somewhere else. But when I looked around and saw several other men eyeing her with the same curiosity, I came to the conclusion that she was a courtesan, whose face was slightly known to them. Being very curious to look close into her face, I crossed the road, going towards her when her eyes happened to be turned another way. But just as I got near her she turned her head and, catching my eye, nodded and smiled. Of course I could do no other than raise my hat, but I did not stop. However, I had not gone ten steps when she was at my side, asking me if I wanted her company. For a moment or two I stood perplexed, not knowing what to say or do. At last I said 'Will you come across the road and have a drink and a chat?' 'Yes, thank you', she answered. With this understanding we crossed the road and entered the best bar of the 'Elephant and Castle', for this girl appeared respectable enough to take her place anywhere. When she was seated and we began to talk. I was not deceived in my first impression, for her voice was gentle, her manners quiet, and her conversation like that of a fine lady.

After we had had one drink, I pressed her to have more, but she firmly declined, saying, 'I drink very little, no more than I can help. I have not accepted your invitation for the sake of the drink, but in the

---

52. Elephant and Castle: a road junction (and, in common parlance, its immediate vicinity) in Newington, central London, only a few hundred yards from the lodgings at Rowton House, Newington Butts, where Davies lived for two years (see 'Chapter XXI: London' in *Autobiography* and included in this book). The area was originally named for a local inn called the Elephant and Castle. This was rebuilt in 1898, and is likely the inn Davies is referring to here, though there were in Davies's time several other such establishments in the area. The current pub with that name is on the ground floor of a small 1960s tower block.

belief that you will now come to my room'. This was quite new, for, as a rule, these kind of women will drink as long as a man cares to pay for it. Being curious to see what kind of a place this interesting girl lived in, I accompanied her at once, for she lived in a side street that was only a short distance down the Old Kent Road.[53] She told me that she was her own landlady, and only one other girl lived in the house, to whom she had let a room.

In a few moments we came to the house, which was very small and stood on a corner. This position was very convenient for her, seeing that she could use either the front or the side door at her discretion. On this occasion she turned the corner and used the side door, for several people happened to be coming up behind us. Not that it mattered much, for no one could tell but what we were man and wife. But it pleased her to be as careful as possible not to get too well known.

When I entered this girl's room and looked around it, I was amazed, for I saw books in every place. There was one hook lying open on a small table near the window, which, no doubt, she had been read-ing that day. I picked it up, being curious to know what it was, and found that it was an old copy of Burns. 'Are you fond of reading?' she asked, seeing what I had done. 'Yes', I answered shortly, for fear I would forget myself and tell her something that would make her inquisitive. 'So am I', she said; 'I am continually buying second-hand books. This copy of Burns was bought yesterday, and all I paid for it was threepence. In fact, very few of the books you see cost me more than fourpence, for they are all old and second-hand. I spend nearly all my time, when I am alone, in reading these fine works, instead of drinking in public-houses with other girls of my class. I go with as few men as I can possibly help. In buying and reading these books, I not only cultivate my mind, but also take better care of my body, which must be plain to you.'

I was quite surprised at meeting a girl of this kind, and respected her as much as though she had been pure. When I looked at her books, I saw that they were nearly all classics and mostly poetry.

I was very curious to know if she knew anything about the work of living authors, so I mentioned a few names, asking if she had read certain books by them. Although she had not, she not only knew the authors' names well, but also knew the names of their books and the nature of them, for she was a great reader of literary gossip and re-views. I asked her if she had ever heard of a certain book by a certain

---

53. About half a mile to the east of Elephant and Castle.

living author. 'Yes', she answered, 'I have heard about it, and have read several small poems by the same author when I have been reading magazines in a free library'. I was very pleased to hear this, and began to wonder whether I should tell her that I was the author of that book and those poems, or not. I was just on the point of giving way to that vanity when a sudden idea made me alter my mind. It occurred to me that she would naturally think that such a famous man must have plenty of money, and I did not want her to make a mistake of that kind, which would have caused her cruel disappointment. However, before I left her I gave her enough money to allow her to remain with her books for two or three days, without being driven by poverty to seek another strange man. She appeared to be quite surprised at this generosity, but I did not tell her anything about myself.

This differs from the three earlier autobiographical volumes in that it concentrates on an aspect of Davies's life after he had achieved literary success. It purports to relate one walking tour across part of southern Britain, a circuitous route from south-central Wales into south-central England. This gives the book a structure that prevents it from being a loosely connected series of anecdotes, though in fact it almost certainly conflates experiences from several such tours Davies made as what he called a 'literary tramp'. Davies liked taking such trips, packing as lightly as possible (he'd buy a second pair of socks after a week and discard the first, for example) and chatting with and giving money to tramps as he encountered them. Though he took the occasional train, on these sojourns Davies mostly travelled by foot – literally, in his case, of course. It speaks to his particular brand of fortitude that his preferred leisure activity involved so much use of his prosthetic leg – he often walked over fifteen miles a day – and that he only ever mentions this a few times, and then generally for amusement. He meets a young boy near Raglan Castle, Monmouthshire:

> 'Have you got a bad foot' he asked with a sudden interest, seeing that I did not walk like ordinary men. This was a question I had expected at the very beginning of our acquaintance. 'How was it done?' he asked.
> 'An engine ran over it', I answered.
> 'Oh, golly! Suppose it had been your head', he exclaimed.

(Chapter X: Playing for Coppers, p. 100)

Surprisingly, there are only very few indications that this travelogue was written during the Great War and that it reports on experiences that occurred during wartime; but this is a book of joyous escape. Davies can be evocative about landscapes, but the people he encounters are clearly of the greatest interest to him, and the book is full of unusual characters and circumstances.

In keeping with the title, some of the chapters begin with a poem or contain snatches of verse, often written by Davies for the purpose.

Chapter II: Children

As the clock struck nine on the following morning, I was leaving Carmarthen,[54] full of joy at the thought of going on and on, the uncertainty of where I would get my next meal, what kind of people I would meet, and where I would sleep that night. Being in this fine mood, I spoke to a little boy, whom I saw playing alone in the road, asking him what he was going to be when he grew up. Of course, I expected to hear him say a sailor, a soldier, a hunter or something else that seems heroic to childhood, and I was very much surprised when he answered innocently, 'A man'. However, I did not question him any more, but gave him a penny and passed on.

I was now without doubt a free man, and did not care whose company I had, whether it was a grumbling farmer or the lazy beggar that had left fleas in the farmer's barn.

When I got about a mile clear of the town, I made inquiries for about the third time, so as to make sure I was on the right road to Kidwelly. 'It is eleven miles to Kidwelly', said the man I inquired of, who was wheeling a bicycle, and whose clothes were shabby and patched. However, the next moment he, seeing me walk with a limp, very considerately reduced the distance, saying, 'It is about nine miles from Carmarthen to Kidwelly'.[55]

'Are there any villages on the way?' I asked.

'None of any consequence', he answered.

'The reason I ask', I said, 'is that I don't want to go hungry or thirsty on my way. If there are any inns, I can do well enough until I get to Kidwelly. Do you mind telling me if I pass any inns?'

'Yes, indeed you do', answered the shabby-looking stranger; 'but if you will take my advice you will keep out of places of that kind. I

---

54. In the first chapter, Davies describes travelling to Carmarthen, and an evening there. Carmarthen is a county town in rural south-west Wales, west of the industrialised South Wales Valleys, and the major Welsh conurbations of Swansea and Cardiff. Newport, where Davies was born, is east of Cardiff, and about seventy-five miles east of Carmarthen.

55. The tiny town of Kidwelly, known for its substantial Norman castle, is actually about ten miles south of the centre of Carmarthen by road, so presumably about nine miles from where the conversation occurred.

have not been inside one for thirteen years. If I had, I would not be the owner of this.'

With these words he pointed to his bicycle, which he at once mounted and rode off. When I was left alone I could not help laughing at the stranger's words, for the bicycle was old and rickety, and was not worth thirteen shillings. If that man, who was so ill-dressed, had nothing more than an old, rickety bicycle to show for thirteen years' total abstinence, it was not much to be proud of. The machine was worth, as I have said, about thirteen shillings, and he had been an abstainer for thirteen years. According to that he had saved a shilling a year, being one penny a month and a farthing a week.

Not long after this I went into a wayside inn and had a pint of ale, where I again inquired if I was on the right road to Kidwelly. On being told yes, I left and continued my journey. But that pint of ale plunged me into such a deep reverie, that it must have been nearly an hour before I came out of it. When I did so, I found that I was in front of another inn, which I entered, and again inquired if I was on the right road to Kidwelly.

'No indeed you are not', answered the landlord's daughter; 'you are now going to Llanelly.'[56]

'What's the name of this village?' I asked.

'This is Minke', she answered. The Welsh pronounce it Minker.[57] When I heard this I knew that I had gone wrong, for I had been told in Carmarthen that I must not go through Minke. However, although Llanelly was fifteen miles from Carmarthen, and it was up and down steep hills all the way, I made up my mind to reach it before six o'clock. I had intended to have made two days of my journey to Llanelly, Kidwelly being one day's walk and Llanelly the next. I was now making one journey of it, under wretched conditions, for it was drizzling rain, and I could not get my feet to grip the slippery road.

I could not help noticing the fine green banks at the side of the road, on top of which the hedgerows were allowed to grow wild. What surprised me was the number and variety of flowers that were

---

56. Llanelli ('Llanelly' is the anglicised and now obsolete form) is a town about nine miles south-west of Kidwelly and over fifteen miles from Carmarthen. The road south from Carmarthen splits just after the small village of Cwmffrwd, and the Black Lion Inn, Cwmffrwd is very likely to be the first inn at which Davies stopped. It is still running.

57. The village is correctly spelled Meinciau, and is over four miles south of where Davies must have made his wrong turn. The pub is probably the Black Horse, Meinciau, now a private house. It is notable that Davies here discusses 'the Welsh' as though he is not one of them at all.

to be seen. All my old favourites were there in abundance: daisies and buttercups, primroses, violets, bluebells, ground ivy, herb Robert, speedwell, milkwort, dandelion and strawberry blossom. There were also a number of other beautiful wild flowers, which I knew by sight, but whose names I could not remember.

When I got to Pontyates, about half-way between Carmarthen and Llanelly,[58] I saw a well-known name on the signboard of an inn, and made up my mind to patronize that house at once. So I entered and, going into the taproom, gave the landlady my order for a small portion of bread and cheese and a glass of ale. She thanked me and, when leaving the room, very considerately closed the door, so that I could not be seen by any others that came in. In a few moments Mrs E— brought me the usual amount of bread and cheese, for which innkeepers charge twopence, and a glass of ale, which costs three halfpence – threepence half-penny altogether. But I was not very hungry, and had only eaten two or three small mouthfuls when I felt surfeited. So I finished the ale, and finding Mrs E— inquired the amount I owed her. When I heard her answer, I was amazed at her impudence. 'Sevenpence half-penny', she said, looking me boldly in the face. I gave her a shilling without a murmur, wishing to God that I was dealing with William her husband.

I had never experienced such a bare-faced imposition in my whole life. It was so ridiculously in excess of the usual charge, that I grieve every time I think of it, in spite of my indifference to money. This woman thought I was a rich man, which surprised me. For not long before this a tramp to whom I had given a penny – he had not begged of me – asked in a kind, considerate voice, 'Are you sure you can spare it?' However, perhaps Mrs E— thought I was drunk, and did not know what I was doing.

I left this inn at an unfortunate time, for on looking down the road I saw about thirty children playing outside a building which I knew must be a school. There were also a number of other children in twos, threes and fours, coming up the road. I did not know how they would receive me, for in out-of-the-way places children often pelt strangers with stones. But when I got in the midst of them they only looked with a mild curiosity, and the oldest among them greeted me respectfully, saying, 'Good afternoon'.

What struck me was, that although they were talking among themselves in Welsh, yet, for all that, they addressed me in English. I asked one of the boys if he always spoke Welsh when he was out of

---

58. A large and well-appointed village a mile and a half on from Meinciau ('Minke').

school and he answered, 'Yes'. 'But', I questioned, 'your school lessons are in English, are they not? 'Yes', he answered.

Having reached Llanelly I went into an inn to have a drink and a rest before I went in search of lodgings. It was a quiet old-fashioned inn, for I was not yet in the business part of the town. When I entered I found it occupied by two very old men, with white beards, who were laughing like two little children. They had had a drop too much to drink, and were now standing up with their arms round each other's necks, and without the least reserve were saying how much they loved each other.

'Jim boy', cried one of them, looking lovingly into his companion's face, – 'Jim boy, I have known you now for forty years, and I have loved you ever since the first day.'

'Tom boy', answered the other with the same fond look, – 'Tom boy, I have always loved you the same. We have had many a drink together, Tom boy, and I hope, indeed, we will have many more.'

'Nothing will stop us, Jim boy; nothing whatever', answered the other, 'for I have never met a man that I loved better. No, indeed.'

I was somewhat confused at hearing two men speak in such a manner, and was very glad that they were too much occupied with each other to take notice of a stranger.

I slept well after my fifteen miles of up and down hill from Carmarthen to Llanelly.

Chapter VI: In Neath Valley

Between two rows of trees,
Here let me take my ease;

To see the light afar,
Shining like one big star.

Is it not fine to lie
With boughs to change my sky;

Alone in this green way,
And let my fancies play?

Now as a growing boy
Will sometimes stand for joy

Tiptoe behind men small,
And raise himself as tall —

So shall my fancy's eye
See none more great than I.

It was very pleasant to breathe the pure air and hear the birds singing on this bright morning in May.[59] I could lie on my belly in the grass like Nebuchadnezzar and feel more exalted than he felt abased.[60] I

---

59. Davies has travelled east, through the heavily-industrialised town (now city) of Swansea and its environs, to the open country beyond.

60. In the Book of Daniel, Chapter 4, we are told about Nebuchadnezzar having a frightening dream, and assembling the wise men of Babylon to interpret it. They do not impart its meaning. Daniel then comes before Nebuchadnezzar, and tells the king that the dream is a warning from God, and urges him to be merciful and humble. A year later, with Nebuchadnezzar showing no signs of increased humility, God banishes his kingdom and casts him among the beasts of the field. Eventually, a God-praising Nebuchadnezzar has his kingdom restored to him. Daniel 4:7 (KJV): 'Now I Nebuchadnezzar praise and extol and honour the King of heaven, all whose works are truth, and his ways judgment: and those that walk in pride he is able to abase.' The historical Nebuchadnezzar II ruled Babylonia from c.605–562 B.C.E., and was the

knew from report that I would pass through fine country on this one day in particular, and seeing that it was only ten miles from Neath to my journey's end, and I had all the day to do it in, I had an enthusiasm that I knew would last till the end. I was in no great hurry to reach Glyn-Neath, so when I came to Cadoxton, one mile from Neath, I stood for a while to admire the beautiful little church at the side of the road.[61] Seeing the quiet little churchyard, with the gate wide open, I went into it for a few moments, to look at the stones and graves. It was very quiet in there, and few people passed on the road to make me feel uncomfortable by being stared at for a stranger. I always like to read gravestones; and a very small stone, that has a grave no more than three feet long, where a child lies buried, always affects me more than large stones and monuments of full-grown women and men.

After reading a few stones I came to a large dark one, which I probably would not have read had I not been startled by one word in large capital letters on top. The word was 'murder', and when I read on I was astonished, for I had never seen or read anything like it before in any churchyard I had been in. Here was no quaint verse to smile at, and no mention of the virtues of the poor girl that lay dead in the earth. The whole writing was a cry of vengeance on the murderer, who had escaped justice and still lived. This is what I read: –

To record
MURDER.
This stone was erected
Over the body
of
MARGARET WILLIAMS
Aged 26,
A native of Carmarthenshire,
Living in service in this parish,
who was found dead
With marks of violence on her person,

most powerful ruler in the known world. He is credited with rebuilding Babylon into the greatest city of the ancient world, and creating its hanging gardens. He was also responsible for the Babylonian Exile of the Jews.

61. The Neath Valley, particularly its wild upper portion beyond Glynneath (as it is usually called), which Davies neglects to visit, is noted for its beauty and its numerous waterfalls. The distance between the towns of Neath (at the foot of the valley) and Glynneath is eleven miles. The village of Cadoxton, with its medieval church dedicated to St Catwg, is just north of Neath, and is now effectively a small suburb.

In a ditch on the marsh
Below this churchyard,
On the morning
Of Sunday, the fourth of July,
1822.
Although
THE SAVAGE MURDERER
Escape for a season the detection of man,
Yet
God has set His mark upon him,
Either for a time or eternity,
and
THE CRY OF BLOOD
Will assuredly pursue him
To a certain and terrible righteous
JUDGEMENT.[62]

When I read the last part of this stone, about the murderer, I was astonished. For up till now I had always seen that space allotted to a peaceful little verse that praised the dead for their virtues, and saying that they had fallen asleep in Jesus's arms, or something else that was tender and beautiful. On very rare occasions I had read something quaint, but nothing so terrible as this. As soon as I had recovered from my astonishment I came to the conclusion that it was the most honest writing I had ever seen on a gravestone, and after reading it again I said 'Amen' three times.

In about half an hour's time I came to the village of Aberdulais, where some very fine waterfalls are to be seen. I had been told of these falls, so when I heard them and located the sound I made my way towards them, for they were not many yards off the main road, although they could not be seen from there. But when I stood in a good position to see them I felt considerably disappointed, because of the scarcity of water. What made my disappointment greater was that I knew, had there been no drought, these falls of Aberdulais would have been magnificent. The great bare rocks which I could now see should have been hidden in a torrent of water; and the pools below them, shallow and quiet now, would have been one great body of dancing spray. The voice of this great waterfall ought to have put an

---

62. The stone is still there. Davies has added all of the punctuation, recorded 'God hath' as 'God has', and omitted the date '1823' at the top of the stone, but otherwise his transcription is accurate.

end to human talk, but now it was no difficult matter for two friends to hear each other without raising their voices. In fact, I could hear the birds singing, and was sorry I had not come when these falls could have been seen in their true beauty with every drop of water turned in to silver by its fierce wild life.

This walk up the Neath valley was wonderful. No doubt in my many travels I had often been in beautiful places, but they had been seen under a dull condition of life, whereas now I had no other object than to seek beauty and, finding it, give full leisure to its enjoyment. I had great hills on either side of me, parts of them being clad with trees and other parts green and bare. These hills were not always so close to the road but that there was room for a meadow or two; and when I came to places of that kind I always stood at the gates and looked at the horses, cows and sheep, and the little lambs that made such strange antics when they ran to suck the ewes. Sometimes I had a canal at my side, quiet and without a ripple, which further on made a loud deep sound as it forced its way through locks. And sometimes I came to dingles[63] that had little streams running through them; streams that were still in active service, in spite of the long drought. Eyes and ears were not the only organs that were tempted by this fine walk, for my nostrils often took in long breaths of air that was scented by the blossoms of May.

My mind was so full of nature that I did not trouble about human nature.[64] Although I had passed quite a number of tramps, I had very little interest in their lives and characters. However, I was not to complete my walk without meeting one that would insist on being heard. As I have said, I had met several tramps, but they had all been men who, seeing that I was not inclined to notice them, had passed on without a word. But this time it was a woman, and as soon as I had caught sight of her I knew that human nature would have to be attended to. As we drew nearer, I saw that she was ill-dressed and dirty, but, of course, I could not expect anything different.

'Kind sir', began this woman, placing a large basket she was carrying on her arm directly in my path, – 'Kind sir, remember that you have had a mother, and whether she's alive or in her grave give me a little help for her sake. When I married Joe Williams, my first husband, I was very young, and I am now old enough to be your mother.

---

63. *dingle*: 'a deep wooded valley or dell' (*OED*).

64. A similar criticism will be levelled, rather unfairly, at Wordsworth, in Davies's 'Introduction' to Robert Burns, *Poetical Works* (London: Collins, 1928). This is included in the present volume.

Give me a penny and God bless you.'

This old woman was so dirty and ill-favoured that I gave her a penny at once, and stepped round her basket so as to continue my journey.

'God bless you', she cried again in a halting voice. I thought the break in her voice was due to disappointment that she had not asked for more, seeing that she got the penny with such little trouble, and not due to grateful emotion. As soon as I was clear of the basket I made off, leaving her standing there and looking after me. But I had not gone three feet when she brought me to a standstill by crying, 'Wait a minute, sonny'. Turning round I saw that she had her hand in her pocket, and was curious to see what she would produce.

'Here', she cried, coming forward as fast as she could, and holding something in her hand. – 'Here sonny, have a pinch of this.' With these words she held out a box of snuff, which I did not accept, but thanked her all the same. 'God bless you', she cried again, as I continued my journey.

When I reached Glyn-Neath, I found it such a tiny little place that it would be difficult to get lodgings without going to a certain large hotel. I did not care to go there, seeing that I had put on old clothes, which were none the better for the rough travelling I had already done. Thinking of these things, I went to the railway station and took train to Aberdare.[65] When I looked from the train windows I was not at all sorry to have taken a ride, for I am sure I caught certain grand scenes that would have been entirely missed on the common road. In fact, some of the views were so grand that I had seen nothing more impressive even in America; and I began to see that we had scenery in our own country that was more than pretty and beautiful – that was sublime. I could see great deep valleys so full of trees that, to my fancy, races of pigmies or giants could live in them without being discovered. The train went up an incline seven miles long, from Glyn-Neath to Hirwain, and that accounted for the long wild distances that passed before my eyes.

I reached Aberdare in about three-quarters of an hour, where I arranged to stay at a restaurant near the railway station.

---

65. About eight miles to the east. Bare mountains rise to the north of both towns, and wooded hills to the south. The railway line was closed in 1964.

Chapter VIII: Welsh Song and Prize-fighting

On the following morning I started for Tredegar, which was about eight miles from Merthyr.[66] But I had three miles of houses before I got into the open country, because of Dowlais on the hill.[67] It was not a very pleasant walk, for I saw the same wretched, dirty little houses of which I had seen so many in Wales.

As soon as I got clear of Dowlais I was on the bleak, bare hills, and was surprised to feel a cold, cutting wind, in spite of its being the month of May. In fact, I had not gone far when I had to cover my left cheek with my hand owing to a stinging pelting of hailstones; and the wind was so strong that I was sometimes almost lifted off my feet. I could now well understand why people often fell and died of exposure when crossing these bare hills on a winter's night and being caught in a storm. It was not very long before I passed Rhymney, which lay to the right of me about a mile off the road. I knew from report that it was a dirty smoky little town, but it looked pleasant at this moment, for the sun made the roofs of the houses shine like silver, and the smoke that went up from the various chimneys was as white as the summer clouds they travelled to.[68] I was very much surprised to hear the cuckoo, seeing that the country was so bare of leaves. My experience of that bird has always led me to place its haunts where there were plenty of trees, and not such a place as this, where bushes were scarce and big trees were entirely absent.

When I arrived at Tredegar it was just about noon. But I was not hungry, and only wanted a glass of ale as a reward for my eight miles' walk. With this thought I entered an inn, where I found only one man present, who was the landlord. However, I had hardly been seated two minutes before another man entered, by his appearance a

---

66. Merthyr Tydfil, a large town in south Wales. Tredegar and Merthyr, both towns with ancient origins, were important centres during the industrial revolution, and grew around their iron and coal-mining industries. Tredegar had been the scene of anti-Jewish riots in 1911.

67. Effectively a continuation of Merthyr, to the north-east of the town.

68. The Rhymney Valley is one of the South Wales Valleys, industrialised for iron, coal and steel. Rhymney is now famous for being the home of the miner and poet Idris Davies (1905–53), who often wrote about that profession and environment. However, he would have been a child when Davies passed by the small town.

collier, smoking a short clay pipe. This man greeted me in a friendly way, and I answered him with the same cheerfulness. However, he did not appear much inclined to talk, and I could not sit there at his side in comfort without saying something or other, but had no idea of what subject to start on. I knew that the poorer classes in Wales have very few interests besides singing, football and fighting, although I had had proof that cricket as a summer game was beginning to create a little interest. Unfortunately the football season was now over, and that subject would not meet the ready welcome I desired. Now I do not know what possessed me that I should start on the dangerous subject of fighting, but I certainly did, almost immediately, saying, 'Have you got a good fighting man in this town of Tredegar?'

'Yes, indeed we have', answered the Welsh collier, looking at me with a great amount of interest.

'What has he done?' I asked, meaning that I was interested in an account of his battles, and feeling very pleased that I had started on a welcome subject.

'He has beaten everything around here', answered the collier. 'He has fought ten battles, look you, and never been defeated.'

Have a drink', I said, to show how well I appreciated his friendly talk.

'Thank you', answered the collier, drinking his ale and pushing his glass towards the landlord to be refilled.

As soon as the glass was refilled he raised it to his lips, saying in Welsh, 'Here's health to us all'. Hearing this I nodded to let him know that I understood, and taking a drink at the same time, which was expected of me.

'So he's a good man, is he?' I began, returning to that most welcome subject. But before I could say another word the Welsh collier said, looking at me kindly, 'Wait here, mun, for one moment, and I will come back'. Hearing this I remained seated, not so much to wait for him as to have a few moments' rest. I had not been seated there more than two minutes when the collier returned with another man at his heels. The stranger, whom I looked at at once, was clean shaven and young, not being more than twenty-four or twenty-five years of age.

'Now, look you', began the first collier, 'here is the man I told you of, and although he is not much more than a boy he will fight you for anything from five shillings to ten pounds.'

'Ay, I will, mun', exclaimed the young fellow, looking at me with a pleasant smile. 'I will fight you for anything you like, and at any time. Ay, indeed I will.'

'You have made a mistake', I said at last, feeling somewhat alarmed at the turn things had taken, – 'You have made a mistake. I have not come to Tredegar to fight, and am not much good at that kind of a game.'

'Indeed, I am truly sorry, mun', said the first collier. 'But I thought you would fight the best man in Tredegar! Ay, indeed, mun – but you have a man that will fight him?'

'No', I hastened to say, 'I am neither a fighting man, nor a fighting man's manager. You have made a mistake, but there is no harm done.'

After the matter was thoroughly explained, the collier insisted on paying for a round of drinks, and made me understand in further conversation that he thought he was doing me a kindness by bringing a man forward to fight me. I could not account for my indiscretion in starting so dangerous a subject, being a stranger in a strange place. Of course I knew that all these little towns had their fighting men, and were proud of them, and that the subject would be popular, but it was quite dangerous for a stranger to show interest in a matter of that kind.

I reached Ebbw Vale,[69] two miles from Tredegar, about half-past one and, having had a good dinner at a temperance restaurant, arranged to stay there for the night. In the afternoon I walked about the town, and found it much more pleasant than I had expected, in spite of the great ironworks that was surrounded with black smoke. It had been a wretched morning – hail, rain and a strong, cold wind – and most likely a fine afternoon, which turned out to be sunny, accounted for my pleasant time in Ebbw Vale. I found a small green space, perhaps a couple of acres, that had seats, and there I sat sunning myself, with the hills all around me. The works close by made a noise like great waves beating against rocks, and made me sometimes think I was near the sea. In the evening I went out again and called at an inn for a glass of ale.

It was all quiet in the front bar, but I could hear several loud voices in a back room. But although I felt strongly inclined to join their company, yet for all that I did not like to walk boldly in to their midst, knowing that they were all strangers. Moreover, they were Welsh, and I have spoken enough about Welsh suspicion. If one of them addressed me in that tongue, and found I could not answer him, my

---

69. A significant industrial town in the county of Gwent (though, like Newport, it was in Monmouthshire during Davies's lifetime). Ebbw Vale was noted for its coal mines and its huge integrated steelworks, making iron and steel. The site of these works was finally closed in 2002.

presence would have been none too welcome. Of course, I knew enough of their nature to know what answer to make if addressed in English. I would not have said that I came from any part of Wales at all, for they would then have despised me for not knowing the Welsh language. And it would not have been safe for my life to have said that I came from an adjoining town, for I knew how these Welsh towns, divided by a mountain only, hate each other, as I will show in the next chapter.[70] If anyone asked me where I came from, and I answered London, I knew well that that answer would mean safety and respect. London is such a great mystery to the inhabitants of small towns that anyone is respected who calls such a place his home.

While I was thinking of these things the men in the back room began to sing. Hearing this, the temptation to join them was so strong that I picked up my glass of ale and walked boldly into the room. As good fortune would have it, there happened to be an empty chair near the door, and I sat down without causing any interest, so I thought. But in this I was wrong, for it was not long before all eyes were turned my way – the eyes of ten colliers – and the next moment not a sound was to be heard, for they were all using their eyes to converse with each other. I never felt so uncomfortable in all my life, for I saw that my coming had upset their comfort. My only course was now to say something to win their confidence. So I began this way: 'Don't let me disturb your singing. Although I am a Welshman, belonging to London, I still have to come to Wales to hear good voices – except when Wales sends good voices to London.'

The London bait took well, as I had expected, for one of the colliers asked at once, 'What is your part of London? I have a cousin there, and his name is David Williams.'

'But look you, Johnny Jones', interrupted one of the others. 'London is a very big place and I will now bet you a quart of beer that this stranger has never seen Dai Williams.'

At this moment one of the others, who appeared to be more interested in beer and song than in me, London or David Williams, began to sing. This was fortunate, for he had not sung a dozen notes before they all joined him.

The singing I heard in this inn was quite remarkable, and I don't know any other part of the world where in a common public-house

---

70. In the next chapter, Davies briefly describes witnessing an altercation between men in Ebbw Vale on the following morning, and asserts by way of explanation that 'there was a steep mountain between Ebbw Vale and Abertillery, and this mountain prevented the two towns from growing and joining together, and for that reason they were bitter enemies' (*A Poet's Pilgrimage*, p. 82).

such fine harmony could be heard. For it must be remembered that these men were no more than rough colliers whose voices had not received any training at all. I noticed with surprise that although one of the singers was small, delicate and consumptive-looking, yet for all that he had a powerful bass voice that was rich and deep; whereas another, who was a giant of flesh, had a voice as soft and sweet as a boy in a cathedral choir.

I always like the old Welsh hymns which these colliers sang, and could have sat listening to them all the night.

There is one thing that must always be said to the credit of the Welsh, and that is, no matter what they do, whether they drink, burn or riot, they never forget to sing hymns, and sing them too with splendid feeling.

After we had had quite a number of serious songs, in which I had joined in the chorus with thorough enjoyment, the whole company looked towards a quiet, very respectable-looking man of about middle age, as a reminder that he was expected to sing. As soon as he became aware of these glances he rose to his feet, and clearing his throat began his song. The song was an old negro melody, which I had often heard before in America and this country.

The words and the music are so good that it still sounds fresh every time I hear it, and it always rouses me to help with my own voice. For the landlady's sake, who had looked into the room and laughed, we sang the chorus several times over. It only consisted of a few simple words, and here they are: -

Make way for my black Venus,
No coon can come between us;
Along the line we'll cut a shine –
That high-born girl of mine.[71]

71. It is hardly 'an old negro melody': these lines are from 'My Gal is a High-Born Lady' (1886), a once-popular 'coon tune' (as the genre was known) written by the white American entertainer and composer Barney Fagan. These songs, which often adopted the rhythms of ragtime, were phenomenally popular in the USA (and, to a lesser extent, throughout the rest of the English-speaking world) from the 1880s until the early 1920s, though their popularity was waning by about 1910. They presented racist and stereotyped views of blacks, were intended to be light-hearted, and were mostly (though not always) written by whites. The titles of other popular 'coon tunes', such as 'All Coons Look Alike to Me' (1896) and 'If the Man in the Moon Were a Coon' (1907), give a flavour of how phenomenally racist these songs tended to be, and 'My Gal is a High-Born Lady' is no exception, though Davies seems impervious to that. Davies (or the group of Welsh miners) has used slightly different words to the original, where the third and fourth lines he quotes are instead: 'Along the line they

Not caring to drink too much, and being ashamed to sit longer than an hour over two glasses of ale, I left that bright company and went down through the town for a walk. However much I disliked this dirty and smoky little town by day, I could not help being struck by a certain grandeur about it when, standing on the hill side at night, I saw the great works in the distance, the fires of which were kept burning day and night. The great volumes of smoke looked very impressive at this time, and it was almost uncanny to see the men moving like black shadows in the fire.

I found the people of Ebbw Vale inclined to be more friendly than in other parts of Wales – with the exception of Neath. The English language seemed to be expected of me and caused less suspicion. In fact, I had not been in the town ten minutes before a man told me his life's history in a few words. This happened at the place where I had had my dinner. After he had gone the landlady came in and appeared very friendly indeed. And when I went back there to tea, after arranging to stay there overnight, she told me all her domestic troubles; of how she had left a drunken husband, how he had tried to take the furniture from her, and how she had won the lawsuit by herself. She appeared to be a good kind woman and I was very sorry to be the only lodger she had that night. Perhaps my own manner had something to do with my friendly reception in Ebbw Vale, for knowing that I was now in my own native county of Monmouthshire I had entered the town with confidence. No doubt my face had a pleasantness that people liked to see.

---

can't outshine / this high-born gal of mine'.

Chapter XI: Tintern Abbey

The following day, being Sunday, was spent in the old town of Monmouth.[72] Judging by the looks of the houses it had altered very little during the last hundred years. This old town was beautiful, very much like Abergavenny, with its wooded hills all around and the fine houses that were to be seen among the trees. In this old town I felt quite comfortable, because I could stand and stare without being stared at. The reason of this was that the inhabitants were well used to strangers, owing to so many people making it their headquarters for a week or two when they visited the many beauty spots that are within easy distance such as Symond's Yat,[73] Raglan Castle,[74] the River Wye, Tintern Abbey[75] and other places. I was told that the town was healthy, there being no factory smoke of any kind.

I was interested in the old castle, where Henry V, one of our finest kings, was born.[76] But I learned that there was very little left of the old castle, only a little of the walls. Unfortunately I could not see even this without first getting a pass, – as hundreds of militiamen were to camp around the castle for three months. However, I was not greatly disappointed, for all these old castles and abbeys are very much alike, – two or three leafy walls, – and to see one is to see them all.

While I was standing on the bridge looking down into the River Monnow a man who was standing at my side drew my attention to a fish just under us, saying, 'Look at that trout; his weight is about a pound and a half. Do you fish?

'No', I answered, 'but I suppose you do'.

'Yes', he said, 'and I have seen some good sport in this river,

72. County town of Monmouthshire, Wales, about two miles from the border with England. On the previous day, Davies had walked from the town of Abergavenny, which is more than sixteen miles away to the west.

73. Village in Gloucestershire, England, famous for the Symonds Yat Rock, which rises impressively above the village in a meander of the River Wye.

74. Late medieval castle in Monmouthshire.

75. In Monmouthshire, and right beside the River Wye, which at that point serves as the border with England. This impressive ruin was, of course, an inspiration for Wordsworth's famous poem 'Lines Composed a few miles above Tintern Abbey'.

76. Monmouth Castle. Henry was born on 16 September 1386. He is sometimes referred to as Henry of Monmouth.

although it is small. Do you see that place down there under the market-house?'

Turning my head in the direction he pointed to, I saw a very old building, whose front was on the street, the back of it being on the waterside.

'Yes', I answered.

'Well', continued the stranger, 'that's where the big trout was caught. There's a slaughterhouse under the market-house, and the fish come there for the offal that is thrown in to the river. Now, in that place there was seen one day a very large trout, a monster for a stream like this. So a number of fishermen came and tried their best, but, do you know, not one of them could land that trout. But on the third day a friend of mine, who was the fattest man in Monmouth and weighed forty-seven stone, brought his fishing tackle, and in less than half an hour that trout, which weighed five pounds, was caught and landed. Now, what do you think my friend's bait was?'

'I don't know much about fishing', I answered. 'Was it a piece of dough, or a grub of some kind?'

'My friend's bait', said the stranger, pleased to think I had not guessed it, – 'My friend's bait was a long tapeworm taken out of a live sheep.'

It was not long before I wished this stranger good-bye, for I did not care to hear any more fishing stories of that kind. The idea of a big, red-faced, fat man, weighing forty-seven stone, handling a long, thin, white tapeworm that would be alive was not very pleasant. As I knew nothing about the weight of fishes, this man could have told me he had caught a trout weighing fifty pounds and I should have believed him. But when he mentioned the horrible sickly-looking tape-worm in connection with a tremendous heavy-gutted man, it was too much for my imagination. However, I could not leave him before he had told me of the big salmon that had been caught in the River Wye, which was the record for that year. I could see nothing to doubt in this. But when he said that on the following day and in the very same hour and in exactly the same spot another salmon of ex-actly the same size had been caught by the very same man – I began to think that my new friend was getting excited. I came to the con-clusion that the River Wye had inspired fishermen as well as poets.

On Monday morning I left the beautiful old town of Monmouth, making my way towards Tintern, which was eleven miles distant. I must say here that these fine walks in a country well known for its beauty, were spoilt by the great number of motor-cars and motor-cy-cles, especially the latter. I can well understand the joy of riding, but to race over the land at such a great speed that cyclists dare not turn their eyes to either side, is surely not a healthy state of joy. Why do these people invade a beautiful country if their only object is to ride with great speed? For any country that has well-kept roads would answer their purpose. The motor-cars were little better, for they travelled at such a rate and made so much noise that they always occupied my mind even when I was on the path near the hedge and in apparent safety. These foolish people have settled places of interest, and have no care for beauty on the way. Of course, if they enjoy that kind of life there is nothing to be said; but it seems a pity that they cannot enjoy themselves without interfering with the pleasure of others. They raise so much dust that the hedges, which ought to look fresh and green, are almost as white as the road itself. And when we go in to the country to smell the may,[77] these people give us a strong, unpleasant smell of oil. Although a poor man, I can get more enjoyment out of life than another man, because of the power of my imagination. For that reason I do not envy the rich having comfortable cars; but I am annoyed to think that they could ride with more joy to themselves and others if they went slow enough to study the things they pass. But when they are in that little iron world of their own they seem to despise the greater world beyond.

My lodgings at Monmouth had been very comfortable. I paid a lump sum in advance for board and lodging up till Monday morning, and had some fears of the consequence. But these people did not take advantage of the arrangement, and I left well satisfied with my treatment. When I was clear of the town, about a mile and a half on the road, I suddenly became aware that I was followed by a big, hulking young fellow about six feet high. Seeing that he was walking slowly like myself, and not feeling comfortable at having him just behind me all the time, I stood still, pretending to admire the scenery, so as to give him a chance to go by. However, when he reached my side, I did not let him pass without wishing him a pleasant good morning. When he heard my voice he came to a standstill at once, but, to my surprise, stared at me without saying a word. One look was quite enough, for, judging by his owl-like eyes and wide-open mouth, I at once came to the conclusion he was daft. Whether that was the case or not, I will leave my readers to judge by the following conversation. It must be remembered that this young man, who was such a big fellow, asked these questions in a simple child-like manner, without the

---

77. An alternative name for hawthorn, the fragrant white blossom of which is often called may-blossom.

least sign of a police examination. Judging him to be quite harmless, I answered his questions in the same straightforward way.

He. 'Where be you going?'

I. 'To Chepstow.'

He. 'Is your mother and your father there?'

I. 'No.'

He. 'Who do keep you, then?'

I. 'I keep myself.'

He. 'How?'

I. 'Somehow.'

He. 'Have you got any money?'

I. 'Yes.'

He. 'Did you find it?'

I. 'No.'

He. 'Did you steal it?'

I. 'No.'

He. 'Where did you get it from?'

I. 'Worked for it.'

He. 'How much have you got, coppers and all?'

I. 'I don't know exactly.'

He. 'Will you let me see?'

I. 'Not now.'

He. 'Will you lend me fourpence?'

I. 'What!'

He. 'Lend me threepence, then; indeed, it is not much.'

I. 'What!'

He. 'Come, lend me twopence, then.'

I. 'What!'

He. 'Lend me a penny, mun, for that is nothing.'

I. 'What, nothing?'

He. 'Well, good-bye.'

I. 'Good-bye'.

However, I could not let this simple young man go without giving him something, so I offered him a penny, which he took with a loud laugh. To my surprise, he had no sooner received this penny than he turned back towards Monmouth. It seemed he had come out of that town on purpose to beg some money. That he should have attempted to borrow fourpence from a complete stranger was extraordinary, for I don't suppose he had ever succeeded in doing that; and how artful he must have thought he was, to tell me that twopence was not much, as though I would not know the value of money.

After leaving this simple young man my road lay side by side with

A Poet's Pilgrimage

the River Wye. It was a dull morning, almost to tears – an ideal time for fishermen, a number of whom were to be seen on the banks, but bad for fishes and poets. However, the sun came forth now and then, and I could see the River Wye shining like a silver blade in a green handle. I had this beautiful companion with me all the way from Monmouth to Tintern, a distance of ten miles, sometimes singing and sometimes quiet; and showing an interesting face all the time.

When I reached Tintern it was still early, but I decided to stay there for the rest of the day and to start for Chepstow on the following morning.[78] I wanted to see Tintern Abbey by moonlight, as I had seen it years before, but this was impossible. For when I went out after dark I saw that the moon was far too young to affect those old ruins. My thoughts had been so busy with the abbey ruins that I had not studied the condition of the moon. As a local poet puts it: –

To see old Tintern Abbey right
Please visit it by pale moonlight.[79]

Although I saw a number of hotels that catered for summer visitors I did not stay at any of these, but preferred to look for a private cottage. After making one or two inquiries I succeeded in finding one. However, I did not scorn the hotels by any means, for I had several glasses of ale before I left Tintern.

When I went out in the evening and stood looking at the abbey ruins, I cannot say that I felt well satisfied with my present state. This discontent was owing to my memory going back to my boyhood days. I remembered that I had come from Newport to Tintern, a distance of seventeen miles, when I was only a boy of fourteen, to see how this abbey looked by moonlight. At that time I was working as an errand boy in an ironmonger's shop, and it was after midnight when I got back home, and I had to rise at six the next morning to be at work by seven o'clock.

As I stood there now, twenty-seven years after, and compared that young boy's enthusiasm with my present lukewarm feelings, I was

78. The town of Chepstow, famous for its medieval castle, is on the Welsh side of the River Wye close to where it flows into the Severn Estuary, and six miles south of Tintern Abbey.

79. Whoever this 'local poet' is, he or she is actually plagiarising Sir Walter Scott's 'The Lay of the Last Minstrel', concerning Melrose Abbey in Scotland: 'If thou would'st view fair Melrose aright, / Go visit it by the pale moonlight'. More likely, Davies knew the origins of these lines, hoped you wouldn't, and wanted them to fit his context perfectly.

not very well satisfied with myself. For instance, at that time I would sacrifice both food and sleep in my travels to see anything wonderful; but now, in my prime, I did not go seeking things of beauty, and only sang of things that came my way by chance. Thinking of this, I came to the conclusion that the boy of fourteen, who came seventeen miles to see a ruin by moonlight, was as a poet the father of the one that stood there in his prime.[80] Judging myself by that wonderful feeling in boyhood, I felt sure that I was only a shadow of what I should have been. However, perhaps this despondent feeling was owing to the absence of the moon, and the fact that the abbey could hardly be made out at all. Whatever it was, I did not feel very happy, and a couple of glasses of ale made me feel more melancholy than ever.

---

80. This phrase is comparable in construction (though almost the opposite in implication) to the famous notion that 'The child is father of the man' in Wordsworth's 'My Heart Leaps Up' (1802). Wordsworth, however, is implying a sense of continuity since childhood in his responses to natural beauty: 'So was it when my life began, / So is it now I am a man'.

A Poet's Pilgrimage

Chapter XIV : Old Acquaintance

Thy water, Alteryn,[81]
Shines brighter through my tears,
With childhood in my mind:
So will it shine when age
Has made me almost blind.

How canst thou look so young
On my fast changing flesh
And brooding cares that kill –
Oh, you sweet witch as fresh
And fair as childhood – still?

When I reached Newport I settled down for a few days, seeing old friends. I made inquiries for one woman I had known in my early days. At that time she was well on in years, but it never once occurred to me now that she would either be dead or at a very advanced and helpless old age. Time had dealt so lightly with me that I forgot the difference in our ages, and expected to see her not only alive but much the same as I remembered her nearly twenty years before.

When I was a small boy this woman had given me so fearful an impression that even now after so many years I should not feel comfortable in her presence. After I had known her for some time I noticed that she never had her head uncovered and always wore a soft cap made for a man. And I, childlike, began to wonder why. One afternoon, when I saw her in a room huddled up asleep in front of the fire, I suddenly made up my mind, being full of mischief, to remove her cap and hide it, thinking she would enjoy my fun when she woke. With this intention I went softly to her side and began to raise her cap, using the most gentle force. But when I had taken it clear off her head, I saw, first to my surprise and then to my horror, that two curled horns were sticking out of her head. To make certain that I was not deceived by her hair taking this strange shape, I felt them, and sure enough the horns were hard and made of solid bone.

---

81. Allt-yr-yn: suburb of Newport.

I don't know whether the cold air coming to her head made her wake, or that she woke by accident, but wake she did, and suspecting or feeling that I had tampered with her cap, which I had now replaced, gave one loud, unearthly screech and made a grab for me. But I had suspected this, and was out of her reach in a second, leaping for my life. I had never seen so evil an expression on a face before, and had never before heard so devilish a sound. I really believe that if that old woman, who up to that time had shown me nothing but loving kindness, had got me into her long, skinny arms at that moment, she would have torn me to pieces.

When I inquired for this strange woman I was told she had been dead for some time. Of course, when I came to consider matters, I was not surprised at this.

One woman, a relative, to whom I paid an early visit, was still hale and hearty in spite of her seventy-two years. On the afternoon of my visit she was also visited by two other women friends who were much older than herself. So I had the honour of being entertained by three elderly women, each one being over seventy years of age. True, there was not much laughter, but notwithstanding that there was a good deal of interesting talk. For instance, the eldest of the three claimed that war could be stopped at once by a special hour of prayer, when all Christians – excluding Roman Catholics, who were an abomination unto the Lord – would kneel for that purpose. 'And now', she continued, 'let us all kneel down and pray for the extermination of England's enemies.' It was very fortunate for all that she still continued to talk, for, after a long speech that lasted twenty minutes, she had forgotten her invitation and said no more about kneeling down to prayer.

'What a spirited woman that was', I exclaimed to my old relative, after her two visitors had gone.

'Yes', she answered, 'but she is not so spirited as she was a month ago, for she has only just buried her mother, and that is a trial for a woman of seventy-eight years of age.'

The town of Newport is, taking it on the whole, very beautiful, owing to a great part of it being built on the sides of hills. Parts of the town are wretched, but no worse than can be expected from a large seaport. But when a man is once on Stow Hill, which can easily be reached in a few minutes from any part of the town, he begins to see at once that the town has a remarkable beauty of position, which could hardly be spoilt by anything man could do. From various parts of this hill the Bristol Channel is to be seen, the islands in it, and the outward- and homeward-bound ships. And this fine sight is to be seen again at the other end of the town, from another hill called Christchurch.

But the most beautiful part of Newport is the green country called Alteryn, which has a clear canal coming down lock by lock, with Twm-Barlum in the distance.[82] I had not been in Newport long before I went walking in that direction. When I was well out of town and stood on a hillside road where I could see down into that wonderful green valley, I became deeply affected at the sight. For there was not the least change; there were the same few little cottages that I had seen so often when a boy. The place seemed to smile at me, and in a little while I began to feel tantalized and tormented that it was still the same, whereas I myself had undergone so many serious changes. 'It will be the same', thought I, 'when I am dead, although my life may be only half over now.' For I could see myself coming here a feeble old man, who was now in his prime, and still finding no difference in Alteryn.[83] For over half an hour I leaned on a gate, looking in all directions, but there was no other life than the cattle in the fields. It is only in the heat of summer when men and boys come to swim in the canal, that this green solitude is made noisy by human tongues.

As I was undecided what move to make next, I went to call on a friend who knew the country for miles round, to consult him about a walk of three or four more days, that would end at Cardiff. So I went to see him, knowing that he was the right man to advise me in the matter. However, when I met him, we began to talk of so many other things, that I clean forgot the cause of my visit and came away without the least idea of where I would go on the morrow.

We talked of a fine mansion that a rich man had built for his bride; but the bride never came and it was turned into stables, and had been stables till this day. Instead of being inhabited by a happy human couple it had become a home for cattle.

After that we talked of Gutto Nyth Bran, which means Gutto of the Crow's Nest,[84] and who was sometimes called 'Gutto the Wind'.

---

82. Twm-Barlum (or Twmbarlum) is a hill to the north-east of Newport. It is a notable landmark: a local nickname for it is 'the Twmp' (meaning 'hump'), because it has an abrupt mound at the summit.

83. Here, Davies perhaps consciously echoes W. B. Yeats's 'The Wild Swans at Coole', first published in 1917 (the year before *A Poet's Pilgrimage*) as the title poem to a collection.

84. Actually spelled Guto Nyth Brân, after his family farm, though his real name was Griffith Morgan – Guto being a diminutive form of Griffith. He lived from 1700 to 1737, and was famed for his running feats. He is reputed to have died from over-exertion and a congratulatory back-slap after winning a race.

He was a native of Llangralto in the Rhondda Valley,[85] and the fastest runner ever known in South Wales. I had heard of one great performance in particular, which happened when Gutto was a boy. One day when his mother thought of making bread she found on looking that there was no barm[86] in the house. 'What a pity that is', she exclaimed, leaving the house to tell her next-door neighbour of her disappointment. It was now that Gutta showed his extraordinary powers, for as soon as he saw his mother leave the house he sprang to his feet and, taking up an empty jug, made off with all speed. The next moment he was running his fastest towards Llantrissant, which was eight miles distant, that being the nearest place where barm could be had for certain. When his mother returned from explaining her trouble to her neighbour she saw, to her surprise, a jug of barm on the table and, guessing what had happened, said, 'Gutto, you are well called the wind'. Her son had run sixteen miles while his mother had been next door to say a few words to her neighbour.

After talking about these things for some time I wished my friend good-bye, having no idea where I would go on the morrow. However, before I settled down for the night, I decided to make Pontypool the end of my next day's journey.

---

85. One of the South Wales Valleys, split into two parts, Fawr and Fach. He was actually from Llwyncelyn, part of Porth, in the Rhondda Fawr.

86. A natural leavening agent.

Chapter XVII: A Long Walk

As my friend's time for rising in the morning was seven o'clock to let him get to work by eight,[87] I asked him to call me at the same time, that I might have a long day for walking. For I had a large stretch of country to cover, seeing that I intended to make Cardiff the end of that day's journey, passing on the way through Machen, Bedwas and Caerphilly.[88] Thus up in good time we left the house in company at a quarter to eight, he on his way to work and I going towards Rogerstone,[89] a little town that was not far away.

I was very glad to get through Rogerstone, for it was even dirtier and smokier than the towns I had passed through on the previous day.[90] There were some very large works there, which not only employed nearly all the men and boys of the district, but even others that came from Risca and Newport, the latter town being three miles away, and where they still kept their homes. These works filled the town and that part of the valley with dense smoke. But when I reached the quaint little village of Bassaleg[91] I saw at once that I had come into a beautiful agricultural country where the sheep's wool was white as it should be. I now began to see stout farmers and their sons and servants with their red faces instead of the pale lean colliers and iron workers of the day before. However, when I got through Bassaleg with its beautiful white church, the home of the Welsh bard David ap Gwillam,[92] I was told that my road to Caerphilly went through Machen, and I knew without more in formation that I was to go through another colliery district. In spite of that knowledge I was not much troubled, for I knew that the road between Caerphilly

---

87. The previous chapter ends with Davies bumping into an old friend in Risca, a small town seven miles north-east of where he had grown up in Newport, and staying at his house for the night.

88. Caerphilly: a town at the end of the Rhymney Valley, Wales, famous for its huge medieval castle and its cheese. Machen and Bedwas are smaller settlements to the east.

89. On the north-east edge of Newport.

90. In the previous chapter, called 'A Valley of Industry', Davies writes: 'This valley was full of collieries and other works all the way from Pontypool to Risca' (p. 150), a distance of about 11 miles.

91. Just to the east of Newport, and south of Rogerstone.

92. Dafydd ap Gwilym, significant fourteenth-century Welsh poet.

would be chiefly open and green country.

Perhaps this was the most pleasant walk I had ever had, owing to the friendliness of the people, for not only did the men greet me but even the women did the same. And when women greet a strange man, the district must have a friendly spirit that is exceptional. In fact, when I went into the inn at Machen the landlady was so easy, cheerful and talkative that I felt like a native of the town. At one time I put this friendly spirit to the test by turning my back on two men that were approaching, and pretending to be deeply interested in Machen Mountain,[93] which was in the near distance. But these men still greeted me and made me turn my face to answer them, which was a real pleasure after all. I did not hear a word of Welsh all along this road, although every name that came under my notice was Welsh without the least doubt. Just before I got into Bedwas one name in particular drew my attention – it was the *Ty-yn-y-Pwll Inn*,[94] which is as surely Welsh as Patrick Flanagan is Irish. I tried to pronounce it, but had to give it up in despair, coming to the conclusion that as there is no accounting for the way such names are pronounced, I should be quite likely to be near the mark if I called it Jones or Smith.

Not long after this I came to the little town of Bedwas, which has the River Rumney[95] running through it. It is always pleasant to be in a town that has a river, and I don't think any place can claim real beauty unless it has this one form of animated nature. I was soon standing on the little stone bridge, resting on its parapet for a while before I continued my journey into Caerphilly. It was on this bridge that Gutto Nyth Bran, the famous runner, whom I have mentioned in a previous chapter, met his death in an unfortunate manner.[96] He was running a race against the champion of all England from Newport bridge to Bedwas bridge, and being the winner, the farmers who had gathered to see the result were mad with excitement. But unfortunately one old dame could not contain her joy, for as Gutto passed the winning post, still going comparatively fresh and strong, she struck him a blow on the back, crying out, 'Well done, Gutto'. When Gutto received the blow he fell to the earth, and when they picked him up he was dead.

After having this little rest, I pushed on towards Caerphilly, a town

---

93. Rises to a modest 362 metres, between Risca and Machen.

94. The building remains, on the main road leading into Bedwas from the west, but it is no longer an inn.

95. The Rhymney River, which begins at the top of the industrialised Rhymney Valley, and reaches the sea near Cardiff.

96. See chapter XIV.

that is so well known for its old castle and a certain good cheese, and also for a market town of some importance. As I did not intend to stay there overnight, and still had a long walk before me, I was very glad to hear that I should pass close by the old castle without going a step out of my way on the road to Cardiff. It was not long before I saw the ruin close at hand, and, judging by its size, the castle must have been very strong in its day. Seen from where I stood, it looked so well preserved that I would not disillusion myself by going in between its walls to see their decay. So, after taking a long, admiring look, I continued my journey, being well satisfied with what I had seen, and without envying the two visitors I saw walking close to its wall.

The road going out of Caerphilly towards Cardiff was very steep and mountainous. For a well-made road it was the steepest I had ever seen. From different parts of this road one could get wonderful views of the town and the surrounding hills. The strangest thing was that this mountain, over which the road went, was a green wilderness without a house of any kind to be seen. In fact, the road went through a country that was open and green nearly all the way from Caerphilly to Cardiff, a distance of six miles. Moreover, the road, well made as it was, did not appear to be used much by either pedestrians, or the traffic of horses and carts, or any other kind of conveyance. With the exception of a few cattle here and there, I seemed to be the only living thing on the mountain. It was not until I got within three miles of Cardiff that I began to see much human life. This walk from Caerphilly to Cardiff surprised me very much, for I knew that the latter was a large city, and I expected its suburbs and outskirts would have reached out so far that there would have been only a couple of miles of green country between it and Caerphilly. Instead of that it was open country nearly all the way.

When I was about half-way between the two towns I was overtaken by a stranger who, without the least reserve, began to walk at my side and talk. I judged this man to be no more than a common worker, in spite of his clothes, which were good and black. It is seldom that the poorer classes of Wales buy any other than black as a change from their working clothes. The reason of this is that they pay so much respect to the dead in attending funerals, that every man is expected to have a suit of black in readiness at a moment's notice. A Welshman loses several days' work every year in order to do this, and often to oblige people be hardly knows.

Judging by this man's clothes, and seeing that it was not a general holiday or Sunday, I came to the conclusion that he was either under the doctor's care or out of work for a little time, but not in straight-ened circumstances.

'Are you a preacher of the gospel?' he asked almost at once, to my surprise. Perhaps it was the large black tie that I wore, so as to cover a shirt that might get dirty, which made him ask this question.

'No', I answered; 'what made you think that?' And then, wonder-ing what effect my words would have, I added, 'I'm not a parson. I'm only a poet.'

'What!' exclaimed the stranger, coming to a halt in the road. 'What, do you mean to tell me that you're a poet?'

Of course I could see at once that this man had some respect for a poet, so I said again, seriously and proudly, 'Yes, that's what I am, a poet.'

After I made this affirmation he stared at me for such a long time that I almost burst out laughing in his face. At last he said, leading the way to a small gate at the side of the road: 'Come and stand here a minute, will you?'

The next moment he was at the gate and looking into a large meadow where there were about twenty cows lying or standing in different positions. I was soon by his side, for I knew no reason why I should not humour him, although I had no idea of what was to come of it.

'Now, this is a beautiful scene', he began, with a rainbow sweep of his arm which took in the clouds, meadow and hedges that were its boundaries.

'It is', I answered, wondering what he would say next.

'Well', he said, 'if you are a poet, as you say you are, make poetry of it and I'll believe you.'

'I couldn't do that at a moment's notice', I answered. 'I must have time for thought.'

He appeared to be disappointed at this, and then asked, 'Are you going to Cardiff?'

I answered that I was, and he said, 'Come, then, and we will talk as we go along.'

It was not long before the stranger again returned to the subject of poetry, saying, 'My wife makes poetry every time someone dies or a baby is born, and she knows a lot of poetry written by other people, as well as what comes out of her own head.'

'Do you remember anything written by your wife?' I asked.

'No', he answered, after a long pause in which he had tried to remember something. 'No, but I know two lines by someone else which she often quotes.'

A Poet's Pilgrimage

'I'd like to hear them', I said, with real interest. The stranger cleared his throat and then began:

Man works from sun to sun,
Bur woman's work is never done.[97]

'Do you know these lines?' asked the stranger.
'Yes, I know them very well', I answered.
'Ha! perhaps *you* wrote them', he exclaimed in a voice of triumph.
'Oh, no', I answered. 'These lines are very old, and seeing that they are of such interest to women, most likely a woman wrote them.'

We went along chatting in this way until we came to an inn, where I came to a halt and invited the stranger to have a drink. While we were there the stranger said in a coaxing voice, 'I wish you would write me some poetry on a piece of paper to show my wife and to prove that I have been with a poet.'

After a little thought I said: 'I will, but only on one condition, and that is that you will not read it until you get home.'

'I'll promise you that', he answered. 'The fact is I can neither read nor write.'

When I heard this I was delighted and lost no time in writing out three little verses which were in my note-book in my pocket. When this was done I gave him the little sheet of paper with the poem on it, which he folded with great care and placed in the inside pocket of his coat. After this we left the inn, and it was not long before he wished me good-bye and good luck, for he was taking the road to Whitchurch, whereas I was keeping the main road to Cardiff.

As I went along after the stranger had left me, I began to laugh and wonder what his wife would think of my poetry, and whether the man would be astonished at what his wife would read to him. For these are the verses, to which I gave a suitable title: –

To the Woman who will read this Poem to her Husband.

I am the Poet Davies, William,
   I sin without a blush or blink:
I am a man that lives to eat;

---

97. An old proverb, the first line of which is usually rendered 'Man may work from sun to sun', making the couplet two neat lines of rhymed tetrameter. This, or variations of it, date back at least to the sixteenth century. It also reflects Proverbs 31.15 (King James Version): 'She riseth also while it is yet night, and giveth meat to her household, and a portion to her maidens.'

I am a man that lives to drink.

My face is large, my lips are thick,
  My skin is coarse and black almost;
But the ugliest feature is my verse,
  Which proves my soul is black and lost.

Thank heaven thou didst not marry me,
  A poet full of blackest evil;
For how to manage my damned soul,
  Will puzzle many a flaming devil.

Soon after this man had left me, I was well into Cardiff with houses on both sides of me. In fact, I was walking on a well-made footpath at the side of the road, which proved that I was now in Cardiff without mistake, and I was passing so many people that I had to keep my mind from wandering, for fear of coming into collision with someone.

Perhaps that is the reason why a small boy who was collecting money in a cigar box took advantage of me. This little boy had held a box in front of me, and thinking he was collecting for some charity, such as the sick, the blind, orphans, the widows of drowned seamen, or the Salvation Army – I dropped a penny through a slit in the top, without the least thought of who or what was to benefit by what I was doing. For I have never, of late years, refused a penny to these collecting boxes, no matter in whose hands they are held or what kind of charity it is. However, before I continued on my way, it suddenly occurred to me that I had seen no letters of any kind on the box to show what the boy was collecting for. So I took a few steps back, and out of curiosity said to the boy, 'What are you collecting for?'

'My birthday', he answered innocently.

'What!' I exclaimed in surprise. 'What! your birthday; suppose a policeman saw you?'

'If he did', answered the little fellow, as innocent as ever, – 'If he did, I'd ask him for a penny.'

'How old are you?' I asked.

'I'm eight years old to-day', said the boy, 'and my father mends boilers.'

'Never mind about your father', I said. 'Don't you know that you can be sent to prison for collecting money for your birthday?'

'Gar'n', said the boy. 'Don't my mother know Mrs Smith who married a policeman.'

A Poet's Pilgrimage

Not caring to waste any more time, I left that innocent little stranger, wondering whether he, being such a good beggar at that early age, would ever become the leader of the Salvation Army. I could not help wondering how he had escaped the eyes of a policeman or an officer in plain clothes, seeing that he was so bold and without the least suspicion of wrongdoing. Judging by the sound when he had rattled the box to draw my attention to it, he must have succeeded in begging several pennies.

Making my way into the business part of Cardiff, I passed through Cathays Park,[98] but it was then the dusk of evening. However, it was not too dark to see the fine public buildings erected there; and their size and magnificence made me think of London.

Although I was now tired, having walked more than twenty miles, I came to the conclusion that it was one of the best day's walks I had ever had, not so much for the beauty I saw as for the friendliness of the people I had met.

---

98. A civic centre in Cardiff, containing a number of imposing buildings dating from the early twentieth century, including the City Hall and the National Museum of Wales, Cardiff (though, because of the Great War, the National Museum building would not open until 1922).

Chapter XXII: The Savernake Forest

When I left Marlborough[99] on the following morning I was struck by seeing so many donkeys, all driven by the better classes, and came to the conclusion that the donkey was held in great favour in that part of the world and had a good time of it. For when leaving that town I heard a noise behind me like a fast-travelling motor-car, and turned my head at once to make sure I was not in danger. When I did so, I saw to my astonishment that it was only a donkey and trap, driven by a young lady. I never thought it possible that a donkey could travel at such a rate, for he was out of sight in a very short time.

Not long before this I had seen a man coming out of an inn, where his donkey and trap were waiting for him. I suppose the man must have had a drop too much, for in stepping into the trap his foot slipped and he fell on the road. The donkey, thinking his master was safe in the trap, began to go, but was soon stopped by a man who had seen what had happened.

'The wrong one was in the shafts', I said to a man who was standing by. The man looked at me, but said nothing, neither did he smile. Perhaps he saw the joke when he had considered a while. I hope so, for I was quite pleased with myself at having made it.

How deadly and mysterious those yew trees look! Just before I reached Savernake Forest[100] I passed a large clump of them, when the sun was for a moment clouded. Perhaps it was the momentary darkness and the loneliness of the place that affected me; for I looked both up and down the road, but could see no sign of any life at all.

> How strange is this: I cannot pass this wood
>   But what its leaves, of such a dark brown green,
> Seem closely knit to hide a deed of blood;
>   And look as deadly as these curtains seen
> In quiet houses, where dark Rumour saith
> Drugged wine is, sudden blows and hidden death.

---

99. Market town in Wiltshire, south-west England.
100. To the east of Marlborough.

However, when I entered the forest, the sun was out again, and I soon recovered my good humour. There were very few large trees with branches over the road, so that my walk was sunny all the way. I could not help thinking what a lucky road the Bath Road was, that it had over two miles of its length in a beautiful forest with so many green, open spaces, and with such a variety of colour in the bark and leaves of the different trees.

After I had been in the forest for a little while I was suddenly hailed by a voice at the side of the road. On turning round I saw a man lying in the grass, who was just in the act of sitting up.

'Have you a pipeful of tobacco?' he asked.

'Certainly', I said, going towards him and offering him my pouch to help himself.

'How far are you going?' he inquired as he filled his pipe.

'As far as Hungerford to-day', I answered.[101]

'But it looks very much like rain, and I fear to get a good wetting before I reach there.'

'Yes', said the stranger, in a disgusted voice. 'Yes, it's sultry enough for rain, but we won't get any until this damned wind goes down. I wish to God the flies would bite, but they don't in spite of the heat.'

When I heard this I looked at the man with some surprise, not having the least idea of what his words meant, and for that reason not knowing what to say. However, I assured him that the flies *did* bite, and that they had been trying all the morning to bathe in the sweat of my neck and forehead.

'I am very glad to hear that', cried the stranger, in a more cheerful voice, 'for that's a sign of rain.'

'Yes', I answered. 'We want rain badly, or there will be a very poor prospect of getting green vegetables in the summer, or fruit either.'

'Oh! to hell with green vegetables! exclaimed the stranger in an irritated voice. 'There are more important things than that. If it doesn't rain soon, it means that I, for one, cannot make a living.'

When I heard this I was more surprised than ever and did not know how to continue the conversation.

In a few moments he continued, saying, 'People are getting stingy and are hoarding their money; they don't prepare for a rainy day.'

'Surely', I began, 'if people are saving their money, they must be preparing for a rainy day. What else are they doing?'

'Good Lord! how dull you are!' exclaimed the stranger testily. 'Can't you see what I am; and if people won't spend their money and

---

101. Market town in Berkshire, ten miles east of Marlborough.

prepare for a rainy day, how in the hell am I to make a living?'

Saying this, he cast his eyes some few feet away, and it was then I saw for the first time a couple of old umbrellas, which he had probably thrown from him in disgust. The stranger was an umbrella mender, or, as he is known on the road, a 'mush fakir'. No wonder he was anxious that people should prepare for a rainy day, by spending their money on umbrellas instead of saving it. Before I left him I gave him twopence, which he appeared to be very glad of.

I could not help laughing as I went along at the way in which the stranger had spoken of preparing for a rainy day, which was quite natural to a man in his trade. To other men the flies were a pest, but they could bite this man and be blessed for doing so. Other men would curse them as they drove them away; but when this man drove them away he gave them kind words and invited them to come again and often.

When I reached a small village about two miles from Hungerford I crossed the border line from Wiltshire into Berkshire. There was a small inn at this village, called the *Pelican,* at which I had a pint of ale.[102] I had been warned that there would be no other inn between Marlborough and it, a distance of eight miles. If there is any news I detest, it is to be told that a country road has no inn for several miles – few and far between. I confess I like to see the inns, even if I do not use them. As I passed through this first little village in Berkshire I could not help being struck by its peaceful looks. There was the little church on the hill, and a small green common at the side of the road. On this green common a donkey was making an ass of himself by rolling about on his back and kicking at the clouds.

I saw several happy-looking old villagers standing at their cottage doors and smoking their pipes. There was no sign of miserable poverty here, and yet I had been told that few of the farm labourers in these parts earned more than fourteen shillings a week. However, they had their gardens and could grow their own vegetables, and the rent of a cottage was only two or three shillings a week. Under these circumstances they were more comfortable than hundreds and thousands of workers in our large industrial towns, who cannot do as well with twice that amount in wages. When I saw these happy-looking old villagers at their cottage doors, I could see that the Old Age pensions had not only made them independent, but had actually made

---

102. Davies is in the small village of Froxfield, on the county boundary but actually in Wiltshire. The seventeenth-century Pelican Inn is still there.

their lives a help to their families.[103] For a country house-wife can make a shilling go a long way indeed.

I had not seen any tramps for more than an hour, and began to wonder where they had all gone to. It must be remembered that I was on the main road from east to west, on which tramps are often met. However, I soon found one who was lying on the grass at the side of the road. I had not noticed him until I had almost reached him. On coming close I saw that he was a very shabby-looking fellow indeed. Although he was now sitting up, I don't believe he was yet aware of my coming. I judged that he had been asleep, for he was now stretching his body and yawning. The way this man yawned frightened me, for he kept his mouth open so long and at such a size that I was afraid something would happen.

I had been told when a boy of a certain man who yawned to such an extent that his mouth refused to close again; and he had to get out of bed at midnight and go in search of a doctor. And now, every time I open my own mouth to yawn, or see others do it, I have a vision of that unfortunate man, and am afraid of the consequence. However, I thoroughly enjoy sneezing, for it never occurs to my mind that I could break a blood-vessel with doing so. Although I am not a religious man, yet for all that I cannot help crying sincerely at the end of a good sneeze, 'God bless us all'. So every time I sneeze it seems to me like Christmas with the whole world.

This man appeared surprised to see me so near him, but soon recovered his wits and, as I had expected, began to beg, asking for a penny to help him on his way. Now, when I had first started on my travels, I had made up my mind to refuse no beggar a penny, and all he had to do was to ask for it. For that reason I gave one to this man, at the same time telling him that many men had begged of me and that I could not afford to give to all.

'Of course not', said the shabby stranger; 'they are not all deserving, and you cannot tell which of them are.'

'Which way are you going? 'I asked, determined to have a few jokes with this man, and make him confess he was a professional beggar.

'To Hungerford', he answered, with a laugh.

'Why do you laugh?' I inquired with some surprise.

'Because Hungerford is well named', he answered, 'and I am certain to go hungry in that town.'

---

103. In Britain, the Old Age Pensions Act (1908) provided 5 shillings per week to those over seventy and with annual means lower than £31.50.

'Well, come along', I said. 'The price of your bed will be four-pence, and I promise to give you that before we get there. I know for certain that you have not been idle all day, and the few pennies you already have will do for food. When I was on tramp, a few years ago, I always had the price of my bed and a penny or two over by this time of the day.'

When my shabby companion heard this he began to eye me crit-ically, not knowing what to say.

'You don't mean to say', he said at last, 'that you have been a real tramp?'

'I have been a real tramp for the best part of my life', I answered shortly – 'and a good one too. One that could get the price of his feather (bed) and a pocketful of scrand (food), not to mention a little skimish (drink), in any place that had people living in it. I used to do so well that I could often afford to take the rattler (train). You ought to be proud of calling yourself a beggar' I continued – 'that is, of course, if you are any good at all at the game.'

When he heard this the shabby stranger was at a loss for words, not knowing whether to take me seriously or not.

'The little work I have done for others', I continued, 'was done in my early manhood, when I had little sense and was too timid to beg. But even then I could not work more than a week without claiming my freedom.'

Although this was the truth, yet for all that it sounded false to even my own ears. Perhaps the reason of this was that I could not openly utter this truth except under certain conditions, and although it was old in thought it was new in speech.

I could see that my new companion was confused and did not care to hazard any remark. However, after we had walked in silence for some time, he began to think some comment on my words was due.

'But you are not a tramp now; how is that?' he asked.

'The reason is very simple', I answered. 'Some time ago I had a small legacy left to me, and it is just enough to keep me from begging and in idleness.'

He made no answer to this, and I could see he was still puzzled as to what kind of man he had met.

Now some time before this I had written a paper in defence of beggars, which a friend had read to a small gathering of people in-terested in social matters. It was quite a foolish thing, meant to cre-ate amusement, and not serious thought. Although the paper had been destroyed, I still remembered two or three points used to prove that the beggar was the dew, and not the blight, on civilization. So, although I could hardly keep from laughing, I said at last, 'You ought to be proud of being a beggar; the beggar is the most religious man in the world, for there is no other man that more truly keeps the ten commandments. He not only does no labour on the seventh day, but he also keeps holy the other six. He never bears false witness against his neighbour, for the simple reason that he is a simple traveller and has no neighbours. He never steals – that is if he is a good beggar. He never covets any other man's goods, because he hates to be tied to any property at all. He is the only wise man, because he is not greedy to own houses or land. He is not vain of his personal appearance, and when he leaves a house where he has begged he never leaves behind him suspicion and jealousy between a man and his wife. People tell a beggar to go to work, but as you know yourself he does very fine work as it is; he works on their best feelings, and there is no nobler work in all the world than that.'

While I was saying these things my companion laughed once or twice and was as puzzled as ever.

'You're very funny', he said at last, 'and I don't know what you really mean.'

'What I mean', I answered, 'is this: I believe you are a true traveller as I have been, and I want you to say so.'

'If I said I was not looking for work you wouldn't give me the price of my bed', he said cautiously.

'Here's the price of your bed', I answered, counting four pennies into his hand. 'Now tell me the truth: are you a true traveller or not?'

'You are right, I am', he said, as soon as he had made sure of the four pennies.

'But', I asked, 'doesn't it trouble your conscience a little when you go begging at the houses of very poor people that have little for themselves? That was the only thing that used to trouble me when I was on the road; otherwise, the life was not too unpleasant.'

My companion looked at me, but made no answer. I could see that he was touched by this reminder of the kindness he had received daily from poor workers that were hardly any better off than tramps.

We were now within a mile of Hungerford and, knowing that I had to find respectable lodgings, while my companion was going to a common lodging-house – knowing this, I thought we ought to part at once. So I sat down at the side of the road, telling him that I was in no hurry to reach Hungerford and would rest awhile. Hearing this, he thanked me for my kindness and hurried off. No doubt he wanted to do some begging in the town before he settled for the night.

When I at last reached Hungerford I was almost afraid I would have to take train to Newbury, owing to the difficulty of finding lodgings. I had tried three coffee houses and six inns, but all without success. However, at the last inn the landlord, who had no room of his own, recommended me to a private house close by, kept by an old widow. So I went there and was accepted as a lodger for the night.

As Davies's first biographer, Richard J. Stonesifer, put it: 'Tremendously impressed by the marvellous success of Nigel Playfair's production of The Beggar's Opera *and its sequel,* Polly, *at the Hammersmith Lyric Theatre, Davies had attempted a task far beyond his powers, the writing of a tramp opera [...] for which he quickly demonstrated no aptitude at all'.[104] A production was never attempted, though in 1923 Cape did publish it in an attractive edition illustrated by William Nicholson. The libretto draws on Davies's tramping experiences, but lacks drama, characterisation and plot – relying heavily on the song lyrics, which Davies could handle with some aplomb.*

---

104. Richard J. Stonesifer, *W. H. Davies: A Critical Biography* (London: Cape, 1963), p. 139.

Characters

Men

JOHN DUFFY	Landlord of a common Lodging-House
DICK, RALPH	Two Rogues
THE PROFESSOR	
MONKEY SAM	
SNIVELLING TOM	
A JAILER	
A LAWYER	
T WO CONSTABLES	
A WORKING MAN, A COLONEL, AND A YOUTH	

Women

MARY DUFFY	Wife of John Duffy
DOLLY	their Daughter
POLL	Wife to Monkey Sam
GYPSY KATE	a Seller of Pegs
A LADY, A LITTLE GIRL, AND TWO SISTERS OF MERCY	

WITH VARIOUS BEGGARS OF BOTH SEXES

ACT 1, SCENE 1
A private room in the Lodging-house. John Duffy and his wife.

JOHN DUFFY
This man, that came a beggar to our door,
Is now worth twenty thousand pounds and more;
And in the kindness of his face I see
Satin and silk for you, pearls for our girl,
And bottles of good wine and ale for me.

MARY DUFFY
Since we're the beggars now, we'll make a plan
To share the fortune of this rich young man.

JOHN DUFFY
Let Dolly pay her loving parents back
All that she owes to them in loveliness,
And fall in love with him before he leaves –

MARY DUFFY

That love of her may bring him back to us.

JOHN DUFFY

That's good – can we rely on the girl to do that? I have, as you know, already lent him twenty pounds to buy clothes with, and to pay the expenses of travel for him and his companion to go North. He has promised to pay me two hundred pounds for my kindness, as soon as he is able; so that my interest will be ten times more than the capital. What proud moneylender, whose coat-of-arms is three brass balls, would not envy me a business like that!

MARY DUFFY

He leaves here this evening.

JOHN DUFFY

In the meantime, let us discuss the house affairs. Have you not noticed that the man 'Trotters' is looking ill, and may die at any moment?

MARY DUFFY

Yes, but when I reminded him of his fishy eyes and his peppery complexion, he said that he felt as strong as a man with double joints and three chins.

JOHN DUFFY

Well, when you see him again, tell him that he has paid us for a bed to *sleep* in, not to *die* in. We have had one inquest here already, and we don't want another.

MARY DUFFY

That was the poor old man that never smiled until he died, was it not? I felt so sorry for the poor fellow that a tear ran down my cheek that was almost as long as a navvy's bootlace.

JOHN DUFFY

Yes, he owed us for two nights' lodging, and, knowing the trouble he was putting us to – for clean linen, and the inconvenience of an inquest – no wonder the scoundrel smiled for the first time, when he knew that he was dying.

Enter Dolly

DOLLY

Here we are again! When are we going to get out of this place? You dress me in fine feathers; you send me to a high school where I sing and play – and this is the miserable nest I have to return to at night.

JOHN DUFFY

You are getting too saucy of late. We have no money to retire, for we spend it all on you. Yes, you have a bird's life, the fine feathers, the music and the play; while I, you ungrateful hussy, have the bird's legs, bony, shapeless and thin. Look at your legs, before you talk to me, fat with a thousand games of sport, and then look at mine!

MARY DUFFY

Listen to me Dolly. You have the power, and you only, to get us all out of this place in a very short time.

DOLLY

In what way, may I ask?

MARY DUFFY

By falling in love with that young man in the kitchen, who is now going North to take possession of a large estate.

DOLLY

I have already fallen in love with him, without a thought of whether he is rich or poor.

Song

I could not love him more –
Though he were richer than
A summer's night
That bubbles over with
A flood of starry light.

I would not love him less –
Though he were poorer than
A winter's morn
That struggles wildly with
A sun that's never born.

JOHN AND MARY

Her love is not a plant that's forced to grow

By any worldly goods that men possess;
  What'er his wealth, she could not love him more,
    However poor, she would not love him less.

JOHN DUFFY
Come, wife, let us go and see if the man 'Trotters' is any better, for we don't want another inquest in this house.

MARY DUFFY
He...he...he!

JOHN DUFFY
What are you making that noise for, like water dropping into a sink?

MARY DUFFY
Don't you remember what fun we had at the other inquest? When the Coroner asked Monkey Sam what he knew of the deceased, don't you remember what he said – 'I didn't know any good of him; to the Devil with him, dead or alive!' He...he...he! How I did laugh, after that.

JOHN DUFFY
Don't be silly – it's no laughing matter, unless it happens to other people.

Exeunt John and Mary

DOLLY
Song

See how the glowworm's light is found
To shine upon a nameless mound:
So, though my lover's life is false,
In being true to none,
And, like that worm's, his beauty shines
Upon a past unknown;
Yet still I ask no more than this –
The knowledge that is in a kiss.

Curtain

ACT 1, SCENE 2

The Professor and Monkey Sam, begging in the street. A street-singer, heard in the distance, also a man playing a tin whistle

PROFESSOR
Sir, that's Snivelling Tom, singing in the distance.

MONKEY SAM
How much have you earned, Professor?

PROFESSOR
Sir. I have in my possession two shillings and twopence three farthings. Hush, here comes a colonel – stand straight, Sir.

Enter Colonel (they both salute him)

Sir, may we have a word with you, as two old soldiers?

COLONEL
(Aside) Two old soldiers, eh; and is that the way they salute? *(To them)* Stand at ease! Shoulder arms! Eyes to the front! Right turn! Quick march! *(They are utterly confused)* Two old soldiers, are you? You are two damn scoundrels!

PROFESSOR
Sir, you are too keen for us. If every officer had your penetration, the British Army would never lose a battle. But I am sure, Sir, you will forgive the imposture when you learn that we are in need of food and shelter for the night. That was the reason, Sir, why we lied to you, thinking that your interest would be more easily aroused to our misfortunes. Sir, we are very sorry.

COLONEL
Well, well, though you are not two old soldiers, I suppose you must live, so here's a shilling between you.

Exit Colonel

MONKEY SAM
This experience has unnerved me.

PROFESSOR
Sir, it turned out well in the end; but if it ever happens again, don't cling to me like a wet towel.

Enter a little girl – she offers Monkey Sam a slice of bread

MONKEY SAM
Thank you, my dear – eat it yourself.

LITTLE GIRL
But I don't want it.

Exit Little Girl

PROFESSOR
Now, Sir, you know your duty, don't you?

MONKEY SAM
What do you mean, Professor? If I had not taken it, she would have only thrown it away.

PROFESSOR
True, Sir, but what about the child's mother? A woman that teaches her child to give food to beggars, instead of throwing it away, must be encouraged to keep alive her tender feelings, and thoroughly deserves to be well begged. For that reason, Sir, you must ask the child for her name and address, and then find the mother. Sir, it is certain that the mother will add silver to her child's bread and butter. Again, Sir, it will be to my future benefit to have the same name and address. Follow that child, Sir, and find the mother!

Exit Monkey Sam
Enter a Youth

Pardon me, Sir, but would you help a poor man with a copper or two towards his shelter for the night? I speak to you as man to man, and if your wife had been with you, Sir, I would not have dared –

YOUTH
I am not married – yet.

PROFESSOR
Sir, I am sorry for the mistake – a thousand pardons. Now, as one man

to another, will you give me a little assistance?

PROFESSOR
Twopence is all the change I have.

PROFESSOR
For that, Sir, I shall be deeply grateful. And when I lie in bed to-night, Sir, I shall say to myself 'To-day I met as fine a man as ever broke bread or breathed the breath of life'. Sir, it is not often that I meet a man like you.

Exit Youth, swaggering
Enter Lady

Pardon me, Madam, but can I be of any assistance to you?

LADY
What do you mean?

PROFESSOR
I would like to do something for you, Madam, so as to earn sixpence towards my rent. A few years ago, I was one of the leading singers at Covent Garden, but my voice failed, and I was soon reduced to calling 'Fish Alivo' in the streets.

LADY
What is your name?

PROFESSOR
My name, Madam, is Smith, but owing to the English prejudice against English musicians, my professional name became Smitherreeno.

LADY
I am sorry to hear this – I will give you sixpence.

PROFESSOR
Madam, I am deeply grateful to you for this kindness, but alas, Madam, I am not so unfortunate as my brother, with whom I have to share this sixpence. My brother, Madam, is not of sound mind – he is, Madam, unfortunately, 'non compos mentis'.[105]

---

105. Davies himself had an older brother, Francis, who had suffered brain damage at birth.

True Travellers: A Tramp's Opera in Three Acts

LADY

Dear, dear, how dreadful! I will give you another sixpence for your poor brother. You are a man of education, I see; and if you call at my house to-morrow morning, I will see what can be done for you. You will not mind if, instead of calling you Mr Smith, I call you Signor Smitherreeno?

PROFESSOR

(With a low bow) I am entirely at your service, I am entirely at your service, Madam, by whatever name you like to call me.

Enter two Sisters of Mercy, who walk slowly and silently across the stage, 'without turning their eyes. The Professor watches them in silence, until they are gone

I must now seek fresh quarters. Those good Sisters are begging for the poor, and I must give them a clear field, without competition.

Enter a mall with a tin whistle, followed by one with an organ

PROFESSOR

(To organ grinder) Sir, you should have been a working-man, and not a beggar – dragging that heavy machine with you all over the country!

ORGAN GRINDER

I am a public entertainer.

MAN WITH A TIN WHISTLE

You are, are you? Any fool could turn a handle, but I am a real musician, and make my own notes.

PROFESSOR

Sir, it would be better for the world if you did *not* make your own notes.

Enter Snivelling Tom

SNIVELLING TOM *(singing)*
    A mother's love, a mother's love
    Comes from the angels above,
    Then cherish her below;
    Let not a mother's instinct smother;

Though roses blow
And violets glow,
Its natural to love yer mother.

Snivelling Tom sings, the other plays his whistle, and the organ man plays —
their several tunes harmonizing perfectly

Curtain

True Travellers: A Tramp's Opera in Three Acts

This is the account of Davies's courtship with his wife Helen Payne, though anonymised to a degree: Helen is called 'Emma' and the author is not identified.

Young Emma *is no simple romance story. It begins with accounts of three of the narrator's temporary 'mistresses', before moving on to the eponymous subject. The narrator was in his early fifties when he was courting 'Emma', a woman twenty-nine years his junior and whom he met at a bus stop. She was not a prostitute, but would quite possibly have become one. In addition to being poor, she was pregnant – though the narrator did not know it at the time – and was to miscarry and nearly die as a result. In portraying Emma's illness, the book provides a grim insight into the inadequacy of medical provision for the poor in pre-Welfare State England. A lot of the narrative is also given over to the narrator experiencing symptoms of a venereal disease: he thinks Emma is to blame, but eventually comes to realise that the cause had been one of the women he had known shortly before meeting his future wife. Emma and the narrator eventually move to the country together and find happiness in a simple life.*

After submitting the typescript to Jonathan Cape, with the stipulation that its authorship should remain anonymous, Davies had severe misgivings. He asked for his original manuscript back and for Cape's copies of it to be destroyed. The MS was returned, but the copies were kept, which is why it survives today. Cape had already experienced his own misgivings by the time Davies contacted him, and had in the meantime approached George Bernard Shaw for his opinion. Shaw replied that 'I agree with you that its publication may do him harm', adding 'if they were both dead it would be another matter'. Young Emma was published in 1980, a year after Helen Davies passed away, with W. H. Davies named as the author.

Chapter IV: The Silk Stocking

When Louise had gone, it was a long time before I could think seriously of taking another mistress.[106] But I found it very difficult to settle down to my work, and went into society more, as much as I disliked doing so. I dislike society, because conversation exhausts my brain more than silent thought – again, I cannot hold my water long enough for a prolonged conversation; nor can I sit in comfort through a political speech or a sermon. People did not seem to dislike me, but my silence must have often bored them. If it were not for having something of a name in the world, I don't believe anyone would have given me a second invitation to their house. What was the use, as far as society goes, of knowing good music from bad, if I could not give some reason? And, although I could tell a good picture when I saw one, yet, for all that, I could not praise it like an art critic. But that I recognised a good picture, when it came under my notice, has been proved more than once. One day, when I looked into a shop window, I saw a picture of still-life – some apples on a small table. 'If I had that picture', thought I, 'I would never be without apples – my favourite fruit – and I would have no need to worry about money, season or crop'. Looking at those apples a little longer, I was so taken with the richness of their painting that I was prepared to give half my fortune to have them in my room. Which meant that I would give ten pounds, my fortune at that time being twenty pounds. But I did not go into the shop, for two reasons. First, I thought the picture would be too much for my purse; and I did not like the idea of raising the shopkeeper's hopes that I was going to buy it and then coming out of his shop without spending a penny. The second reason was this: I always like to spend my money as though I am worth plenty more, and did not want the shopkeeper to think that I was too poor to pay the price he asked for his picture. The picture was by F——. Now as I had never heard of such an artist – although I know now that he was one of the greatest masters of that kind of work – it must be seen from this that I know a good work of art when I see one.

---

106. Bella and Louise, two previous mistresses of the narrator, are named in the titles of earlier chapters of *Young Emma*.

It was now that I met a certain strange woman, whom I would have cause to remember for a long time. One night I had gone out to have dinner with a friend, at his own house in the West End.[107] Other friends came in for coffee after dinner, and then we all began to drink brandy. This went on for some time, and it was long after midnight when I parted with him at the door, and began walking towards my own home, which was about a mile away. With the exception of two or three policemen, standing quietly in doorways, there was no sign of human life anywhere; and the sound of my own feet on the hard pavement was an annoyance to my nerves. Under these circumstances, the reader will judge of my surprise when I say that a woman suddenly stood at my side, coming from I know not where. And when I saw, at a first glance, that she was well-dressed and ladylike in appearance, I was more surprised than ever. 'Surely', thought I, 'this woman is not homeless; and her presence here, at two o'clock in the morning, can be no other than an accident.'

'Where are you going?' I asked, not knowing what else I could say.

'I am coming home with you', she answered, taking hold of my arm.

'No, no', I said hastily. 'You have made a great mistake. If you do not look for richer customers, you will soon be in rags – and my home is only the home of a poor man.'

'Come along', she exclaimed, with a light laugh – 'I have not asked you for money. When I do, we can discuss the matter then.'

As we walked along, she began to explain matters, and I did not see any reason to think her story improbable. She told me that she had been drinking heavily, and that she had finished by drinking six strong liquors within an hour of closing time. Then, being in a high state of intoxication, she had walked the streets, not caring to return to the hotel where she was staying. And although she was now in a fit state to do so, it was too strange an hour, and she preferred to wait until the rest of the world was well awake.

'I am living apart from my husband', she said, at last; 'but he is rich and makes me a generous allowance. For that reason, I have no need to go home with you or any other man, to make a living.'

Not long after this we reached my home, which was in a mean little street – although a stone could almost be thrown into one of the most fashionable quarters of the world. And when I opened the front door, and we both clattered up the narrow, awkward stairs that

---

107. The West End refers to largely fashionable areas of central London to the west of Charing Cross.

did not have one straight step, I made my companion some apology. But she only laughed, and said – 'How interesting'.

When we were in the room and seated, I asked my companion if she would have a glass of wine, which was the greatest mistake I could have made. To make matters worse, the bottle was almost empty, and I had to open another. I could not fail to see the eagerness in her face, and I knew at once that I ought not to have opened a full bottle of wine, especially at that hour. Before I had half finished my drink, hers had gone, and yet I could only remember seeing her slowly taking one or two sips, like a bird at a fountain. But when I was slow in refilling her glass, it did not take her long to remind me that it was empty, and that she would like more. So, when I saw it was a case of finishing the whole bottle, I was determined that we should not sit too long over empty glasses. When we came to the last two glasses, she said, half stupidly – 'Open another bottle'.

'This bottle was the last', I answered – 'and we were very lucky to have it.'

'What's in that bottle on the shelf?' she asked, pointing to a far corner.

'Vinegar', I answered.

Bring it here and let me see', she said.

By this time, I began to see that there was going to be trouble. However, I brought her the bottle, and she was not satisfied until she had not only smelt it, but tasted it too.

But I will now go back to our earlier conversation over the wine, which was so interesting to me that I began to wonder if I had found a kindred spirit, and the proper companion for a literary man. For it was not long before she had told me that her husband was the brother of a well-known author, and mentioned his name, with other well-known authors she had known. It was now that I told her that I was something of an author myself, but not with a very big name.

'Do you know the work of—?' she asked, mentioning an author with a world-wide reputation, who had died a few years ago. 'He', she continued, 'was a great friend of my husband's and I have often had tea with him at Thirty — Street.'

I have known a number of strange coincidences in my time, but this was the strangest of all. For I had had dinner in that very house a few hours before I had met her. And when I studied the whole case from beginning to end, I did not know what to make of it. For instance, why did she mention that very house, with the thousands and thousands of other houses in London? And why should we two, both connected with literature, be brought together at that strange

Young Emma

hour, and the only two human beings in the streets and awake? But my first thoughts that, getting a divorce from her husband, she would then marry me and put an end to mistresses and strange women, was to have a severe check, and soon too. For when she saw no sign of more wine, her mood changed suddenly, and she became hard and quarrelsome. Her voice was raised to a higher pitch, and I began to think of my neighbours who were now asleep. At last my patience gave way altogether, and I told her in a cold quiet voice that if she did not want to settle down quietly until daylight, she could go: and that she was not only welcome to the wine, but also to the money I had given her. For I had already given her a certain sum, which she had not asked for, and which she took with the utmost indifference, and threw, in a crumpled state, into her bag.

'Do you want to go?' I asked, leading the way towards the door and expecting her to follow me.

But the only answer she made to this was to take off one of her shoes, and then the other.

The next moment she began to take off her stockings, which were of fine silk. While she was doing this, in silence, she was looking at me all the time, and I thought I saw a strange, mad light in her eyes. Her face was smiling, but I felt certain that her joy came from some wicked thought, which was soon proved to be correct. For she suddenly threw one of the stockings into my hand, and cried, in a sharp voice – 'Are you going to murder me with that?'

'Nonsense, what nonsense!' I said gently – 'What brought such a foolish idea into your mind?'

Without making a direct answer to this, she began to swish the other stocking around her own neck, saying, at the same time – 'Now is the time; the work is already half done'.

It was now that I began to feel really angry, for it was four o'clock in the morning and I needed sleep.

'Do as you like', I said, 'stay or go; but I am going to sleep here, in this chair.'

With these words, I closed my eyes, folded my arms and settled down.

What happened after this I can only guess. I must have gone off to sleep immediately; and she, no longer having anyone to talk to, probably did the same. As I did not hear her make the least movement, she must have been very quiet; or was I myself in such an exhausted state that I could sleep through thunder? All I know is this – I opened my eyes, in changing my position, just long enough to see two things, that it was five o'clock and that my strange companion was lying curled, almost in full dress, on top of the bed, as though she had been too sleepy to undress. 'Thank God I will soon have a sober woman to deal with', was the quick thought that went through my brain before I fell asleep for the second time.

When it was eight o'clock, I was determined to sleep no more until I had got rid of my companion, although I felt stupid and limp from insufficient rest. Now, although I am a rough man in some ways, that can boast of neither college nor club, yet, for all that, I have been called more than once 'one of Nature's gentlemen'. Which means, I suppose, that I am a gentle man. If the term could not have been applied to me on the present occasion, I would have regretted it to the end of my life. For when I woke my companion and offered her a cup of tea, the change in her was so great that she appeared to be a different woman altogether. Her gentle voice, with its finely balanced accent, so surprised me that I said to myself – 'Surely this is not the woman who only four hours ago used foul language and talked of murder!'

And when she began to apologise for any trouble she might have given, and hoped that I would forgive her, I, not to be outdone in gentleness, said, 'You have given no trouble at all, and I hope you have rested well'.

Soon after this she was dressed and ready to go. Although I had no desire to see her again, I certainly wished her no harm. In fact, I felt pleased to know that she was not poor, and had more money coming to her every week than I could earn by my work.

But she had scarcely shook hands and said goodbye, when she saw my morning paper, for the first time, lying unopened on the table. I had brought it upstairs from the letter box while she still slept.

'Do let me see that paper before I go', she cried suddenly, holding her hand out eagerly.

'Certainly', I said, feeling rather awkward at her silence, while she stood near the window, reading, for what appeared to be a long time. However, it was not long before she was in the street and going, I suppose, back to her hotel lodgings.

When she had gone, I picked up the paper and the first thing I read was of a woman that had just been found murdered, strangled with her own silk stocking. This cleared up the whole mystery. My late companion had been reading of that murder the night before, and that accounted for her strange behaviour. But as I had not seen an evening paper, I knew nothing about it.

As soon as I was left alone to think of what had happened, I said to myself – 'No wonder some of these strange women are found murdered!'

I was reminded of another woman, whom I had met some time before, and gone with her to her rooms. And I remembered how she had taken up a board in the floor and shown me two bundles of treasury notes, which must have contained something like two hundred pounds. If she had done this with some men she would have been murdered in her sleep. The circumstances were very peculiar at that time. For treasury notes had only just come out for the first time, and caused so much suspicion for a week or two that some people trembled like guilty thieves when presenting them in payment. To make matters worse, shopkeepers, not having sufficient silver in hand, were refusing to cash them. This woman who now had paper money for the first time in her life, and who was poorly dressed, was so much afraid to tender these notes in payment that I believe she would have gladly sold me the whole lot for five pounds' worth of silver. Before I left her I gave her thirty shillings in coin, in exchange for two notes, advising her, at the same time, to buy a new hat and coat, and then spend her paper money without fear of being arrested. I did not ask her where the money came from, whether it was stolen or found, but told her very seriously not to show it to strange men, if she valued her own life.

Chapter V: Young Emma

My only fear in writing this book is that my readers will think I am something of a woman-charmer; one who is always bending over a woman's shoulder, devoted to her every whim and flattering her with soft words. This is entirely wrong, for I would much prefer the company of men to women. First of all, I am a great smoker of strong tobacco, and I like to blow my heavy smoke where I like, without consulting my friends, and for that reason I often find women a nuisance. I am also fond of strong drink, and a suspicion that women count my glasses makes me feel uncomfortable. However, I have never once, in all my life, been rude to a woman. But I am so conscious of lacking the charms that please a woman that I don't think it possible that any woman could fall in love with me at first sight. Yet, strange to say, many a woman would have trusted her future life with me, after she had known me a little time. Perhaps they have thought, on a closer study, that I have enough kindness, good humour and patience to make a good husband.

My experience with Bella, and then with Louise as mistress, had taken up twelve months of my life and I was as far off as ever in getting one woman as a life companion. And after my experience with the woman with the silk stockings, I began to see that I could easily make a bad mistake that would ruin me for ever. The whole question seemed to be this – whether a woman drank or did not. Although I was a drinking man, I was very particular about this; for I did not expect any woman to have the same willpower and control as a man when it comes to taking drugs. And if it came to having children, when a tin mother would be of more value than a silver father – what would happen if she drank and neglected her home? No, no; I could live with a slovenly woman, an extravagant woman, and with a woman with a sharp tongue; but with a woman that drank I could never live. The effect of drink on men is strangely different, it makes devils of some men and angels of others. But the effect of drink on women is to make devils of them all.

I began to wonder, at this time, whether it would not be wiser to go more into society and try to get a wife that way. But the very thought that I would get a woman who would drag me into the limelight gave me an unpleasant feeling. For I hated society, and all my thoughts were set on a quiet life in the country. Every day I was thinking of green lanes, and woods with their own heaven of blue-bells; and pools where I might see a kingfisher dive, to brighten his jewels with water. Not a day passed without my having such thoughts as these.

One night, about two weeks after my adventure with the silk stockings, I went forth again on the old quest. Having this idea in my mind, I had stayed at home all day – with the exception of an hour to lunch at a restaurant – so that I might be in fit condition to tramp the streets all night, if it should be needed. For I had made up my mind to make a great effort, on this particular night, to find a young woman who was not too demoralised to be saved from the streets – if someone gave her the chance.

The war had been over for some time, and the streets were no longer full of soldiers. Women were now casting their eyes on civil-ians, in the same way as they did before the war, and they no longer felt uncomfortable at the side of a man who did not wear the King's uniform. If a man was well-dressed and looked prosperous, he could take his choice of glad eyes and winsome smiles, followed by friendly nods. Many a strange woman who passed him by would give him the invitation; and he could raise his hat and speak without fear of accost-ing a respectable woman. On this occasion I was dressed smartly in a light overcoat, which was almost new, and it was this that probably made a number of women smile and come to a very slow walk, to enable me to make the next advance. But here I must make another confession which may appear strange indeed. It is this – I am a very shy man. For instance, if one of these women did not actually come to a dead halt and speak to me first, it was not at all likely that I would have turned back and followed her, however much I might have been impressed by her beauty, and however cordial might have been her greeting. Time after time have I gone out looking for a woman, and time after time have I returned home alone, because I have not had the courage to take advantage of a woman's encouragement. This is the reason why I never made a mistake in accosting a respectable married woman, in spite of my dealings with scores of other strange women, through a number of years as a single man. As far as I can remember, every woman that I have had dealings with has come up to me boldly and told me why, before I could express any thought of my own. But what I have said before, about having an honest-look-ing face, has stood me well in cases of this kind; for women have, more than once, given me far more encouragement than I could have expected from them.

This shyness is sometimes so painful that I have to take two or three strong drinks before I can look at a woman, in spite of having gone out on purpose to meet one. I am very pleased to be able to make this confession; otherwise in the following adventure I would appear like the strong, crafty, designing man of middle age on the look-out for a young and innocent girl.

It was now eleven o'clock, and I was standing at the end of the Edgware Road, near the spot where the Tree of Tyburn had stood.[108] There were quite a number of women and young girls walking to and fro, but none of them seemed to take my fancy. Some of them were the worse for drink, and I was determined to have no more to do with a woman of that kind. All at once a bus stopped right in front of me, and I looked, half wondering what kind of passengers would alight. There was only one; and that was a young girl who could be anything between fifteen and twenty years of age. Thinking of her youth, I began to turn my eyes away, but the smile on her face would not allow me to dismiss my interest in that way. Not only that, but it soon became obvious that the smile was meant for me. If I had any doubt, it was to go at once, for, in passing close by, she nodded slightly, and almost came to a halt. But although I raised my hat in acknowledgment and returned her smile, my old feeling of shyness came back to me, and I made no effort to overtake her. However, when she turned her head and saw that I was not following her, she, apparently liking my appearance too well to lose me, stood looking my way, and waiting to see what I intended to do. When I saw this, and knew that the hour was late and that the streets would soon be almost empty of human life, I mustered up enough courage to approach her and to ask her where she was going.

'I have spent the evening with some friends, and am now going home', she said.

'Will you come to my home instead?' I asked, knowing what her answer would be, for I had only approached her after much encouragement.

'Yes', she answered simply, without asking any questions, and with absolute trust.

With this simple word, she took hold of my arm. I believed, at that time, that she took my arm because of a little fear of older women

108. Tyburn was once a Middlesex village, near to where the Marble Arch now stands in central London. The 'Tyburn Tree', a gallows, was erected in 1571, and public executions took place there until the late eighteenth century.

who glanced darkly at her in passing; jealous and angry that she – a young and simple-looking little creature – had succeeded in getting a male companion and they had not. But when I knew her better, I came to the conclusion that natural affection had as much to do with it as any fear she might have had of her own jealous sex.

As we passed the Marble Arch, going towards Holborn,[109] I cannot say that I felt comfortable. I began to wonder what people thought of seeing a well-dressed man of middle age walking side by side with a young girl that was poorly dressed. Her age was twenty-three, but with her short skirt and a soft, saucy-looking little velvet cap with tassels, she did not look a day more than fifteen. I seemed to have a fear that some inspector of morals would come up to us, and say to me – 'What's that child to you, and where are you taking her?' And I had to admit, in my own mind, that if this happened, it would be a right and proper thing to do, and a credit to the country – even though it had no sympathy with me. Thinking of this, I took my companion through the back streets, which made the distance to my home a little longer, but not much.

As we passed under the street lamps, I looked sideways at my companion, and was well satisfied with her appearance; and once or twice I stopped and lit my pipe, when we were in dark places, as an excuse to look into her eyes. But what struck me more than anything else was the softness and tenderness around her mouth. I was very pleased to see this; for it was a sure proof that my companion had had very little to do with men, and was not a professional street-walker. If she had been that, it would have been certain that her mouth would have been firm and hard, and no softer for a smile that was forced and false.

When we reached my rooms, I asked my companion if she would have a glass of wine.

'No, no', she answered, quickly – 'I never touch strong drink in any form, but I would like a cup of tea, if it is not too much trouble to make it.'

'This is a good beginning', I thought, thinking of Bella and the woman with the silk stockings.[110]

Soon after this she began to tell me, in answer to my questions,

---

109. They are walking east along Oxford Street, one of central London's main thoroughfares. In 1921, Davies had moved to small and unglamorous lodgings at 13 Avery Row, Brook Street, Mayfair, generally one of London's more fashionable and expensive districts.

110. In Chapter II, Davies recalls Bella stealing his possessions, including a clock from his mantelpiece and the contents of a bottle of whisky (which she replaces with water).

something about her own life. First of all she surprised me by saying that she was in steady work, in the city; but that the place closed on Friday night and did not open again until Monday morning. For that reason she had to live with some friends during the weekends, and pay them for her board and lodging. However, she did not like the place very much, and intended to give a week's notice on Monday, when she returned; as they did not pay her sufficient wages.

When I heard this, I understood a good many things, or, at least, thought I did. This poor girl was one of a great number of others, who worked for a starved wage and was forced to occasional immorality. Such were my thoughts, but they were not altogether right, as will be seen later on.

It was not long before I made up my mind to try and win this young girl's love, with the object of marriage. I flattered myself that she had already taken a liking to me. As she did not have to go back to work the next morning, I promised myself a long conversation with her, in which I would make her certain offers. What that conversation was about, and its result, will be told in the following chapters.

Chapter VI: The Complaint

The next day was Saturday, and young Emma, my new mistress, was away from work for the weekend.

'What will your friends say, when you go to them this morning, to know that you were away all night?' I asked. 'Will they suspect you of leading a fast and a double life?'

'Not at all', she answered, 'I will say that I have stayed with my other friends, whom I had just left before I met you. And as my friends do not know each other, the truth can never be known.'

On further conversation I found that she was a country girl, and had no relatives in London; and the only friends she had were the people she had visited the night before, and the people she should have gone to after, instead of going home with a strange man.

During the night I had lain awake for a long time, and made my plans. But now, when the time came for speaking them, I began to doubt their wisdom. It did not seem to me a right thing that I, a man who was old enough to be her father, should try to bind her young life to mine. And yet it was quite obvious to me that she could do much worse; that she would take to a fast life and die young. In that case I, though twice her age, might very well survive her by a quarter of a century. However, there was no time to be wasted, for she would be leaving me soon, and I did not want it to be for ever.

So I began in this way – 'You are giving your employer a week's notice on Monday, but you do not appear to have any prospect of another place. Now, if you care to come here and look after my comfort, you will be certain to find a kind and an easy master.'

'Very well', she answered, with a soft laugh – 'we'll try our luck together. You can expect me here in a week's time, on Saturday morning, about ten o'clock. Will that do?'

It did not surprise me in the least to hear her say this; for, after all, she would always be free to leave me at a moment's notice, if she was not satisfied with my treatment. And as I would have to trust her with money for housekeeping, there would be no need for her to go away without a penny in her pocket.

In case she should alter her mind, thinking, from my present squalid surroundings, that I would be too poor for any luxury that was not a dream, I gave her a little more account of myself, and what she could expect.

'I am not so poor that I cannot live in a better place than this', I said, 'but in these days it is very difficult to make a change, owing to the shortage of houses. But as soon as we are able to move', I continued, 'we will; and we will buy more furniture, and take a pride in making a better home.'

Not long after this I wished her goodbye, and she left, with the promise to come back to me in a week's time. Strange to say, I had looked forward to her going, for I wanted to sit down for an hour alone, and enjoy her in the spirit and as a pleasant dream. However, it was not long before my feelings changed entirely. I soon began to ask myself – 'How can I live without her for a whole week?' And I began to think of what a fool I had been in not asking her where she worked, so that I might be able to see her. In the end I began to curse myself for letting her go at all. 'Why should she give her employer a week's notice?' I asked myself. He, with his low, starvation wages, had no consideration for her, then why should she study him? She had already told me that she kept nothing there that was worth bringing away, and that all her clothes were at her weekend lodgings. For that reason it would be quite as easy for her to leave at once as to leave empty-handed in a week's time. What annoyed me was this – if I had suggested such a thing, no doubt she would have agreed. 'If, through this stupidity, I lose her altogether', thought I, 'I have only myself to blame.'

But these thoughts were gentle compared to the one that followed. For I suddenly had a vision of that young girl – not working quietly in a shop or warehouse – but parading the streets and attracting the notice of men. I saw her walking lightly and shaking the tassels on her velvet cap; as proud of her grace and beauty as a black horse, when he prances at a funeral. Smiling here and there, her actions seemed to cry out – 'Who'll buy, who'll buy a thing dainty and young? You there, smoking the large cigar, shall I say, "Sold again and got the money"?'

This thought became so terrible at last that I could no longer remain indoors, writing; in spite of having certain other thoughts that were eager for expression and whimpered at the long delay. 'If she's guilty of this kind of life', thought I, 'I am sure to find it out. She will not be able to keep away from her old haunts for a whole week; and if I am there, night and day, how can she escape me? Although she may not come close, my sight is wonderful for seeing a long distance off.'

With this thought taking full possession of my mind, I left the house, and made my way towards the Marble Arch. But I walked very slowly, for my eyes began to work at once, searching in every direction, to find a young girl with a velvet cap. This velvet cap had become more important to me than my father's waistcoat, which is all I can remember of him. My father had died young, when I was very small, and I cannot remember whether his face was bearded or smooth, or whether he was lean or fat. All I can remember of him is the soft velvet waistcoat, on which I could lay my face and sleep; loving him for that warmth and comfort, while he was loving me for myself, and giving me the care of a father. He was a small man, I have been told – like myself; but he had a weak chest, and coughed like a giant.

In about half an hour I reached the Marble Arch and, passing it by, stood at the end of the Edgware Road, in the exact place where I had met young Emma. But not seeing any signs of her, it was not long before I began to reason with myself. For instance, this young girl would not have the strength to keep walking day and night; and, if she walked at night, she must rest by day. With this thought, I crossed the road and went into Hyde Park, where so many of these unfortunate streetwalkers take their daily rest. But although I saw scores of girls and women sitting in chairs and on the free seats, I could not see one that resembled in any way the girl I was searching for. However, I decided to sit down myself, taking a position that would command a long distance through the Park, and trusting to my eyes to make no mistake. Once or twice I trembled with excitement as I caught sight of a blue cap in the distance; but it was not long before I decided that the woman was too thin or too fat, too tall or too short to be the one I searched for, and dreaded to find. However, I made up my mind to remain in that neighbourhood until midnight, and have my meals there, before I returned home. The hours seemed to go heavily and slow, no matter what I did. It was all the same, whether I sat on a seat in the Park or drank tea in one place or ale in another – the time did not pass any the more quickly. At ten o'clock I was standing at the end of the Edgware Road, but none of the buses that stopped there discharged a young girl with a velvet cap. But all at once I saw a couple of people in the distance – 'That's her', thought I – 'I have found her at last'.

I stepped back against the wall to let them pass. In doing this I had turned my eyes away, for not more than a second, but when I looked again, the both of them had vanished. 'They are gone indoors', thought I, walking up the street.

It was not long before I came to a public house. 'They are in here', I said to myself. The door was wide open, and I looked in, but only saw a number of men. However, I went inside and called for a drink, so that I might be able to see into every corner of the place. Yes, there was one woman there, sitting in a corner at the side of the door; but while I looked, she was joined by a man, who had just been served with drinks and was carrying them from the bar. I could see at a glance that this woman had not the remotest resemblance to the one I sought. Her hat was not only not of velvet, but was also of an entirely different shape, and she was old enough to be young Emma's mother. 'Surely', thought I, 'I must be going mad, to make a mistake like this.'

It was very fortunate, at this time, I was reminded of an adventure in the past, when a similar state of feelings had possessed me. On that occasion I was crossing a desert, which I had been told could be crossed in four days. So I took enough food with me to last three days, thinking a fast on the last day would do me more good than harm. But I was wrongly informed for, on the fourth day when my provisions were all gone, I could still see no sign of a house, much less a village or a town. The consequence was that when I did see a house, at last, in the far distance, I was in a bad state indeed, being lightheaded with hunger. My eyes were playing me such bad tricks, that I began to pounce on objects to the right and left of me, mistaking them for various forms of food.

Thinking of this adventure had a good effect on me, on the present occasion, for it brought back my common sense. I knew that if I was not careful, the same state of feeling would come again. And, even as I once mistook stones for hunks of bread, so would I now, if I did not restrain myself, see velvet caps in every direction, and tassels hanging to them all.

With my thoughts under better control, I began to make my way home, for the hour was getting late. But never once, until I was indoors for the night, did my eyes forget my morning command – to search the streets in every direction for a young girl wearing a blue velvet cap with tassels hanging to it.

I spent the next day in much the same way, and also the days that followed, until Saturday morning came at last; when I was to expect young Emma at ten o'clock. As I lived above a shop, the front door was opened early in the morning, and left open all day; and visitors could walk straight up my stairs and knock at my private door, without waiting for an answer in the open street.

The great morning came at last; the morning that was to alter the whole course of my future life. But instead of feeling proud and happy at the prospect of meeting a new love, whom I had even hope of making my bride – instead of this, I was sitting limp in a chair, and in a wretched state of unhappiness. My breath, which, owing to a feeling of sickness, made every effort to groan or sigh, came either too fast or too slow, and I was trying to get it under proper control. 'What a fool I have been', I muttered to myself, bitterly. 'To think that I, with all my experience in life, and all my years, have learnt nothing, nothing at all.'

I looked at the clock, but cannot say why; for time did not matter now – it was quite certain that I would see no more of young Emma and her velvet cap. She would keep away in fear of her life. For when one of these girls gives a man a venereal disease, she is even afraid to meet him in the open street, where thousands would protect her from violence, and she would be foolish indeed if she did not change her haunts for a while.

'No wonder', thought I, 'she was not to be seen anywhere near the Marble Arch; she was more likely to be found at Charing Cross or near St Paul's.[111] It is quite certain that she will not come here and meet her victim all alone, in his own room.'

But although I had these thoughts, it must not be imagined for one moment that I would do this poor girl any harm. On the contrary, I pitied her, as much as I pitied myself at having lost her. Although I was certain that she would not dare to come again yet, for all that, I still remembered her with a strange pleasure. I was still concerned about her more than about myself.

It was not long before all my thoughts ended in sorrow for her, and I cared nothing for my own life. It did not take me long to come to the conclusion that I would soon be all right again, as far as the body was concerned. My constitution was strong, and my health had always been good. Knowing this, I had every confidence that this complaint would not do me much harm, and would only cause me a little inconvenience for a month, or perhaps a little longer. 'To a doctor', thought I, 'this will not be much more than a laughing matter, and I already know his advice – 'Don't drink, and don't worry'.

My experience with women, after all this time, had led me nowhere; for I was now as far off as ever in getting a companion for life. Bella was a thief; Louise was an invalid;[112] the woman with the silk stockings was a drunkard; and now, young Emma – But I had no

---

111. The immediate vicinity of St Paul's Cathedral is not especially known for that, but in the early twentieth century, Charing Cross Road had a reputation for being the haunt of prostitutes.

112. Bella had stolen his clock; Louise had proven prone to jealousy, and had left him for another man.

sooner come to this name than there was a gentle knock at the door. When I heard this, my heart leapt in my body, and for a moment I could not believe my ears.

The next moment a young girl, wearing a velvet cap, walked into the room, without waiting for the door to be opened for her, and as though the place belonged to her and she only knocked from politeness. It was young Emma, with her smiling face, and the trim tassels on her shoulder. But what amazed me most, was the innocence in her face.

Chapter VIII: A Night of Horror

It did not take me many days to know that my illness was going to be stubborn and long, in spite of rest, medical treatment, and young Emma's care.[113] Although I no longer suffered pain, except for aching bones, caused by lying so long in bed, yet for all that, my foot was still fat and bloated, and still showed no sign of being different. Unfortunately I was suffering something worse than pain; it was a sick feeling which came over me occasionally, when my life felt sinking lower and lower, until I thought the very end had come. My courage always failed me then, and I could no longer try to make young Emma laugh. And when my great little nurse realised for the first time, that her patient was unusually quiet and asked, 'Are you sleeping, Bunnykins?' – she received no answer, for I had no courage to say, 'No' and give the reason why.

At this time I was lying on a couch in my sitting room, my bedroom being the room below. And every night young Emma brought up a mattress and bedclothes and slept on the floor at my side, so as to be near me through the night. These things she removed in the morning, in case anyone came to see me. For some reason or other, she seemed to need my company almost as much as I needed hers, and would not sleep in the room below all alone.

One night, when I woke about the middle hour, I saw to my surprise that young Emma was sitting up straight, with her head bowed, and her two hands clasping her knees. 'Surely she is not dreaming', thought I, 'and going to walk in her sleep, while I look on helplessly, and without power to reach her.' But just as I was about to speak to her, she unclasped her hands and began to lie down, making a few light sounds, which might have been either moans or talking in her sleep. But although I lay awake for more than two hours after this, she did not move again.

The next morning I told her what had happened in the night, and asked her if she had any knowledge of it. 'Yes', she said, 'I sometimes

---

113. In the previous chapter, Davies describes finding that he has contracted a venereal disease, which causes, among other things, rheumatism – and especially a swollen ankle. He assumes this has been contracted from Emma. She nurses him back to health.

have severe pains in my back, but they soon pass away. I had a bad attack of influenza during the epidemic,[114] and since then those pains come on me occasionally. But I would not like to walk in my sleep – unless I walked to my Bunnykins.'

When I heard this, I told her to go to my doctor at once and be treated for her complaint. This she did, and returned with a box of pills and a bottle of medicine. So now we were two invalids, under the same doctor. We made a great laughing matter of our race back to health, each one determined to come in first. She claimed an advantage from youth; while I swore by a life that had been toughened by years.

Not long after this her attacks not only became more frequent, but also became more painful, and it was not long before she broke down altogether. One afternoon she had gone downstairs to prepare tea, about four o'clock. But she was so long away that I began to wonder if there was anything serious the matter. And when I heard her at last on the stairs, she was walking with so much labour that I became alarmed. To make matters worse, she halted halfway, and I did not know, when she moved again, whether she would succeed in climbing the stairs or fall backward and break her neck. It was a great relief when she reached my door and entered the room. But I saw at once that there was something wrong with her; and there was no need for her to say, as she did – 'There you are, Bunnykins, you must now help yourself, for I can do no more'. The next moment she staggered to the door, and while I was lying there without the power to stand on my feet, I could hear her groping her way painfully and slowly down the stairs to the room below.

Needless to say I did not help myself, and the tea remained there, at the side of my couch, for hours, until it was removed at last by a strange woman. 'We are now at the mercy of strangers', thought I, and wondered what would happen next.

Not long after this, I began to hear groans and cries of pain coming from the room below me. These sounds became so loud and violent at last, that I could hear the people in the street coming to a halt under young Emma's window, to listen and talk. It was not long before one or two of them, at the risk of interfering in a private matter, entered the shop, and said to the woman in charge of it 'There is a woman here in great pain. Can nothing be done for her?'

This woman, who had not been very friendly towards us,

---

114. Probably the London flu pandemic of 1918. The events Davies relates occurred in 1922.

suspecting that young Emma was more of a mistress to me than a housekeeper, became alarmed at this, and answered that she would go at once and make an enquiry.

As soon as she had seen young Emma, she came hurrying up to me and said – 'Your little housekeeper is in a terrible condition, complaining that something in her inside has fallen down, and she is suffering great pain. Shall I go for a doctor?'

But there was no doctor to be found; they were either out of town or visiting other friends. I suspect too that my address in a small, narrow alley, did not appeal to one or two of them, in their fine West End mansions when their servants announced it. Strange to say, it did not occur to me to send for my own doctor, and hers too. However, when the woman told me of her failure, I thought of it then. But when she reached his house, she heard that he was not at home and would not be back for an hour or more. So there was nothing to do but wait.

It was almost two hours before my doctor came, and the poor girl was in agony, and crying for help all that time, while I lay upstairs listening, without any power to move. This was no fault of the doctor's, of course, for he had come at once on hearing that he was wanted at my place. But every time the poor child cried out for the doctor, it seemed to me like a cry in the wilderness, where it would be impossible to get even an echo for an answer. I expected every cry to be the last, and imagined her to be drowning and sinking for the last time, with one little hand above the water, and no one to see or take hold of it. 'To be tortured here all this time by another's agony, while in this helpless state', thought I, 'is a cruel thing indeed.'

When the doctor arrived at last, he was only with her a few minutes, but seemed to have given her instant relief, as far as pain was concerned. But as he had to hurry away to attend another serious case, he did not come to see me, and only sent a message to say that he was to call on me professionally the following day.

It was six o'clock when the manageress came upstairs with this message. She also had something to say of her own – 'Your housekeeper must now go to the hospital', she said, 'before she bleeds to death. The doctor has only rendered first aid, and there is more serious trouble to follow.'

With these words she left the room, with the object of getting young Emma to the hospital as soon as possible.

But at eight o'clock that night, two hours after the doctor had gone away, young Emma was still lying on the bed, and losing blood all the time. The manageress had been in communication with several hospitals, without any success. They were either full of patients or did not take in cases of that kind. When it was nine o'clock, the woman came up to me again and said – 'What are we to do? I have every fear that she will bleed to death if something is not done at once.' At last it was decided to go to the police station and see the inspector in charge, and explain the matter to him. But when the inspector had heard the whole story, he nodded his head and said – 'I am very sorry, but this is not a case for the police.' It was now half past nine, and the woman did not know what to do. However, when she was returning she accosted a police constable, who was on duty near us, and insisted on him entering the house and seeing the girl for himself. She had no sooner done this than he came up to me at once and said – 'The girl looks dying, and something must be done. Now, if I have the police ambulance brought along, to remove her to the hospital, are you willing to pay the expenses, which will be a pound or more?'

'Certainly', I answered, 'I will pay more than that, if it is necessary.'

'It is a very difficult case', continued the police constable, 'because she is inside a house. When we pick up a woman in the open streets, we generally manage to get her into a hospital in twenty minutes or half an hour.'

'We have made a mistake', I said. 'If this poor girl had been thrown into the gutter or placed on someone's doorstep, she would have been sure of hospital treatment in a very short time – is that right?'

'That's quite right, sir', answered the police constable as he left the room.

It was now ten o'clock, and there was not a sound coming up from the room below. The silence to me appeared to be much more terrible than the sounds, when young Emma had cried in a loud voice, for someone's help. But there was nothing to be done, only to wait patiently for the ambulance. It was almost half an hour before it came, and the clock at Westminster was striking the hour of eleven when young Emma was being carried downstairs. This made it seven hours since she was taken ill, and she was not in the hospital yet.

Another unpleasant feature of the case was this: the sight of a police ambulance standing at my front door caused fifty or sixty people to assemble there; and as the public houses had only just closed, more than half the people were the worse for drink. So that when young Emma was being put in the ambulance, she was greeted by a Babel of sounds, some crying a drunken pity, others making the sound of hissing with their lips, and others uttering ribald jokes, all of which I heard as I lay helpless on my couch. What a pity this beautiful, green world should have become verminous with humanity.

Young Emma

It was certainly a great relief when I heard the ambulance going off, although I had a fear that it was too late and that young Emma would not recover from the long delay. But the trouble was not over yet, it seems; for when she reached the hospital, they refused to take her in, in spite of the doctor's letter saying it was an urgent case. And it was not until one of the doctors had come out to see her, and reported in her favour, that young Emma was admitted into the hospital. I am only giving the bare facts, as things happened, and make no comments.

I will now go back a little way, to the time when the ambulance was at my door. It was then that the woman who managed the shop below came up to see me for the last time, to get money from me to pay the ambulance men when it was all over.

'I don't mind speaking to you on this matter', she said, 'because I am a mother. Your housekeeper has gone with a six months' child, which the doctor has removed. But although the child is dead, it is certainly an awkward position for you – if anything happens to the mother.'

My surprise at hearing this almost took my breath away, for I had never thought, for one moment, that young Emma was in that delicate condition, neither did the woman below, for that matter. And that that woman did not suspect anything of the kind is most surprising; for she did not like young Emma, because, I suppose, of her great youth and beauty. She would have been very glad to know that the plumpness of young Emma's body was her shame and not her pride; and that that fair body was rounded off by an unborn bastard. But the woman had no more suspicion than I had, and was as much surprised as myself when the truth became known.

When I began to weigh these words, after the woman had left my room, a good many things became clear to me, unless I was much mistaken. I have already said that I sometimes had an impression that young Emma had something on her mind; and here it was, a serious thing indeed for a young girl without any prospect of marriage.

As I sat thinking and thinking, the whole mystery seemed to unfold itself. One lighted part seemed to light another, until very little was left to provoke my curiosity. For instance, it was quite clear to me now why she intended to leave her situation.[115] It was not because of low wages, but because she was about to become a mother. She was giving her employer notice to save herself the shame and

---

115. When he had first met her, Emma had made it clear that she intended to leave her poorly-paid job as soon as possible. She had since done so.

mortification of receiving notice from him, which, if she remained there any longer, must soon happen. When I had reasoned as far as this, it also became clear why young Emma had taken to me, and so affectionately too. She had left her situation because she was about to become a mother; and she had taken to me because she was in search of a father. And now, no longer in fear of becoming a mother, and no longer in search of a father – what will she think of me, when she is fit and well, and her worst trouble is over? Will she still think that a man who is old enough to be her father is the kind of man to be her lover? The answer I made to this question was certainly not in my own favour; but I could hardly blame young Emma if she changed her feelings under the different conditions that were coming.

But there was still a little hope, when I remembered how her mother had married a man much older than herself; for there is nothing stronger in the world than a mother's example. What I wanted was not her gratitude for anything I ought to have done for her, but her love, and as strong as she liked to make it. If I could not have that, there was no reason why we should ever meet again.

It was not long before I began to think of our first meeting and how strange it was. We had come together with as much ease as two drops of rain on a leaf, when the wind shakes it. One look into my face and one look into hers, and we trusted each other immediately. 'If, after all', thought I, 'young Emma never comes back, and thinks I am not worth seeing again, even for a few minutes – if this should happen – what am I to do with this foolish face of mine: why does it look so kind and honest that everyone takes advantage of it; that even this young girl from the country could see at once her chance to play her own part, without any question of what became of me in the end?' At this time I was thinking rapidly, and I soon came to the most terrible thought of all – suppose young Emma was dead: it would not have been a very serious case, I believed, if our civilised state, with its numerous doctors, hospitals and police, had moved at a reasonable pace; but a delay of nearly eight hours, when a person is losing blood all the time, is a great temptation to Death. When I came to this thought, I was none too hopeful, and feared for the worst.

It was now that I began to think of the words used by the woman below, when she had said – 'It is certainly an awkward position for you, if anything happens to the mother.'

Yes, the position would be painful indeed, and I was distracted with the thought of it. I could see her mother, a plain simple creature up for the first time from the green country to enquire into the particulars of her daughter's death. This woman would come to me and charge me with causing the death of her child. It would be no use trying to persuade her that I had only known her daughter for a month; and she would scorn the idea of her daughter being employed as a housekeeper by a man who lived in two small rooms in a squalid little alley. What could I say? For young Emma had given me no address of any kind – not of a relative, or her employer in the City, or her friends at Chelsea. I knew of course that they would ask young Emma for her mother's address as soon as she was taken into the hospital, in case anything serious should happen. However, they would probably not use it unless they saw some sign of real danger.

These thoughts were having a bad effect on my own health; for, although I was not suffering much pain, I was still in a very weak state, and still had no power to leave my couch. It was not long before I came to the conclusion that my condition now depended on one thing – whether young Emma was alive or dead. If she lived, I too would live; if she was dead, I too must die, from having lost the will to live.

from Chapter XIII: The Green Country

The house we went to live in consisted, as I have said before, of eight rooms, and was semi-detached.[116] A little house of four rooms, and standing in its own grounds, would have pleased me much better, especially if the rooms had plenty of breathing space. It may be necessary for a king or emperor to live in a palace whose windows number the days in a year, because of his large household and public receptions. But as a lonely man of dreams, I would be quite satisfied if my windows numbered the months that are in a year, and I only had the choice of two small doors to come and go.

However, the house was well-situated, and had a small narrow lawn at the side, with a row of six large trees overlooking a high wall. At the back was a large garden with fruit trees, shrubs and evergreens, flowers, and a summer-house in a sunny corner. This garden interested me as much as the inside of the house interested young Emma. For while she was indoors, looking at the rooms, I was in the garden, trying to name the trees, and thinking of their summer glory, for it was now October. And what a dream of leaves I had: I wanted to cover the whole house all over with green leaves; around every window, all over the roof, and even around the chimney stack.

But this, of course, would take years and years; and life would be generous indeed, if I ever saw that done.

As soon as we were settled in our new home, it was necessary for me to get another doctor, for I still suffered from my complaint and my ankle still refused to let me walk for more than a quarter of an hour or twenty minutes.[117] This doctor no sooner came than he proposed a course of inoculation, which would last three months, to which I agreed. 'It is not very painful', he said, 'and there is no danger – although you may feel a bit feverish for an hour or two after each

---

116. In the intervening chapters, the narrator describes the return to health of both Emma and himself; Emma eventually comes back from the hospital and explains that she had fallen pregnant to a man she had refused to marry. The narrator asks her to move with him to the country (though the location remains unspecified), and she agrees to do so. They move. The narrator is still experiencing some fever and rheumatism after several months.

117. It should be remembered that Davies initially intended to publish *Young Emma* anonymously. If his particular writing style would not have indicated the authorship, the focus on the author's *one* rheumatic ankle might have provided a hint.

inoculation'.

But the truth is this I – I felt so feverish after each visit that I was afraid I would either go mad or die. At the end of this treatment, I found myself no worse and no better than at the beginning. So, after I had paid my bill, I made up my mind to see another doctor, and to be wily in the way I approached him. For it suddenly occurred to me that the rheumatism in my ankle was due to my venereal complaint and, if I was cured of the latter, the other would go away. My rheumatism was due to poisoned blood, and not caused by old age or a constitution weakened by a hard life of exposure in the open air. 'My next doctor's bill will be the fourth', thought I – and it must be the last.'

These thoughts had no sooner taken possession of my mind than I went to see another doctor and told him of my complaint, which had lasted several months. 'What have you been doing for it?' he asked, after an examination.

When I told him, he said – 'You have been doing the right thing, but you have not done it thoroughly and properly, and that is why you are not cured. It seems to me that your doctor should have known this, after all this time. Can you come here tomorrow evening, at the same time, and we'll see what can be done.'

'By the way', I said, as though it were an afterthought – 'by the way, I suffer from a little rheumatism too, and, after this thing is over, I would like you to treat me for that.'

'Very well', he answered, 'but when this affair is cleared up, I don't suppose there will be any more rheumatism.'

This was the same conclusion as I had come to myself, and I was delighted to hear a doctor say the same thing. When I left him I was full of hope that something would be done at last. The result of my second consultation with my new doctor was good, so he said. It consisted of a quarter of an hour's massage, and then my own treatment. The latter I had not done properly, he said, and showed me how to do it.

'If this had gone on much longer', he said, 'it would have led to a serious surgical operation, but I am hopeful now that it will not be needed.'

When I heard this, I was considerably alarmed, for I had never realised that there was as much danger as that. In fact, I had been under the impression that if I cared to wait long enough, time would have purified my blood and brought back my health, without a question of doctors at all.

After this I paid him three more visits, and went through the same treatment, and that was not only the end of my venereal disease but also the end of my rheumatism.

[...]

Young Emma would not have been a very good companion for the ordinary literary man, and yet she pleased me well enough. It did not worry me in the least to be asked suddenly, when my brain was struggling with what some people would call 'lofty thoughts' – 'Why is a bar of soap like the Bible?' She was fond of riddles, and I was not good at solving them, to her joy. And when she asked me one evening, in her simple, childish way – 'Are you as great as Shakespeare, Bunnykins?' I did not think it worthwhile to take a too modest view of the matter, and answered her in the same simple way – 'Sometimes'.

Her questions sometimes fed my imagination, and had a peculiar interest to me as a literary man. This was one: 'Suppose a man had come up to you when in your thirtieth year, and said – "Your wife has just been born"; would you have believed him?' Or – 'Did it ever occur to you, when you were thirty years old, that your future wife was only a small baby, and you would have to wait until she was a woman before you could marry her?'

I always tried to give some pleasant answer to these strange questions, knowing what pleasure it gave her in asking them.

No, young Emma was not a brilliant talker, by any means; but it was restful and soothing to feel one's self in the presence of a great heart and an affectionate spirit, and not a great brain. For that reason, our language was often nothing more than cuddles and kisses, and making love in silence; in the same way as I would hold a flower by its stalk and bend down to smell it, without a word to follow.

Strange to say, I had never wanted anyone to share my literary dreams; and that is why young Emma, not being interested in them, suited me so well as a companion. When I gave her a book that was written by myself, all she did was to take a knife and cut the leaves carefully. After doing this, she kissed its cover, and then kissed me, before she placed it among her own books, to be read – any time.[118]

---

118. In the rest of *Young Emma* (chapters XIV to XVIII), the narrator describes his simple marriage to Emma. All the while, however, he thinks she is to blame for his venereal disease. A doctor sees Emma and informs him that this cannot be the case, because there is no sign of her ever having had it. He concludes that the woman with the silk stockings, described in Chapter IV, is to blame.

Young Emma

Later Days, *a strange mixture of bravado and honesty and Davies's last major prose work, is an account of life since he had found success as a writer. There is a fair amount of name-dropping and a bit of score-settling, as is shown in the following pages, but many of the anecdotes are rewarding in spite (or because) of this. Moreover, the book offers some excellent if not always reliable insights into the British literary and art worlds in the decade following the outbreak of the Great War, especially in self-conscious London, from the perspective of one of its most unusual and self-conscious members.*

In this book, Davies regularly draws on his ostensibly incongruous experiences of begging and tramping to shed light on his current circumstances and those of the people he now meets in relatively high society. The book ends in a stripped-down but flat and anticlimactic account of how Davies met his wife, whom he calls 'Young Dinah'. This was Davies's solution to having spiked his far more candid account, Young Emma, *the previous year. Every chapter begins with a poem.*

from Chapter I: The Camp

[...] My first book caused a little sensation, as much from the strangeness of my life as from any merit it might have.[119] But Edward Thomas, who gave me a fine boom in several influential papers, knew that a poet could not live by poetry alone, and became a practical friend, finding me a small cottage in the Weald of Kent, where I was able to live on my small income of eight shillings a week, owing to my rent, coal and light being paid mysteriously by Thomas and his friends. Unfortunately, my second book of poems was something of a failure, because of my foolish haste to publish again, as is usual with new authors.[120] So that I felt considerably disappointed when Edward Thomas began to tell me how so many authors sing themselves out in their first book, and then have no more to say. But when my second book was followed by *Nature Poems* and my *Autobiography*,[121] Thomas was then delighted to find that he had made a mistake.

The first poet I ever met was, I believe, Walter de la Mare. This happened on one of the rare occasions I accompanied Edward Thomas on a day's visit to London.[122] But as I am refusing to make this book a catalogue of well-known names, I am not to mention a great number of poets and society people whom I have met and parted from without anything particular happening. For instance, de la Mare, as a number of people know, is a very charming man, but in thinking of him I am completely at a loss for copy. Every time I have met him, often at his own home, he has plied me with so many strange questions that I cannot remember anything we have been talking about. And when I get home and consult a dictionary about a word he has

---

119. At the beginning of this chapter (and of the book) Davies recalls some aspects of his life before he found literary success, in particular his experience of being a tramp in America.

120. *New Poems* (1907), which is dedicated to Helen and Edward Thomas. Thomas thought this collection 'painfully mediocre', as he put it in a private letter. See Lawrence Normand, *W. H. Davies* (Bridgend: Seren, 2003), p. 54.

121. Both published in 1908.

122. Walter de la Mare (1873–1956), poet. It may seem strange that Davies does not name Thomas as the first poet he ever met, but of course Thomas only started writing his own poems in 1914.

used in his questions, I find the definition to be even more confusing than the word, and impossible to apply to the question in hand.

On one occasion a man who had come to interview me asked me if I knew de la Mare, and whether he was easy to approach, as he wanted to get him for his next interview. But although I said all I could in de la Mare's favour, I certainly warned the man that he would come away as the interviewed and not the interviewer; that he would never interview de la Mare, but that de la Mare would interview *him*.

Up to the present time, I should think quite a hundred people have asked me if I knew Walter de la Mare. And when I have answered 'Yes', I don't believe there has ever been one case, whether the questioner was a man or a woman, where the question was not followed by these words – 'Isn't he a charming man.' But of the hundred people who have asked me if I knew Yeats, not one has discussed him as a man before they have said something about his work. No wonder a certain poet-editor ignored me altogether when I told him how difficult I found things because my pension, which at the time was only £50, was too small. 'How Walter de la Mare can live and educate his children on less than two thousand a year is a mystery', he said, ignoring my more modest claim altogether – 'and the Government should see that he gets it.' When a man's charm is so great that his friends say things like this, it seems to me that his life is dangerous, although he may be a fine writer, and he should be shut up for safety.

On one occasion de la Mare asked me how I wrote my poems. This being a plain and simple question, I began in this way – 'First, an idea comes to me.' But I had no sooner said this than de la Mare asked quickly – 'What do you mean by "an idea comes to you"?'

The reader will understand my confusion in trying to explain a thing that was so obvious.

Shall I mention the name of a well-known poet who was so modest, when he went to America, that the natives could not hear what he had to say – his voice was so quiet and low. But after three months of American hospitality and adulation, the natives could not hear his words for another reason – the voice had increased so much in volume.

There is another well-known poet who is so rich and well dressed that when I met him the other day in Charing Cross Road, I was afraid to speak to him for fear of being arrested for begging. And yet I knew him well and liked him too. I did not even dislike him when, not recognizing a friend and a fellow-poet, he held out his hand at Piccadilly Circus to prevent me from passing before his gorgeous car.

But although this fine fellow is not very great as a poet, I have heard that when he entered a certain place in America, hundreds of the natives bared their heads in reverence. Why do the Americans think so much of our worst writers? It is very consoling to think that as soon as my power as a writer begins to fail in England, I shall begin a new life of greatness in America.

Later Days

from Chapter III: 'Authors of the Sea'

[...] Conrad,[123] who happened to be in Town, came to the Mont Blanc to meet some of his old friends.[124] But although his face lighted up when we were introduced, to show that my name was known to him, he simply made an expressive sign with his hands, saying something about not being able to talk to me there. From this I understood that he would have liked us to be alone together. When he left he made this idea certain by inviting me to pay him a few days' visit any time I liked, and just to drop a line in advance to say that I was coming.

Some time after this, when it was near Whitsuntide, and I needed a breath of purer air, I remembered Conrad's invitation, and wrote to him. I judged that I would be less likely to interfere with his work if I went there at holiday-time. Back came an answer, by return of post, saying that he would expect me, and meet the train.[125]

When I arrived Conrad was on the platform waiting, and it was not long before we were shaking hands. But after this Conrad looked around, saying that he was also expecting a young countryman of his, who had come over on political matters relating to England's attitude towards Poland. It must be remembered that the Great War was now on, and every place was full of the movement of troops.

Hearing Conrad say this, I felt sorry that I had come, for I did not want to meet Conrad the politician, but Conrad the sailor and writer. And when Conrad and his young countryman began to complain that a certain sum to help Poland could not be raised, and yet England was doing all she could to help less deserving nations; when it came to this I began to feel uncomfortable, and did not know what answer to make. But although I nodded my head in agreement, I

---

123. Joseph Conrad (1857–1924), Polish author resident in England, who wrote in English.

124. A number of writers assembled at the Mont Blanc restaurant, Soho, every week. Here Davies met the likes of Hilaire Belloc, Ford Madox Ford, G. K. Chesterton and John Galsworthy. Davies was living in London at this time.

125. This is almost certainly the visit alluded to in Robert Frost's anecdote, quoted in the 'Introduction' to the present volume.

believe I said something about the English people being the most generous in the whole world; and that our papers were every day praising the gallantry of Scotch, Irish, Welsh and French troops, and saying very little about the achievements of their own.

That evening, when we all sat down to dinner, Conrad and his young countryman talked in their native tongue, while Mrs Conrad and myself at the other end of the table, had enough to say in English. In a few moments we had both found a subject to our liking, and had become so animated that Conrad forgot all about the troubles of Poland and asked once or twice – 'What are you saying?' On being told, he would smile approval, and would then return to the heavy, serious subject of their own. However, Mrs Conrad was a charming woman, and full of ideas; and I felt that no conversation that I could have had with her husband would have pleased me more than the one I had with her.

On the following day I had Conrad to myself for an hour or more. His young countryman had complained of neuralgia, and was either resting in his room or had gone out for a walk. But I made a bad start indeed, as soon as we settled down to talk. Some time before this a man had told me that although Conrad had his Master's certificate and was a Captain, yet, for all that, he had never been in actual command of a ship, having retired from the sea before that time. As this man had asked me to put the question to Conrad, if I should ever meet him, I did so at once. But when Conrad heard this, he appeared to be quite upset, and offered to go upstairs for his papers to show me, and to mention the names of ships he had commanded. As soon as I saw Conrad's distress, I assured him at once that the man meant no harm by that question and that he was one of his greatest admirers. On hearing this Conrad appeared more pleased and satisfied.

Soon after we began to talk of our contemporaries, and Conrad began to question me about the work of a certain writer, saying that one of his prose books had been strongly recommended to him, but that after reading one chapter he had to give it up as impossible.

Just before this we had been talking of Civil List Pensions. So that when Conrad, with rather a worried face, asked me about that writer, I came to the conclusion that he had been asked to sign a petition to that effect. Conrad, I believe, wanted to be honest in the matter, but was troubled by an overkind heart. So when I praised the writer as a poet, Conrad smiled happily, and in a more settled mind – the petition was already signed. However, I may as well say here that the writer in question had so many influential friends, from the Prime Minister down through the most aristocratic ranks, that it would have made no difference at all whether Conrad had signed the petition or not.

The next thing, I believe, was to discuss the works of Masefield; not to discuss it as literary men, but as sailors. Conrad seemed to suggest that Masefield was not altogether true to life in his description of ships and sailors. On hearing this, I said that 'Dauber', instead of being rejected and despised, would have been the most respected man on the ship; respected even by the captain and first officers, because of his unusual gift of being able to draw and paint pictures.[126] I mentioned several cases of this kind, where the illiterate and poorest classes had respected a man of gifts, when he had accidentally been thrown into their own life. 'If the Dauber', said I, 'was not respected by those honest seafaring men, it must not be put down to spite, disrespect, or jealousy of a gifted man, but because they disliked him for his personal conduct, or because they thought he was a sneak and carried tales to the captain. If that was the case', I continued, 'he should have been made the villain, and not the hero of a story.'

Conrad agreed with all this, and said he had known cases of the same kind, where the life of a quiet dreamer like that would have been safer than any other life on the ship, or in the camp – wherever it might be.

These things, of course, had nothing at all to do with the poetical value of the 'Dauber', or any other of Masefield's poems – we were only discussing their relation to real life; and both Conrad and myself were men who knew that life well, and had a perfect right to criticize any other man who should make it the subject of literature.

If anything equals my admiration of Masefield at his best, it is my admiration of him at his worst. At his worst he is extraordinarily good, as the following verses will prove –

'Her father struck
  Jane on the head,
Young Will upped
  And shot him dead.

'Jane died soon:
  At high tide,
At high noon
  Jane died.'

---

126. John Masefield (1878–1967), English poet, who would later serve as Poet Laureate from 1930 until his death. Masefield's long narrative poem 'Dauber' had been published in 1913.

I have a sincere and honest admiration for those two verses, for they are the two best bad verses that I have ever read. The flatness of that last verse is probably one of the finest things in English literature. Time after time have I tried to match those verses with lines of my own, and still I fail. Even the following sounds tame in comparison —

'Little boy,
   Big gun;
Loud noise
   Life done.'

So although I share the honour with Masefield of being included in the anthologies of the best poems, yet, for all that, I have a great fear that I shall never be able to write anything good enough to be included in an anthology of the best bad poems. I have such a dread of being left out of that book that I have made quite a number of efforts to match those two little verses of Masefield. Sometimes I think I have succeeded, as in the following lines from my opera, 'True Travellers.' It is about an old midwife called Martha, and is chanted by her great admirer Poll.

Not all the revels, Martha, we have been to,
Can give us, when we're old, a peace like yours —
Due to the corpses you have gone and seen to.

Although my readers may think this verse is not bad enough to be compared to Masefield's, I would still like to hear that I have made a good attempt. As I have said before, I am quite sincere and honest in saying this; for I do not bother my head much, or lecture the public on 'The Great Mission of Poets'; and do not care whether I am called a poet or a rhymer.

Probably those two little verses of Masefield and the above lines of my own, have given me as much delight as anything else in Literature. They are to me a joy for ever, in the same way as the best passages in Shakespeare, Coleridge, and Keats.

When we were discussing other authors, I was rather taken by surprise to hear Conrad exclaim emphatically — 'Hudson is a giant!'[127] I had never had the least idea that this was so, for, as I have said before, I had not read any of Hudson's books up till then. So hearing Conrad

---

127. William Henry Hudson (1841–1922), novelist. *Green Mansions* (1904) remains his best known novel.

say this, I made a mental note of it, with the intention of reading something of Hudson's as soon as possible.

I may as well say here that in the course of a few days I got hold of a copy of *Green Mansions,* and found it one of the most fascinating books I had ever read. What a pity I had not known that extraordinary book at the time I was meeting its author! And why was I not told of it during the whole twelve months I was meeting Hudson, week by week?

But I was never to tell Hudson personally of my high opinion of his work, for the meetings at the Mont Blanc were now coming to an end. Owing to the illness of his wife, who had been an invalid for a long time, and who now did not like to have her meals alone – owing to this, Hudson was one of the first to be absent. Two or three others died, and then the coming of the Great War did the rest.

But although I was never able to tell Hudson personally how much I admired his work, I certainly was not backward in telling others; for I have sent many a reader to *Green Mansions,* and have never heard of a disappointment.

Strange to say, I was in the same position exactly when I visited Conrad – I had only read one thing of his, and that was a newspaper article. And if that had not been sent to me by a Press Cutting Agency, because of my name being mentioned in it, in which Conrad had said that a certain poem of mine would be read when radium would no longer be a wonder – if it had not been for this, I could have said that I had never read a line of Joseph Conrad.

That night, when it was getting late, I saw Conrad in such a way that I do not care to remember him under any other circumstances. We were all standing at the time, to wish Mrs Conrad good night. And when Mrs Conrad still continued her conversation with me, her husband stood there silently, holding his two hands, and with the most wonderful smile I had ever seen on a man's face. It was a smile full of kindly amusement and indulgence, as though he were the great father and we were his little children. He stood like this for a minute or two and then said – 'There, there, say good night, you are keeping the gentlemen standing.' Saying this, he bent his head, and, after kissing his wife's hand, he led her gently to the door. We will leave Conrad at that – standing with his face in the full light, the full light of his own spirit.

When I left Conrad he presented me with his last book, *Victory.* But although I thoroughly enjoyed it, I must confess that it was more from my low taste in Literature than my better taste; in the same way as I enjoy beer as well as wine, and am a good judge of either. For I found *Victory* to be sheer melodrama, and not a work of high art. And when I tried to repeat that wonderful dose of melodrama, by getting a copy of *Lord Jim,* I found that, although I struggled to the fortieth page, I could not get one page farther. So I am now waiting to read *Typhoon, Chance* and the *Nigger,*[128] to find the hand of a master.

---

128. *Victory* (1915), *Lord Jim* (1900), *Typhoon* (1902), *Chance* (1913) and *The Nigger of the 'Narcissus'* (1897) are all novels by Conrad. Why this wait to read the latter three should take at least another decade, and whether Davies ever did read those novels, are not clear. *Heart of Darkness* (1899) may seem a surprise omission from Davies's list, but it only became Conrad's most popular work in the later twentieth century.

Chapter IV: The Philosopher

Who knows the perfect life on earth?
   It lies beyond this mortal breath;
It is to give the same kind thoughts
   To Life as we bequeath to Death.

It is to show a steadfast love;
   As faithful to our friends that live
As our dead friends are to ourselves
   Sealed up from gossip, in the grave.

But who can lead this saintly life,
   When friends are false and men unkind;
And every man will cheat a man
   Whose trust, like faith in God, is blind.

Hang this pale fool, Philosophy!
   Kind hearts obey themselves, no other:
Why like a saint can I take pain
   And not inflict it on another?

I had now been living in London for several months, and met quite a number of literary men. But as some of them have left no striking impression on my mind, and seeing that I am not writing this book for the sake of mentioning names – this being the case, I will remove them gently from my path, without giving them the cold shoulder.

On one occasion, when I had called on my publisher, my conscience was made to feel uneasy by his suggestion that I should call on the Shaws, to thank them personally for what they had done for me.[129] Now, I had always wanted to do this, but had always been afraid of Shaw's gluttony for work. This fear was soon justified, for

---

129. George Bernard Shaw (1856–1950), Irish playwright resident in England. In 1908, Shaw had written the preface to *An Autobiography of a Super-Tramp*.

when I sent him a line proposing to call on him, he answered at once, inviting me to have tea with Mrs Shaw and himself on the following day. But he finished up by saying that he was attending rehearsals, and would not have much time to spare. 'I am leading a dog's life', he said – 'not that any dog would or could stand it.' On the following afternoon I was at Adelphi Terrace and, seeing a small gate at the front of the stairs that led up into a flat, I rang the bell. It was not long before I was confronted by an Irishwoman who, before I could say a word, cried in a savage voice – 'He's not in!' Although I tried to explain that, in spite of not knowing either Mr or Mrs Shaw, yet, for all that, they had proved great friends to me, and I felt certain that they would be glad to see me. But the woman's face became harder and harder, and it did not even get softer when I said that I was expected there to tea. Strange to say, this bad beginning was followed by the most extraordinary welcome I have ever received anywhere; for the next minute a woman's head appeared over the banisters, and a simple, spontaneous voice cried – 'Is that you (calling me by name)? Come on, come on.' It was all so natural that I felt at home at once, and went up the stairs as though they were my own.

After this cordial greeting, it will not be surprising to hear that Mrs Shaw and I were soon on the best of terms and talking without the least difficulty. This went on for some time, until Mrs Shaw suddenly looked up into the air and said – 'This is Mr Davies.' Turning around at these words, I saw, to my astonishment, that a tall, bearded man was standing like a stone statue at my side, with a long arm extended in my direction. How he came there was a mystery, for I had not heard the least sound and, I may as well say here, my hearing is distinctly good. I had lived in lonely places where it was always wise to be on the alert for sounds, and to investigate – although it might only be a beetle crawling under the leaves.

But when I saw that man standing there, I had not the remotest idea of three people being present in that room. I began to think of trapdoors in the floor, which worked with wonderful ease, or the same kind of doors in the ceiling, to let people down on invisible wires. However, the grip of his hand proved that there was no illusion, and it was not long before he was saying how much we knew each other – through correspondence and mutual confidence – although we had never met until then.

Just before this meeting, I had been reading the poems of Clarence Mangan, and began to tell the Shaws of my great admiration for the

'Dark Rosaleen', and some of that author's other pieces.[130] 'Yes, yes', said Shaw, when he heard this, 'but Tom Moore has written some good things too.'[131] He then began to quote from Moore, and when his memory began to fail, Mrs Shaw prompted him. And when Mrs Shaw's memory failed, her husband came to the rescue. In this way they managed between them to recite quite a number of poems by Tom Moore.

I was rather surprised at this, to find that Shaw was one of the most poetical men I had ever met. I had always looked on him as a human philosopher and a master of Political Economy, and, on that account, had been in some fear of meeting him. And when at last he began to talk of his visit to a lonely lighthouse and its one lonely inhabitant, the silence of that perilous journey in a small boat, with only the sound of the waves beating its sides, and the rhymic splash of the men's oars as they rowed away from the wild coast – when I listened to this, I was more dumfounded than ever. 'Where', thought I, 'is that cold practical thought, which is only commonsense, but which, coming at the psychological moment, when other people have lost their heads, reaches the height of a divine philosophy? Why is it that this one man in particular has the power at times to utter a little common-sense and make us see it for the first time?'

Shaw was there for about twenty minutes, and then had to rush off, having to attend a rehearsal of one of his own plays. But although he had come in a silent, mysterious way, as I have said, I was determined to keep a sharp eye on his departure. However, I am not quite certain how he left the room, for he appeared to glide and thin away, and I am not sure whether he opened the door at the end of the room, or passed clean through it like a ghost. With the exception of hearing his voice, I am positive that he made no other sound; either when he sat down or got up; either in his coming or his going, or in

130. James Clarence Mangan (1803–1849), Irish poet. His later works, including 'Dark Rosaleen', often had a strong Irish nationalist bent. This is a version in English of the 'Róisín Dubh' (literally 'Black Rose'), a political song in Irish dating back at least to the sixteenth century. It is actually a song about a woman: to avoid prosecution by English censors, many Irish songs describing the fate of Ireland employed such metaphors.

131. Thomas Moore (1779–1852), Irish poet and songwriter. Moore is accorded a similar status as a national bard by some in Ireland as Robert Burns is by the Scottish. His most famous works include 'The Last Rose of Summer' and 'The Minstrel Boy'. He supported Catholic Emancipation in Ireland but, like Shaw, he spent most of his life in England. He was harshly critical of injustice, and not only in Ireland: he wrote mocking portrayals of American life and the institution of slavery, and supported the Greeks in the War of Independence.

his use of the tea-things.

The Shaws had been very good to me as an unknown author. Not only had Shaw written a preface for my *Autobiography of a Super-Tramp*, but Mrs Shaw had also done everything she could in the matter of getting the book published. She paid for the type-setting and casting, and told me it was my own property. But when the Great War came, and I had no money to pay for the paper, printing and binding for a new edition, I had either to lose all my type and plates or let the book go out of print altogether. So I gave the machinery to my publisher, who then supplied the paper and covers for a new edition, paying me a royalty on each book that was sold. However, the raising of my pension in that very year more than made amends for the loss of my plant.

Soon after the Shaws had done me this great kindness, I wrote to Mrs Shaw, saying that I would like to dedicate a book of poems to them both. But Shaw did not like the idea of dedications, and here is his opinion, coming through his wife, who said that if her husband had been writing to me directly, he would have put it to me more nicely.

'Dedications be damned! Poetry is a very big thing, addressed to the whole world, and it should not be labelled with the names of individuals. It is like giving a soldier a cross for valour and then belittling it by putting the name of Queen Victoria on it. Besides, Davies doesn't understand about dedications. When my mother first came to London she innocently dedicated one of her songs to a certain officer who had sung it when it was only in MS. To her horror, he acknowledged the compliment by sending her a very nice letter enclosing a £10 note, and formally covering up the gift by asking her to give him credit for copies to that amount, in case he should need them. My mother, of course, sent back the money; and she took good care not to dedicate her songs to people again. Only yesterday there was an account in the papers of an Italian priest committing suicide because he dedicated a book to the Pope, and the Pope only sent him £4. The only dedications that are not liable to be misunderstood in this way are those dedications to a wife, or mother, or father, which have now become hackneyed. Davies mustn't dedicate his book to anybody. We should not misunderstand, but lots of other people would.'

As I have never had any idea or intention of writing a book of this kind, I have no notes in hand, and have to rely entirely on my memory. But I have been fortunate in finding the above remarks in a letter from Mrs Shaw, which I had placed in a book she had sent me – *Selected Passages from the Works of Bernard Shaw*. With the exception of the Shaws, I have never in all my life written to anyone proposing a meeting, with the intention of writing about them afterwards; and that will account for a number of well-known names who are not mentioned in these pages.

Whatever people think of Shaw, judging by his work, it is certain, judging by the great number of young authors that have had their work read and criticized by him, that he is one of the most sympathetic men living. The only other heart I knew to match his is the heart of a woman – Alice Meynell.[132] When I consider the number of writers who have told me of letters they have received from Bernard Shaw and Alice Meynell, I am amazed. Everywhere I go I meet them; some of them have had success, and others have failed. Only the other day a poet wrote to me from the country, sending me a little volume of poetry. And when I returned a few lines of encouragement, he wrote back to say that it was only once before that he had met with kindness – the other time was when Alice Meynell had written to him.

I did not meet Alice Meynell until a short time before her death, when a friend took me along with him on Armistice night. She had just finished a review of one of the older poets, and asked me if I did not think his work was sustained. As I did not have as good an opinion of that poet's work as I had of Alice Meynell's usually sound judgment, I answered – 'Yes, there is certainly something in his work that is sustained, but I don't know exactly what it is.' This caused her to give a slight laugh, but she did not press the matter more closely.

I may as well say here that I had never had the least wish to meet Alice Meynell, because of the great number of writers who had forced themselves on her, regardless of her own work and time; and the same thing applies to Thomas Hardy. It seems to me that the best respect we can show to a great writer is to keep out of his way and not waste his time, making it of no more value than our own. How often have I heard great beggars complain of their wasted time, when they have been detained in conversation by people who were more inquisitive than generous.

---

132. Alice Meynell (1847–1922), English writer and editor, perhaps best remembered for her poetry. Meynell's support for other writers was indeed notable, and not only through her work as a magazine editor. With her husband Wilfrid Meynell, she gave assistance to the opium-addicted poet Francis Thompson, and published his 1893 book *Poems*.

from Chapter V: A Poet and His Dog

Still do I claim no man can reach
　His highest soul's perfection,
Until his life, from day to day,
　Deserves a dog's affection.

We will now go back to the Mont Blanc, where Edward Garnett presided over the midday meal.[133] Now, after that meal, Edward Thomas and myself would go along to the St. George's Restaurant in St. Martin's Lane, where there would be another gathering to tea, presided over by Edward Thomas. The regular attendants were Edward Thomas, Ralph Hodgson,[134] myself, and one or two others. Strange young writers came occasionally, being invited by Edward Thomas after he had reviewed their books in the various papers.

Hodgson was a man to my own mind, for we both preferred to talk of dogs and prizefighters instead of poets and poetry. He was very seldom seen without his dog, and the same words could be applied to him, with a little difference, as to the Mary of our childhood days, when we read –

'And everywhere that Mary went,
The lamb was sure to go.'

The sight of Hodgson and his dog always reminded me of those words, altered to fit his particular case –

'And everywhere that Hodgson went,
The dog was sure to go.'

Not only did I like Hodgson for that – that I could exchange ideas with him on the noble art of self-defence – but that there was

---

133. In London. Edward Garnett (1868–1937) was an English writer, critic and editor.
134. Ralph Hodgson (1871–1962), English poet.

another strong bond between us, which was that he smoked the same common strong tobacco as I did. For that reason we could help each other out, in case one of us ran short. I may as well say here that I have now changed my tobacco, for I have discovered a tobacco that equals my old tobacco in strength and has the advantage of a fragrant odour. So that I can now puff big clouds into a lady's face, and cause her to smile instead of suffocate. But Hodgson, I believe, still sticks firmly and faithfully to the same old weed, saying that he would rather change his friends than change his tobacco.

But although Hodgson said, 'I would rather change my friends than my tobacco', it must not be thought that his conscience was always satisfied with that. On one occasion, when we were both invited to meet some ladies at their club, Hodgson's conscience behaved so cowardly that he even betrayed one of his best friends. For when the ladies told us we could smoke, Hodgson, knowing the strong odour of his tobacco and mine, said, as we were filling our pipes – 'Don't mind Davies' tobacco, it is awfully strong.' This remark, of course, acted as a restraint on my smoking, and I had to puff too gently for my full enjoyment. Whereas Hodgson, who usually puffed enough smoke for two men, had his courage increased by my timidity, and made enough smoke for three. The only satisfaction I could take was to break up the party by leaving early, knowing that Hodgson must follow before the truth came out as to which smoker caused the most annoyance.

Only once, I believe, have Hodgson and I not agreed in our opinions. We had been talking of coloured men, and I, with the prejudice I had brought with me from America, was not speaking of them too kindly. On hearing this Hodgson said something about 'prejudice', and giving them 'fair play'. When I heard this I was astonished, for even Hodgson had admitted that we in England were more lenient to coloured people than to our own. So I said, 'If I am prejudiced against them, you are prejudiced in their favour, and that is much worse. So when you say "fair play for coloured men", let me answer, "fair play for white men".'

However, this was a dangerous subject, and we changed it almost immediately. […].[135]

---

135. The rest of the chapter is largely devoted to a description of Hodgson's relationship with his troublesome pet dog.

from Chapter VII: The Journey

[…] Yes, life is continually on the change, and it is almost impossible, in these days, for any man to keep his own individuality. If he writes love songs about cuddling a pretty girl, he is told seriously to avoid those pretty toys and study the deeper problems of life; and yet the cuddling of a pretty girl has often led to a serious problem indeed. If he writes too much about humanity, his work is called sordid and dull; and if he writes too much about Nature, it is called lifeless and pretty. Not only that, but so much of this criticism is false and not to the point. For instance, if I sent the following poem to the press, it would be returned, and I will tell you why – although I must say that most of my things are accepted by either one editor or another:

Come away, Death, make no mistake,
   There's no one in that house to die;
She's young and strong, though suffering pain,
   And waits to hear her first-born's cry.

'Nay', answered Death, 'there's no mistake,
   I've been to this same house before;
Though no one saw a corpse come out,
   Or any mourner at the door.

'I've been to this same house before,
   I know it well from any other:
And now I come again, to see
   A dead-born child destroy its mother.'

Now if I sent this poem to an editor it would probably be returned, and another, whose subject was a butterfly or bird, a daisy or a tree, would be accepted. The reason for this is that I have been labelled as a Nature poet, whom the deeper problems of life does not concern. For that reason I am not allowed to give my critics the lie, but must stick to my butterflies, my bees and my birds. The above subject is one for Thomas Hardy, with his interest in the deeper things, and not for a Nature poet – but why? Every poet is a man of moods, otherwise he would be dull indeed. […]

Later Days

from Chapter IX: Reading for Charity

[...] One scheme to get funds towards the War, which was started by these ladies in high life, was particularly successful. It was to get together a number of poets to read their own work in some large drawing-room, which would be lent for the occasion. Tickets would be sold at a high price, so that at the end of the performance there would be a clear sum of several hundreds of pounds. For, of course, there would be no expense, unless it were a few pounds for printing programmes. But even these little sheets were sold for twenty and thirty times their worth, and it was all a part of the scheme to realize a larger sum.

The first meeting of this kind was held at Byron's old house in Piccadilly, with Augustine Birrell in the chair;[136] and among the readers were Yeats and Belloc, who read their own poems; while two or three well-known actors recited the works of others.

Now it must be remembered that I am a very shy man, but not having courage to refuse help in a good cause, I allowed my name to be entered for that event. I had not the remotest idea of what would happen, for up till then I had never once read my own work aloud to anyone. However, I had the consolation to think that although people might think that I was a very bad reader they would not be able to say that I was a very bad poet.

At last the terrible day came, and it was not long before I was a part of that packed audience, waiting for my name to be called as the next reader. The meeting had opened with a witty speech by the chairman, after which Yeats read some of his most beautiful poems, which made the beginning a great success. Others followed, and then came two or three bad readers – who were not bad poets – and the audience began to show less enthusiasm. And when my name was called at this critical time, I was almost in a state of collapse, because of the failure of the men who had just read and the coldness of the audience. For, seeing that I had never before been on a public

---

136. Augustine Birrell (1850–1933), academic and Liberal politician. Birrell was Chief Secretary for Ireland 1907–1916, resigning after the Easter Rising (1916).

platform, and had never once taken a lesson in elocution, how could I feel otherwise?

However, it was not long before I was on the platform and, setting my eyes on my manuscript, was determined not to raise them again until my reading was over. But I had no sooner finished reading my first poem than the audience began to cheer, a thing they had not done before; and the chairman, who had been sitting silently in his chair, during the other readings, began to show his approval by saying every now and then – 'Yes, yes; ah, yes', with almost as much excitement as the audience. One of the poems caused such a stir that I did not know what to do. A small group of young men began to cry out my name, and two or three ladies raised their voices to a higher pitch, crying – 'The Moon! The Moon!' which was the name of the poem I had just read.[137] I need hardly say that when I had finished there were loud cries of 'Encore', and I was sent back to read again, just as I was escaping through an open door.

When I was standing at the back of the audience, after I had done reading, and ready to slip away, a tall lady came up to me, and, saying that she was Clara Butt,[138] congratulated me on my successful reading, and asked me if I would give her my MS. poems. But I told her that two of the poems were new, and I had no other copies of them, which disappointed her, I believe. However, I sent her a book of poems in a few days after, but have had no cause to think she ever read them.

[...]

Some time after this I was at another fashionable drawing-room, where I read for an hour, and was the only reader. On that occasion the War benefited, I believe, to the extent of a hundred pounds. At the end of the reading, I was approached by a tall, graceful old lady, who introduced herself as Lady Ritchie.[139] I was so charmed with her that I accepted at once an invitation to lunch with her on the following day: although I did not know that she was Thackeray's daughter, or that Thackeray ever had any daughters, for that matter; and I was certainly not influenced by her being a lady of title. I accepted the

---

137. From *The Bird of Paradise* (1914).

138. Clara Butt (1872–1936), English contralto. During the First World War, Butt organised concerts for service charities, and was in 1920 awarded with the title Dame Commander of the Order of the British Empire (DBE).

139. Anne Isabella, Lady Ritchie, née Thackeray (1837–1919), English writer and eldest daughter of William Makepeace Thackeray.

invitation because of a wonderful charm in her voice and manner which did not seem to belong to the present age – and in spite of my dislike of these social engagements.

When I was there on the following day it seemed a strange, old-fashioned little world that I had discovered. I was at the house of Thackeray's daughter and I met there one of Dickens's daughters too. And it was strange indeed to hear Lady Ritchie talking so naturally of Tennyson and Browning, and other Victorians, without any reference at all to the living writers whom I was there to represent. It was quite obvious that Lady Ritchie knew nothing of my work, and her only interest in me came from two things. First, I had impressed her as a reader of poetry. Secondly, she was delighted to meet an author for the first time in her life who had actually worked with his own hands; from necessity, and not with the object of writing a book. 'And you', she said, looking at me with wonder and interest, 'you have actually worked with your own hands for a living, like the common men we meet in the street. How extraordinary!'

I could have said that I had always done my best to avoid doing that and had only done so when forced by circumstances, and that I was far from being proud of what I had done in that way – but I did not like to destroy Lady Ritchie's world of wonder.

[…]

These readings soon led to others of a different kind, where one or two poets would be invited to dinner and, when the dinner was over, others would come in until there was a large party. At last I began to think I was being used as a public entertainer, and came to the conclusion that I could be better employed at home in writing new poems instead of reading old ones for the pleasure of others. However, I was not justified in this, for wherever I went other people, as well as poets, tried to do something themselves to make the party successful. For instance, at one of these houses Lord Crewe[140] took the floor and tried to remember and recite a poem he had written in his youth, but without much success.

Up to the present I have only dealt with literary men, for I did not meet many artists and painters until later in my life. But to give this book some variety, I will finish my chapters on literary men by

140. Robert Offley Ashburton Crewe-Milnes, 1st Marquess of Crewe (1858–1945). Liberal politician and occasional writer of verses and non-fiction prose.

mentioning Arnold Bennett and Arthur Symons,[141] although I did not meet them until after the War. These two writers were the last literary men of consequence that I have met; while St. John Adcock[142] was the first, closely followed by Edward Thomas.

The first time I met Adcock I judged him to be a very young man; and when he began to talk of his children I came to the conclusion that he would not have many, and that they would be young and small. So when I paid him a visit on the following day, I had my pockets full of penny toys – a monkey on a stick, a couple of tin trumpets and a penny whistle. But when the first child came in I saw to my alarm that she was a young woman of sixteen or seventeen years of age; and even her younger sister, who came after, was far too big and old to welcome my toys. So I said nothing about them, and gave the toys to some poor children whom I met on my way back home.

The first thing I did on meeting Arnold Bennett, was to thank him for the early encouragement he had given to my work when he used to write reviews under the name of 'Jacob Tonson', in his own early days of journalism. This was a splendid introduction, and we were soon at ease, sitting side by side and well pleased with each other's company.

'Whatever I have said as Jacob Tonson', said Arnold Bennett, 'you are at liberty to repeat under the name of Arnold Bennett. Tell your publisher that.'

But while we were talking in this way, the gong, which we had not heard, had gone for dinner, and people were waiting for us to move into the dining-room. So we had to be reminded. Strange to say, nothing went right after that, and I began to see that Arnold Bennett was not the same man in a mixed crowd as he had been when we were together. For when I said something at dinner in praise of a certain play, he said emphatically 'I don't agree with you, Davies, the thing is bad.'

Hearing this I waited, of course, to hear him give some reason, but to my surprise, he said again, after a long pause – 'the thing is bad.'

Still giving him another chance, I waited again and, after a second long pause, out came the same words – 'the thing is bad.'

---

141. Arnold Bennett (1867–1931), English novelist. Arthur Symons (1865–1945), Welsh-born poet, critic and editor.

142. Arthur St. John Adcock (1864–1930), English novelist, poet, Fleet Street journalist and editor of the monthly magazine *The Bookman*. He is now remembered for writing the first article on Davies for the British press. See 'Introduction'.

Now if he had only increased his vehemence, such as – 'the thing is bad, the thing is rotten, the thing is damn bad' – if he had only done this, I would have felt much less disappointed.

My first meeting with Arthur Symons, at the beginning of my literary career, had to be postponed owing to his serious illness, which lasted for years. And although I have met him since, I prefer to think of the man in his full powers, when he was the greatest critic of his day. I shall never forget how his one voice silenced all our literary professors when they were comparing Stephen Phillips to Shakespeare and Marlowe,[143] and the way he did it, too! Not by quoting the poet at his worst, but by taking the very passages that those professors were raving about, and showing that they were little better than rhetoric.

To be praised by Arthur Symons in those days meant the favour of the whole Press, which I was not long in finding out. His words were quoted everywhere, and every journalist I came in contact with told me of my good fortune in being praised by Arthur Symons.

143. Stephen Phillips (1864–1915), English dramatist and poet.

from Chapter X: Politics and Society

[…] In writing this book I had intended not to mention any of the younger men, and to confine myself to established names. But I must make an exception of one young poet, because it was the sensation of his death that set half the world writing poetry and the other half reading it. This young poet was Rupert Brooke who, through his great personal charm and his own personal connections, made his death the most extraordinary thing in the history of literature.[144] He was made to represent Literature in the Great War; and his early death proved he had so many friends that, had he lived, he would have needed superhuman strength to have made himself a great poet. If Rupert Brooke had not died, it is hardly likely that poets would have been asked to read their work to the public and that the interest in them would have been so great that people paid guineas to see and hear them.

To be honest and sincere, I must say certain things now that a good many people will not like. First of all, Rupert Brooke was not only not a great poet – his work shows not the least sign that he would ever have become one. For instance, all our great poets achieved greatness in their early work, either in passages or single poems, which they could never surpass in after years. Look at the fine things in 'Endymion.'[145] And what of Shakespeare's sonnets, the first songs of Burns and the early poems of Milton? The only difference between their early work and their later was that their greatness was more sustained and they had less failures. But there is not the least sign in the work of Rupert Brooke to justify us in saying he would have become the first poet of his age, above Hardy, Yeats and

---

144. Rupert Brooke (1887–1915), English poet perhaps best remembered for his patriotic sonnet 'The Soldier' ('If I should die, think only this of me…'), written before he went to fight in the Great War at Gallipoli. He never took part, however, developing sepsis from an infected mosquito bite and dying in a French hospital ship moored off Skyros, Greece.

145. Presumably this is a reference to John Keats's famous poem of that name, written in 1818. Considering Keats died less than three years later, and at the age of twenty-five, this is perhaps not the best example Davies might have offered to illustrate his point.

Bridges.[146] No, we must look on the death of Rupert Brooke as the passing away of a charming and a gay young spirit; and to talk of a severe loss to English poetry is all sentimental cant and humbug. Even his sonnet, which has been quoted as his best piece, 'If I should die' – even this is not very great as poetry; but seeing that he *did* die, it takes the significance of a prophecy and upsets our judgment. Not only that, but it is peculiarly dramatic and suitable for recitation, and, coming from a rich, fluent tongue, sounds large and impressive.

On one occasion, when I was dining out, a young writer came up to my table, and said 'Have you heard the latest news?'

'What is it?' I asked, judging that it would have something to do with Literature.

'Rupert Brooke the poet', said the young writer, 'has committed suicide in the Pacific, and is now a journalist.' He was referring, of course, to Rupert Brooke's articles, describing his travels, which were being published in the *Saturday Westminster Gazette,* and which were not of much value as literature.

After saying these things, judging Rupert Brooke as a poet and man of letters, I will now come to him as a man, and in this I have nothing but praise. When I heard the news of his early death, it came to me as the first great blow of the War. The second blow came on the death of Edward Thomas, my first and oldest literary friend. I met Rupert Brooke about a dozen times, I believe, and was always struck by his sound common-sense and his strong sense of humour. And, seeing that he looked up to me as a kind of master, I took full advantage of that fact and gave him what I thought was good advice. For instance, I knew that he was seeing too many people, so I preached the gospel of work. He always agreed to this, being well aware of that danger; and always said that he was going away to a quiet place almost immediately. On one occasion when he had repeatedly mentioned the name of a certain great lady and her views on different matters, I told him that it might be necessary – if he was to become a great author – to hear the opinions of Matilda Jane Ann and Doll Tearsheet as well, which he would probably find interesting.[147] He was not accus-

---

146. Robert Bridges (1844–1930) was at the time Poet Laureate (1913–1930).

147. Doll Tearsheet: a prostitute in William Shakespeare's *Henry IV, Part 2.* Matilda Jane Ann is perhaps the 'Matilda Ann' of *Matilda Ann's Story: A Romance of Osteway* (1902), a ballad poem advertising Ingram's Milk Weed Cream, marketed in America as 'The natural tonic food for the skin'. In the poem, a fifty-nine-year-old farmer's wife sneaks some eggs into town, sells them in order to buy a jar of the cream, uses it 'faithful, every day, / For a full good month', and becomes 'purty as can be' to her husband. However, though this is precisely the sort of tale one can imagine Davies

tomed to this straightforward talk, but seemed thoroughly to enjoy it.

One morning he called at my house, on the chance of finding me at home and free to go out to lunch. So we went to a small restaurant in Soho, where he was to meet another friend. All I can remember of that lunch was this – the three of us did nothing but laugh all the time. Rupert Brooke and his friend were brimming over with gaiety, like two schoolboys. He was so boyish in his happiness that I had an impression that he had been saving his money for a month or more, and was now determined to spend every penny of it on food, drink, and rides. And that is how I like to remember him, wishing me good-bye and standing in his bare head, for he had come out without either a hat or a cap. Soon after that I heard the news of his death.

If this charming young man had lived, he might have become a good critic, even a great one, for he had excellent taste in poetry; but a greater poet than Hardy, Yeats, or Bridges – there is not the least sign of that.

enjoying, this poem was published after he had left America for the last time and it is not certain he would in fact have known it.

Later Days

from Chapter XI: Works of Art

[…] While I am writing of Sickert,[148] I must mention one of his best friends, Harold Gilman,[149] of whom I once saw a great deal, because we used the same haunts. Gilman called to see me quite a number of times, and every time he came he criticized a certain portrait of mine which, I must admit, was feeble in every way. Gilman hated it, and every time he saw it wanted me to sit to him for a portrait to show how much better it could be done. But as he was then in an experimental stage, and had strange ideas of colour, I thought I would wait – on the advice of a friend – until his ideas became more settled. For I did not want Gilman to paint my face bloated and purple, like the face of a drowned man who has been found after many days in the water.[150]

One night, when I was sleeping on my couch in the front room, so as to be better able to hear if there should be an air-raid – this picture fell off the wall and almost stunned me. The very first words I heard on the following morning were these – 'Harold Gilman has died suddenly of influenza.'

Now as there had never been any other than friendly feeling between Gilman and myself, I could only account for this in one way. That in his delirium, when dying, he was thinking of that portrait which he had so much detested; and, in his imagination, had struck it off the wall. But the connection between these two facts – the imagination of a dying artist and the solid substance of a real picture – is

---

148. Walter Sickert (1860–1942), influential early modernist painter of German descent, who became a British citizen and a prominent member of the Camden Town Group of artists in London. Davies and Sickert were good friends, and Sickert sketched Davies on several occasions. His painting *The Blackbird of Paradise* (1896–8), depicting a buck-toothed and smiling young woman wearing a black hat with feathers, may have been a tangential inspiration for Davies's poem 'The Bird of Paradise' from the 1914 collection of the same name.

149. Harold Gilman (1876–1919), English painter and founding member of the Camden Town Group.

150. For those unfamiliar with Gilman's work, looking up paintings such as *Sylvia Gosse* (1913) and *Mrs Mounter at the Breakfast Table* (1917) will give some impression of what Davies feared.

left for others to explain or to suggest some meaning.

I have already mentioned sitting to Epstein for a bust.[151] This was before the War became so serious that the age-limit had to be raised to fifty years. The Tribunals were not only brutal, but often ignorant men. This is what they said to Epstein – 'you have made a great name as a sculptor, and we are going to give you a chance now to make a name as a soldier.'

Epstein was a man of few words, but there was always strong matter behind them. On one occasion, when I asked him what he thought of a certain picture in the Academy, done by a contemporary, he simply shrugged his shoulders and said – 'It is one of the horrors of the War.' And when I told him about a certain one-armed artist, whose work impressed me as being very clever, Epstein answered astutely – 'If you had told me that you had met a very clever artist, I could have believed you; but when you say he has only one arm, I must have my doubts about his cleverness.'

When I heard this I was brought at once to a better understanding, and knew that I had been under the influence of sentiment. For of course an artist only works with one hand after all; and if he had a hundred arms his work would be none the better.

As I am not an art critic, I will say nothing of what I think of Epstein's work. But I would like to say that nothing I have ever seen before, in the world of dead matter, has given me more delight than the small head of a baby, which I once saw at one of the galleries.[152] There it was, with its little, open mouth, pleading – as I heard a lady say maliciously – for sixty guineas. However, she meant no harm by this, and was only annoyed that she was not rich enough to possess it. If I had been a rich man, that baby's face would not have pleaded in vain, even for twice that amount.

I got on very well with Epstein, as I always do with Jews, or, for that matter, anyone else. But it was quite obvious to me, right at the beginning, that he had a mind that was easily poisoned by other people, and what he needed, more than any other man I had ever met, was a good friend to tell him that he did not have as many enemies as he believed. However, he was not suspicious of me, and I already had the good opinion of most of his friends.

When I sat for Epstein he had just bought a large, strange-looking

---

151. Jacob Epstein (1880–1959), highly influential American-born British modernist sculptor. In 1916, Epstein produced a bronze head of Davies. In return, Davies was given a cast, which he kept on display at home.

152. Perhaps *Baby Asleep* (1902).

figure, which he had found in a second-hand shop and bought for a few shillings. He had thought, right at the beginning, that the thing was very old and of great value; and when he had brought it home and examined it more thoroughly, he was positive that that was the case, and made up his mind to sell it to the British Museum. 'Now', said Epstein, 'the British Government has always been mean in buying works of art, and when they take this they will have to pay me a good price for it. What sum do you think I ought to sell it for, Davies?'

'I wouldn't take a penny less than £2,000', I answered.

'We will see', said Epstein. 'I may let it go for less, but don't know yet.'

Not long after this Epstein was called out of the room, to see three representatives from the British Museum, who had come to examine a great treasure and make an offer for it. In about a quarter of an hour they had gone and Epstein returned to the studio, looking sad and disappointed.

'They have not persuaded you to sell it for two or three hundred pounds, I hope', I began to say, with some alarm.

'No', answered Epstein, 'but what they said was this – "it was a splendid thing as a copy, but there were certain signs to show that it was not old and genuine, and was only an imitation. It was worth", they said, "about ten or twelve shillings".'

'But surely', I said, 'you are not going to take their word for it, are you? Why can't they make a mistake?'

'Of course, they have made a mistake', answered Epstein, his old confidence returning to him.

When I left Epstein I was very pleased to see that he was still as confident as the cannibal in the story. Do you know the story of the cannibal who was brought into court to serve as a witness? When the judge said – 'There is nothing to prove the death of John Summers, no grave, no stone and no monument', this cannibal pointed to his own round belly, and exclaimed proudly – 'I am the grave! I am the stone! I am the monument!'

Some time after these meetings with Sickert and Epstein, I had been invited to spend a few days with William Rothenstein,[153] down in Gloucestershire. He wanted to do a portrait of me, and said that

153. William Rothenstein (1872–1945), English painter, best known for his work as a war artist and for his many portraits. A collotype of Rothenstein's very flattering 1916 pencil portrait of Davies appeared as the frontispiece of *Collected Poems* (London: Fifield, 1916).

he would not have asked me to make so long a journey had he not thought I would enjoy the change of air and different scenery.

When I reached him, I found that he was spending all his mornings in painting one tree, which stood all alone in a meadow. His studio was full of this tree, seen under different conditions of light and in different seasons.[154] The position of that fine tree was so solitary and unique in being planted right in the centre of a large green meadow – that I could quite understand the fascination to the mind of an artist. And when I think of some of his fine studies of it, I always feel sorry that Rothenstein had never made me a little present of his work, for sitting to him – as every other artist had done, from John,[155] Epstein, Sickert, Nicholson,[156] Laura Knight,[157] down to a number of younger artists who are not so well known. Rothenstein is the one name I miss on my walls in spite of sitting to him for portraits on two different occasions.

In the afternoon Rothenstein spent his time in working at a large oil portrait of himself. Now Rothenstein is certainly no better looking than I am. I have a distinct recollection of my grand-mother saying to me once – 'you are ugly enough to please any woman, no matter how particular she might be.'

So when I saw Rothenstein standing there, with a large fat smile on his lips, as he painted himself by looking into a mirror – when I saw this I felt that I must either rush out of the room or strike him a heavy blow on the back of the head. However, Rothenstein's smile in the evening, when he sat with his three children, and was a father instead of an artist, was a different thing altogether.

The evenings were spent in Rothenstein reading the poems of Tagore, the Indian poet, whom he had drawn and painted a good many times. But although I offered a little criticism, Rothenstein did

---

154. Almost certainly a wych elm close to Rothenstein's home in Far Oakridge, Gloucestershire. Rothenstein painted this tree many times, and in all seasons. It was eventually destroyed in a storm in 1937.

155. Augustus John (1878–1961), Welsh painter and etcher, and one of the most famous and popular artists of his day. Davies came to dislike John's 1918 portrait of him, which has a rather substantial chin, exaggerated quiff, and dreamily 'artistic' countenance.

156. William Nicholson (1872–1949), English painter, illustrator and wood-engraver. Davies and Nicholson were good friends. Nicholson illustrated a number of Davies's books, and drew Davies on a number of occasions (for instance, sleeping at his desk with images depicting his thoughts floating overhead, for Davies's collection *The Hour of Magic and Other Poems* (1922)). Nicholson's later (1927) portrait of Davies hangs in the National Portrait Gallery, London.

157. Laura Knight (1877–1970), English artist. Knight's 1920 etching of Davies appeared on the cover of *The Song of Life and Other Poems* (1920).

Later Days

not mind in the least, but still went on reading.

Some time after this I met another great admirer of Tagore, who was a lady this time. 'I wonder', said I, 'what Tagore, being an Indian, thinks of Kipling's fine stories of Indian life.'

'He would never think of him', answered the lady in a lofty voice.

from **Chapter XII: Artists All**

[…] When I arrived for dinner that evening I found on entering the room that nearly all the party was known to me, and it was only necessary to introduce me to one man, who was Max Beerbohm.[158] Now when I saw that little and small great man standing there, dressed perfectly in the white and black of evening dress, I thought he was, as a man, the most harmless and gentle creature I had ever seen; the kind of man who would go through life with his eyes on the ground, to give worms their right to cross his path. And when I heard his quiet little voice – full of small hesitations and stammers – this idea impressed me more than ever. However, it was not long before I found that Max not only had something to say, but could say it with some force too. What I mean is this – he was just as powerful with his tongue as with his pen or pencil.

As soon as we were seated for dinner, someone raised the question of an attack on Shaw, which had just been written by one of the younger generation. The only thing that could be said in favour of that young writer was that he was ill and suffering from the severe strain of the war, and had lost all reverence for a man who was not only greater than he would ever be, but was also old enough to be his father. This was the opinion I expressed at the dinner party. But Max objected to my words at once, for he did not like 'old enough to be his father.' 'For', said he, 'there is no age in art; and it makes no difference whether the young attack the old, or the old or young attack each other.'

But it was not much good to continue this subject, because Max had not read the article, and looked on it as a clever work of art; whereas it was feeble, unpleasant and ill-natured.

Not only that, but I now began to see that Max was very exact and particular in the choice of words, and that though he might agree with one's opinion, it was not certain that he would agree to the way

---

158. Henry Maximilian 'Max' Beerbohm (1872–1956), English caricaturist, essayist, and novelist, best known for the novel *Zuleika Dobson* (1911). Davies is recalling a dinner given by William Nicholson in London.

it was expressed.

A few years before this dinner I had met another man, an art critic, who was exactly like Max in this. He argued about nothing at all, just for the sake of making you express an opinion in the exact terms he would use himself. On one occasion, when this man had called at my place, he gave me one of his little books, which consisted of short stories and a few articles on Rembrandt and others. The first sentence I read, on opening his book, ran like this - 'It was eight o'clock exactly, and Marie, etc.' Exactly!

As soon as dinner was over, Max made his way toward me, and I advanced a step or two to meet him, without the least suspicion of what was to follow.

'How long is it since Shaw discovered you?' he asked, in a gentle voice.

Now when I heard this I felt at once that there was something wrong, and that I was being asked a question that would be dangerous to answer. The question reminded me of when I was asked by a certain woman – 'How much money have you got, coppers and all?'[159]

However, the question called for an answer of some kind, so I said – 'About fourteen or fifteen years ago, I believe.'

'Oh dear, dear!' exclaimed Max, in an aggrieved voice. 'Oh dear, dear – and has it been going on all this time!' – implying, of course, that it was about time I was forgotten.

'Yes', I answered, adopting the same serious and aggrieved tone – 'yes, and it is likely to go on much longer too' – implying that my name would not be forgotten for a long time to come.

This round went in my favour, I believe, but I will leave others to judge that.

The next moment Max began again in a gentle, soothing voice, and Nicholson had now drawn near, to hear what we were talking about.

'Shaw', began Max, hesitating and stammering – 'Shaw saw at once that you were – a real poet; and – of course – being a decent fellow – like a good many more – just lent a hand – the same as most people – would have done – and – and helped a lame dog over the stile.'

Saying this he edged away quietly, and Nicholson, seeing that

---

159. In Chapter XI of *A Poet's Pilgrimage*, included in the present volume, Davies actually reports this question being asked of him by a young man with 'owl-like eyes and wide-open mouth'.

the battle was over, went off to speak to some one else. This blow knocked me out completely, for I *was* lame, and the expression was not figurative, as it would have been with others. There I stood dazed and half-stunned and wondering as to what had happened; in the same state as a man when he is washing, and the soap-suds in his ears are whistling like birds.

When I mentioned this incident to a friend, some time after, he said – 'Davies, you were hit below the belt and fouled. It was not a clean blow.' However, when I appealed to Nicholson, who was the referee of that last and second round, he says – 'No, I don't think so.' But perhaps he wants to be faithful to *two* friends, instead of one.

However, I soon recovered, and it was not long before I was seated at the side of Fanny Pryde, and talked with her for the rest of the evening. Once or twice I looked around to see what the other people were doing; and saw that Max was in a far corner poring over a book. But I don't know whether it was a printed book and he was reading, or a blank book in which he was making sketches of the company.

Max is a very clever man. Of all our living celebrities, his mind is the most subtle; and his knowledge of human nature is almost un- canny and diabolical. For instance, why did he go from place to place and speak of a certain actor in this way – 'What a pity it is that A—, who is such a nice fellow, should be such a bad actor!' Max knew, of course, that to call a man a nice fellow is not worth repeating, as nice fellows are common, but to call a man a bad actor is to be sure that the words will be repeated everywhere. And if these words come to the ears of A—, what then? He would not give a pin for being called a nice fellow, but to be called a bad actor –

And why did Max call another man a Japanese Jew? Speaking for myself, I like Jews, as I have said before; and of all the coloured races, I certainly like the Japanese best. And yet, somehow the very thought of a Japanese Jew makes me think of freaks and abortions. I can no longer enjoy a little quiet laugh, as when I think of a Scotch Jew. Now if the thought of a Japanese Jew has this uncomfortable effect on me, who has no prejudice against either Jew or Japanese – what would the effect be on others who do not like either? [...]

This book is largely a work of re-editing, with some chapters taken verbatim (or almost verbatim) from his previous books Beggars *and* The True Traveller, *sometimes with previous anecdotes or chapters being run together to create 'new' chapters, retitled, and threaded loosely into a narrative. Effectively a shameless potboiler, it is the weakest of Davies's tramping memoirs, and the last of them.*

Foreword

A few people, perhaps a very few, will remember that my *Autobiography of a Super-Tramp* was followed by three other books of prose, two of them dealing with my own tramping experiences, and the other being a novel. We will say no more about the novel, and regard it as a pest to be exterminated at sight.[160] I will go so far as to offer two-pence for every front page that comes my way, in the same way as we offer a penny for the tail of every rat that is killed. If any of my readers are fortunate enough to get possession of a score or more of that particular novel and send the front pages to my publisher for a reward, they will be doing more good to the community than any rat-catcher that ever lived, although he boasts of twenty thousand tails.

But when I come to mention the other two books, *Beggars* and *The True Traveller*, it is a different matter. To the younger generation those two books are unknown, nor were they known to any great extent to the readers of that time. On reading those two books some time ago, I decided that if they did not deserve to be better known it would be a wise thing to close my mouth for ever as a writer of prose. For those two books belonged to a day when I could tackle a subject with as much ease as a bee can open a flower, and I certainly cannot do that now.

However, there was one strong point against them – the essay-form was used more than the narrative, and people preferred the latter. In doing this book, *Johnny Walker, Tramp*, I have used the experiences selected in *Beggars* and *The True Traveller*, but I have destroyed the essay-form, and made the book run as a story. This has been done successfully, I hope, without injury to the material contained in the two earlier books. And as this book is arranged in an entirely new way, with some new material added, I have every hope that it will get the welcome of a new book, even by those who remember the earlier ones. To the younger generation it will of course be a new book, and should come between the *Autobiography* and *Later Days*.

---

160. *A Weak Woman* (1911). Critics have almost exclusively agreed with Davies about the failure of this novel. Davies would soon try his hand at longer fiction again, though his second and final novel, *Dancing Mad* (1927), met a similar response.

The Adventures of Johnny Walker, Tramp

I am very pleased at the reception given to my last book, *Later Days*. The first two Press notices frightened me, and my self-confidence, which – with the exception of my liver – is probably the strongest part of my constitution, was shaken severely. The first notice appeared in a well-known evening paper, when the book was still hot from the Press. This great haste to write unkind words made the matter sound personal, and

'Fe, fo, fi, fum,
I smelt the blood of a clergymun!'

This attack was followed by another, where my book was said to be too dull to read. But seeing that the lady wrote still another long article in another paper, to say the same thing, proved that the book was far from dull to her, but was of some intense interest. However, after these two writers, who thought to guide both the Press and the public, had done their unkind work, a change followed quickly, and the book's fortunes improved.

And now, ladies and gentlemen, by your kind leave, I will introduce you to *Johnny Walker, Tramp*.

Chapter XVI: Nicknames

Even in this strange lodging-house, which was well conducted and clean, there was always a certain amount of mild excitement going on, owing to the quaintness and simplicity of its many strange characters, nearly all of them being known by a nickname. I was present in the kitchen on the day that one man arrived as a stranger, nameless and alone, as far as the other lodgers were concerned, for they did not know what name he had entered at the office. He was in rags and tatters, and 'Rags' or 'Tatters' should certainly have been his name. In fact the name was offered to him, but he returned an unsatisfactory stare. He was preparing his tea at the same table as 'Punch', and the latter being in need of a pinch of salt, and seeing none of his friends at tea, asked this stranger to oblige him, saying: 'Would you oblige me, "Rags," with a pinch of salt?' The man stared at 'Punch' for a moment, and then walked away without giving an answer. He was at that time cooking a herring at the fire. Now, it so happened that a few moments later this man was pouring out tea, when all at once there was a loud cry of 'Whose herring is this?' The man turned quickly at the sound, and saw his herring making a few spasmodic motions, as it dangled on a long wire. He immediately ran to the rescue, but, alas! too late; for the tatters of his loose and broken clothes encompassed him like a deadly plant, and when he arrived the herring was lying motionless under the grate. After great care he managed to bring it to the light, covered with ashes and cinders. Still, with great care, he washed it and, after placing it flat on a plate, returned it to the fire. 'I hope you do not blame me for that accident, "Cinders"', said kind-hearted little Punch. 'Oh, no', answered the man newly named 'Cinders'. '"Cinders" has too much sense for that', said Red-Nosed Scotty, who happened to be sitting near. 'Whose teapot is this?' cried the kitchen-man, who was about to build the coke fire and wanted all food and teapots removed. 'It belongs to "Cinders"', cried a number of voices. From that day to this his name is 'Cinders', owing to the accident to his herring when he first came, alone and unknown. If he was arrested, it would be – 'Cinders is in jail'; and if he died it would be – 'Cinders is dead'.

If a man who goes to live in a common lodging-house does not utter his own name in a very short time the lodgers will give him one. Brown had a large nose, and would most certainly have been named 'Nosey' had he not on the first day recorded a simple anecdote of his childhood, in which he had cause to call himself William Brown.

I remember the day well when the 'Dodger' – a man who gladly helped others to spend their earnings on ale and, when they sat penniless and hungry, sat himself down alone to beefsteak and onions – I remember the day well when this man caused a never-to-be-forgotten sensation in the lodging-house kitchen. A letter was at the office for Algernon Dudley, and the manager had been in the kitchen several times in quest of that gentleman. It was near seven o'clock in the evening when he came into the kitchen for the fifth time and cried, 'Is Algernon Dudley here?' 'Yes', answered a man in the corner, and coming quickly forward. All eyes turned towards him, and who do you think Algernon Dudley was? No other than the common 'Dodger'. 'Fatty', who claimed to be a fighting man, whom no man had ever succeeded in knocking down, said to the lodger named Brown, 'You could have knocked me down with a feather'.

Brown's remarks on this occasion were very sensible, as they usually were. 'It was, is, and always will be the custom, said he, 'for a woman who gives birth to a child to name it. For this reason she is no sooner on the trot again than she begins scheming to that end. Now', continued Brown, 'we must not picture the "Dodger" as he is – God help him! – but as he was, a little innocent child in the arms of a doting woman. Such was the case, and has been the same with others, including ourselves, and will always be. Now, this poor woman – some people would call her foolish – no doubt had great respect for the "Dodger" as a baby and, to distinguish him from the common race of mankind, named him in the manner we have just heard. Perhaps I am right, perhaps I am wrong; but if the true facts were known, you would probably find that I am not far from the truth, But in spite of all this, I quite agree with our friend's remark, that it fills us with astonishment.' The 'Dodger' had lived in the house for more than two years when this incident caused so many comments.

But let us return to the man 'Cinders', for that gentleman was no helpless wreck in a doss-house; he was really a gay spirit and capable of love. He was a man with a long, melancholy face, seeing no humour in life and, if the truth must be told, he was positively ugly. Yet this man 'Cinders' had been seen on several occasions walking the streets with a woman on his arm. One of the lodgers said her looks were passable, and another said that they were more than passable compared to 'Cinders'. Brown had seen them together, and, said he, 'Although a man ought to believe his own eyes, I would never believe such to be the case, had not "Cinders" said, "Good night, Mr Brown". And if a man is not to believe both eyes and ears, then what is he to believe?'

Of course there could be no union between these poor souls; for she was in service, and he did odd jobs at the market, earning a shilling, or a little more on lucky days. As the manager said, it was amusing and could not amount to anything serious. They could go on walking arm in arm all their lives, for they would never be able to marry and walk apart.

This courtship had been the talk of the house for over three months when, one night, it was brought to an end in a strange manner. 'Cinders' and his love had been all the evening drinking ale in the 'Borough'. He, seeing some smoked haddock, fancied some for his supper, and, after making a purchase, rejoined his fair companion. It was near midnight when it suddenly occurred to 'Cinders' that the manager closed the house at twelve o'clock, and if he – 'Cinders' – was not there by that time he would be out for the night. Reminding his lady of this, they both started for home, her road lying the same way as his. The manager was just closing the door when 'Cinders' arrived.

Now, goodness knows what demon put it into this woman's head to cook her lover's fish, but this she seemed determined to do. 'I am coming in to cook your supper', said she. 'No', answered the manager, 'this is a house for men only, and we do not allow women to enter, except on special occasions. Not only that, the kitchen is now closed, and I would not open it again for "Cinders" or any other man. He will have to go supperless to bed or come home earlier; he must do this, or seek lodgings elsewhere'. The lady then started to abuse the manager in a loud voice, but that gentleman, not heeding her, caught 'Cinders' by the shoulders, saying, 'Go to bed, you old fool', at the same time shutting the door in the lady's face.

The next morning, when 'Cinders' was cooking his haddock, the manager lectured him severely on what had occurred the previous night: telling him that if he could afford to keep a lady cook he must seek better lodgings. Brown, who happened to be within hearing, gave evidence that he distinctly heard a woman's voice say, 'I am going to cook his fish', but thought he must be dreaming. Even now he believed it was all a dream, and he would like to hear the truth from the manager's own lips, as to whether it was an actual fact or not. On being told that it was, Brown turned his eyes towards

'Cinders' and, seeing that gentleman hold down his head in wordless shame, Brown was forced to believe it all. Probably that was the end of their courtship, for they were never seen together after that.

I was forced by circumstances to live at this lodging-house much longer than I had expected, and saw quite a number of changes, on account of death coming to some of the old lodgers. One of the strangest and quaintest of them all was old Scotty Bill, the fly-catcher. Consumption did not claim him as a victim, for he died at the advanced age of eighty-three, which was wonderful for a man who had spent the best part of his life in a common lodging-house. No doubt if he had lived under better conditions he would have reached a hundred years with ease. All his interest was in flies. While other lodgers were discussing the abundance of fish in Billingsgate, or the scarcity of vegetables in the Borough market, Scotty could be seen counting the flies in the kitchen, as a sign whether he should go out with his fly-papers or not. His language was very strong, and the last words he was heard to utter surprised even those who were accustomed to him, by their unusual weight and speed. He was a stubborn invalid, and fought hard against going to the hospital. His death was quite characteristic, and I can hardly imagine it to have been otherwise. He, like many another one, was found one morning helpless in bed, and the manager, seeing that he was very ill, in spite of his assurance to the contrary, sent at once for the doctor. But when the latter arrived he and the manager were surprised to find the bed empty. On making inquiries they were told that Scotty was in the kitchen, and it was there that they found the old man, reading a newspaper. In spite of this the doctor saw that Scotty was not in good condition and tried to persuade him to go to bed, but this the old man swore that he would not do, and demanded some reason for such a request. Then there was a whispered consultation between the manager and the doctor, and it was decided to send for the ambulance and have him taken to the hospital whether he would or no. Now, Scotty had lived in that same lodging-house for over thirty years, and for that reason was well known in the locality. Therefore, when the ambulance arrived at the door, and a woman outside inquired of a lodger as to who the ambulance was for, and was told of Scotty Bill, the news soon spread abroad. In less than five minutes between twenty and thirty women had assembled at the door. These women of the slums were never very clean, and at the present time not one of them was in a fit condition to answer her own door; but they forgot this in their anxiety to see poor Scotty Bill and wish him a speedy recovery. At last the old man appeared, and it staggered him to see the number of women at the door. But when he heard them say, 'Poor Bill', and 'Good luck to you, Scotty', his fury knew no bounds. Standing with one foot on the step, he paused, and then poured forth such a torrent of abuse that some of the women lost all sympathy with him and feebly retaliated. He told them to go home and scrub their dirty faces, instead of coming there to watch him – and other things not fit to mention. It was, they confessed, the worst language they had ever heard, and more than one of them was capable or using very strong words. That was the last seen of Scotty Bill, and that was his dying speech, for he died on his arrival at the hospital.

I have heard of the death of a number more, men that lingered with such determination that it almost seems as if they have taken advantage of my absence and died; for they all seem to have gone one after the other since I left. 'One-eyed' Jim is dead. A terrible cough he had, but his face and neck were always like raw beef. That one eye of his blazed with such power that I have often imagined the devil hard at work shovelling half a ton of coal a minute to supply its fierce light. He also went off suddenly, walking the kitchen on Monday, and lying cold and dead on the following day.

'Rags' is also dead, the great drinker: the man who when abroad complained that whisky made him totter, whereas it was an earthquake that tumbled the city's towers, and made the firm-footed houses reel. 'The whisky's in my legs', said Rags, not knowing that it was a great earthquake.

Monkey Sam and the Dodger are both dead, and there is no doubt but what the Dodger's death hastened Sam's. These two were the slyest pair of men that I have ever met. I believe they understood each other's thought so well that when one's body itched the other could, without seeing his friend make the least motion, scratch his own body in the exact place. These two men conversed by looks, and uttered very few words. They were so well matched and thought so much of each other that something more than accident must have brought two such men together. It was always clear that if anything happened to part them neither one would seek friendship elsewhere.

I had seen some of these men fighting against death day after day, but with such determination that I can hardly believe the report that calls them dead: especially as there is no proof of lettered stone, seeing that they are all in a pauper's grave. All these poor invalids in common lodging-houses are under the impression that doctors, when they find that their patients have no friends, and cannot be cured thoroughly, kill them. And that is why they are so stubborn, and fight till they can no longer move, before they will enter a hospital.

The Adventures of Johnny Walker, Tramp

I have already mentioned my habit of writing, when in this common lodging-house, but it was over two years before this writing came to anything and I could publish my first little book.[161] So that it was not long after this event when I was to be found living in a small lonely cottage in the country, sometimes very happy and sometimes very sad. I had been thinking all day of my strange companions of the past, both in America and England, and that accounted for my dream at night. In that dream I had invited them all to a grand supper, for I was now leading a different life. I was seated at the end of the table, which was full of fine things, and Brum, of America – the greatest beggar I had ever met – was seated at my right hand. After making them a short speech, in which I commended them on their way of living, and expressed deep regret that I had ever been cheated to follow Literature, who had led me into a treacherous swamp in which I stood up to the knees, with little power to either return or advance – after making this short speech, I invited them to help themselves, and to receive my undying friendship.

They then began to assist themselves with a hearty goodwill, all except Brum, who, to my surprise and confusion, sat motionless, glancing with scorn at his companions. 'There', said he, with deep disgust; 'do you call these men good beggars? See the way they rush at the food, as though they had starved themselves all day in anticipation of this meal'. Saying this, he began slowly to feel the lining of his coat, and, after much trouble, took out a greasy paper parcel, placed it on his knees and began to make room for it on the table. This being done, he spread the contents before him and began to eat in a very slow and indifferent manner. As for myself, I could not eat for joy, to see all these dear faces before me, and sat smiling at one and another, laughing and sighing in turns. Sometimes I closed my eyes, and opened them again on my companions, endeared to me by a past that had few cares and worries.

By a strange coincidence, Irish Tim of London was paired with Oklahoma Sam of America. Now, the latter was a man of very few words, and he always had in hand a long dangerous-looking knife, with which he trimmed his nails, whittled sticks, or threw at cracks in the door, flies, or any other object that caught his eye. But he never allowed that knife to remain long out of his hand, for, if he threw it at a door nine feet away, he was sure to recover it in a couple of leaps,

---

161. *The Soul's Destroyer* (1905), Davies's first collection of poems. The circumstances surrounding the publication of that collection are discussed in the 'Introduction', and are also the subject of much of the latter part of the *Autobiography*.

and before it had finished trembling in the wood. When I have seen him asleep at the cattleman's office, he always had this knife between his teeth.

As I have said, Sam was a man of few words, but on the subject of war he was more talkative than an old man. His memory on that subject was extraordinary: knowing the dates of battles, the number of their forces, names of regiments and generals, and the exact position of their entrenchments. Tim must have unwittingly broached this subject, for I was suddenly startled by hearing Oklahoma Sam say, 'This is Napoleon'; at the same time down went his knife over an inch into the table. I had noticed from the first that Sam had scornfully pushed aside my table knife, preferring to use his own, although he had retained the use of my fork. Looking at once in that direction, I saw Tim's face turned my way, with sarcasm trembling on his lips, which only needed a little encouragement, and he would then utter one of his scathing comments, thinking to blight at once the newly-opened flower of Sam's eloquence. 'Don't look that way, look at me', cried the man from Oklahoma, placing his left hand on Tim's shoulder and speaking in a voice terribly quiet and firm. 'I see', answered Tim, leaning back, with his two hands resting on the table – 'I see; this is Napoleon'. 'Yes, and this is Blücher',[162] continued Sam, taking the knife out of the table and quickly planting it dangerously near to Tim's right hand. 'And this', cried Sam, forcing his words between his teeth and holding the knife suspended in the air, 'is Wellington', and down it flashed between the two big fingers of Tim's left hand. Tim grew much paler as he removed that hand to his knee, and it was at once apparent to me that for the rest of the evening he was a spell-bound man, afraid to hazard even a civil question for fear it would be misunderstood.

Next to Sam and Tim sat Chicago Slim, who was relating to Bony – an English beggar – his awful suffering for a week in the State of Utah, where a beggar had no other food than bread and milk confronting him on every threshold he approached, and how travelling in that part was known to all beggars as 'the bread-and-milk route'. Such were his awful sufferings, related to the sympathetic ears of Bony, who, in exchange, mentioned his own disappointments in England, 'where', said he, 'I find public-houses to be the easiest, quickest, and most profitable places'. He was just about to relate instances when the Curly Kid, who had been listening to their

162. Gebhard Leberecht von Blücher (1742–1819): Prussian field marshal, and prominent opponent of Napoleon I.

conversation, asked Chicago Slim this question: 'How is it that, when I was in Utah, the citizens did not baby *me* with bread and milk?' 'Don't know', answered Slim, uneasy and disconcerted. 'I went to no houses, but begged on the fly', cried the Curly Kid, 'and people had to give money or nothing. Slim, I reckon no true beggar would allow himself to be fed day after day on bread and milk'. Chicago Slim did not answer, and at once fell in the estimation of Bony, who now considered him to be unworthy of further attention.

'I shall never forget', said Bony to the Curly Kid, who had by his remarks proved himself to be a beggar equal to any emergency — 'I shall never forget my disgust when, one Sunday morning, I found myself accidentally in a town where public-houses are shut on the Sabbath Day. I had to beg of proud, neatly-dressed church-goers, for the good-natured drinking man had not the heart to come out of doors, and you can imagine my ill success. How I wished all these people who were carrying Bibles and prayer-books had bottles and jugs instead!'

How the hours passed, looking on these delightful companions! The first to leave was Tim, for Oklahoma Sam had become personal about his rough beard, and wanted to shave him, there and then, with his knife; and, in fact, was sharpening it on a stone for that purpose, which I had often seen him do before. Tim civilly but firmly refused this kindness at Sam's hands, and, being afraid that he might be forced to undergo such an operation, got up and, saying 'Good night all', left the room.

Others followed, one by one, and two by two, until at last I was left alone with Brum. 'Yes, and I must go, too', said he; 'for I intend to call on a dentist who is good for twenty-five cents'. Saying which he also departed, leaving me standing alone, sad and motionless, at the end of the table.

'Here', said I, walking up the room and looking affectionately at an empty chair — 'here sat Wee Scotty; here sat Monkey Jim, and there sat Never Sweat; here sat Rags, and there sat Cinders; here sat Irish Tim, and there sat Oklahoma Sam'.

Indeed, there could be no mistake as to where Sam had sat, for he had used his knife to such purpose, in describing the tactics and manoeuvres of Napoleon, Blücher, and Wellington, and their rapid movements in the heat of battle, that the table-cloth was all in tatters, and that part of the table was in splinters for nearly two feet square.

I stood undecided, for I had tasted their life, and, I knew that it was after all far better than the chained life I was now leading. In an instant, I made up my mind to follow Brum, and again enjoy the open-air camp fires, and saunterings in strange towns, and lying under shady trees in quiet woods within the sound of fresh springs. But I had scarcely moved when the room turned into a stone cell, and the wooden door became steel, and thick iron bars crossed the window. It must have been the strong feeling, incident to such a great change, that made me wake.

I then found myself sleeping alone in a small, poorly-furnished cottage, a stranger newly arrived in a strange village; and I had to admit, as a man in possession of all his senses, that I had far less cause to be happy than when I was a nameless wanderer with Brum in Louisiana, with Australian Red in the State of Michigan, or cabined with Wee Scotty and Oklahoma Sam on the cattleship *Tritonia*.

My Garden and My Birds *(1939) runs together Davies's last two prose books (*My Birds *and* My Garden, *both 1933). These attempts at domestic naturalist writing are slight to say the least, and demonstrate a distinct lack of knowledge about flora and fauna. Included here is the last chapter of* My Garden, *which demonstrates a continued peculiarity of mind, if also Davies's enthusiasm for talking his way around a subject about which he knows almost nothing.*

Chapter XII: Last Remarks

Bewitched

Give me a night in June that's clear and quiet,
  That I may stare at Heaven until I see
Her face all twitching to her farthest star —
  Conscious of one true man's idolatry.

I stare at dewdrops till they close their eyes,
  I stare at grass till all the world is green;
I stare at rainbows all their precious life,
  Till nothing's left to prove what I have seen.

I stare at Robin Redbreast on his bough,
  Till he comes down with many a pretty dance:
I stare at my own Self, and walk the earth
  With half my spirit in a wonder-trance.

There is a great difference between a London fog and a country mist; the one sticks in the throat and burns the eyes, while the other is as sweet and wholesome as the morning dew. But although I have no more desire to see a London fog, I must confess that I saw one once that made life more romantic than I have ever known before or have experienced since. I remember one day when walking up the Kingsway, during a very black fog, how thoughtful I became at the apparent unreality of my surroundings. I could see nothing solid and substantial — all I could see were stars shining over my head; and all these stars were the lights that were shining in the windows of tall buildings, where men and women could not see to work unless they had artificial light. But every kind of iron, wood or stone, was invisible, and life appeared unreal and ghostly. For the first time in my life I became interested in the sound of my feet on the hard pavement — it was the only thing that seemed to prove that I had a body, and that a solid earth was under me. I remember well how I went into a doorway to light my pipe, and saw that the place was already occupied by another.

My Garden and My Birds

'Madam', I said, raising my hat – 'this is an exceptionally bad fog, is it not?'

'Well, Mr Whatsyername, ' answered the lady, slowly – 'you can believe me or believe me not, but as far as I can see it is getting thicker and bloodier than ever. I can feel it in my eyes, throat and bones – believe me or believe me not.'

These fogs, which were once the pride of London, are now getting rarer and thinner, they are not jet-black, as they used to be, but are more like a creole or mulatto. The last one I saw was only a common half-breed, which Day would despise and Night would be ashamed to call his own. You could see the light of day through its dark ribs, and there was no confusion in one's mind as to whether it was twelve o'clock at noon or twelve o'clock at midnight. It was not the real thing at all – it was only a chimney-sweep fog, or the fog of a coal-man, dirty but not black.

Although I have always known that birds resent the presence of a cat, yet, for all that, I have never until this day seen them do any more than scold and occasionally follow at a safe distance. But to-day I have seen my cat Pharaoh actually running home for his life, even though I am here to protect him. I have now seen that there is one bird in particular who is so spirited and fierce in the protection of his young that he actually attacks a cat at close quarters. In fact the whole scheme of my life has been thoroughly reversed; for instead of protecting the birds from my cat, I am now in the position of having to protect my cat from the birds. This has surprised me very much, for at other times of the year this Thrush appears as inoffensive as a Wren, although his stripes and marks bring the tiger to mind. However, this spirited attack of a Thrush, and his success in driving my cat home, is certainly a great boon to the other birds who also have young ones, which they are not so able to protect. But it is very difficult to forgive this bird for his wicked temper, even in the consideration of his duty as a parent.

I suppose there is no joy in life that equals the hearing of a certain bird for the first time – the real living voice of a Cuckoo or Nightingale, whose names are so well known to us. I remember asking a friend to give me some hints, so that when I heard the Nightingale I could make sure it was her, and that I was not listening to some other bird. I had never heard this bird before, and had gone to a place where the voice would certainly be heard, providing the night was quiet and warm, and without wind. Well, I heard that bird, with no mistake: and even the first few notes brought the cry to my lips immediately – 'The Nightingale!' And I was surprised to think that I had asked such a question, that I was likely to mistake the bird's voice for another's. It was the richest bird-music I had ever heard in my life, and the confidence of the bird was amazing. Even the first few notes, which were only a matter of practice, were the work of a master, without hearing the full song that was to follow.

I have just been studying the difference between the hedge-sparrow and the house-sparrow, who are so much alike in appearance and are so different in their nature. For instance, the house-sparrow chirps, while the hedge-sparrow sings. The house-sparrow, too, is untidy and rough in appearance, while the hedge-sparrow is almost a rival to the Robin in daintiness and grace. The house-sparrow believes in war, and at least one battle a day, whereas the hedge-sparrow is all for peace. The hedge-sparrow is of more gentle nature, and much better behaved.

In fact the house-sparrow does nothing but scratch and eat; when he is not scratching he is eating, and when he is not eating he is scratching. But whatever the hedge-sparrow may do in private, he can be watched closely all through the day and never once be seen to scratch himself in public.

Sparrows, it seems to me, do not care much for individual fighting but, like the Irish, prefer riots.[163] And the result of much noise, bluster and wild blows, is no more likely to lead to a dead sparrow than it is to a dead Irishman. If such a thing happened, that one of these sparrows was killed, would the living not hold a wake, like the Irish, and renew their battle? I remember, when a very small boy, being taken by an aunt to an Irish wake. We kept a small public-house, at that time, and the people who held the wake were customers. In fact, most of the beer drunk at this wake came from our inn. When we reached the house of death, my aunt recognised it at once, because it was more noisy than any other house in the street. But although she knocked three times, the door was not opened. So my aunt, knowing the people inside, opened the door herself and walked in, dragging me in by the hand. As I have said, I was a very small child at that time, but the impression left on my mind will last for a lifetime. In fact, I spoilt the visit altogether for my aunt, for in less than five minutes I was clinging to her body and screaming in terror, and she was forced

---

163. In addition to the prevailing derogatory stereotype, Davies's indecorous generalisation here is probably influenced by circumstances surrounding the birth of the Irish Free State: the Easter Rising of 1916, the growth of paramilitary organisations such as the IRA and the UVF, the violence leading up to the Government of Ireland Act 1921, and the Irish Civil War of 1922–23, had formed part of the backdrop to much of Davies's writing life.

My Garden and My Birds

to take me home immediately. There was another reason for this — she was afraid that I might receive an accidental blow which might kill me, and what would she do then?

But in that five minutes I saw a lot. It seems that one of the party, who was showing the most emotion, had been unkind to the deceased in life, and was now accused of being false, which soon led to a free fight. Two people were fighting in one corner, and two others were fighting under the table. Two others were just beginning a fight, and, in their struggle, had knocked the corpse over and fallen on it as it lay on the floor. It was now that I began to scream, and did not stop crying until I was safe at home and in my own bed.

The next day these people were at our house, drinking, and in a wonderful state of quiet beneficence. It seems that nothing very serious had happened, and probably the only one who had sustained a fractured bone or a broken skull was the corpse. And as he was already dead, and could neither bleed nor groan, and would be buried shortly — what did it matter?

I have mentioned this case, one of my earliest impressions, to show that the sparrow can have his wild riot, as the Irishman can have his wake, and all come well in the end.

Miscellaneous Prose

Especially in later life, Davies was invited to contribute a small number of articles to magazines and introductions to books, as well as being asked to edit and introduce anthologies. Some of the more interesting of these shorter prose pieces are collected here.

How it Feels to be Out of Work [164]

It is generally in spring or summer that a man out of work takes courage to leave his friends and seek work in strange places. He can, and does, somehow manage, with the assistance of relatives, friends and landladies to get food and shelter in winter, but no sooner does the air begin to brighten in spring than he must feel more independence; and if he still cannot get work at home, he obeys the old lust to wander, even as a dog goes hunting. His hands begin to itch for something to do, and it is now a matter of chance whether he is to be a working man or a real beggar. So he takes to the road, not doubting but what he will soon find work and settle, until such time as better trade in his native town beckons him to return.

Very well then; he has a shilling or two in his pocket, which his friends have mustered for him, and he leaves his native place. He is quite happy, for it never once occurs to him that work is not to be had – if honestly sought.

At this stage of his career the man no sooner hears of work being done than he hastens in that direction. If he sees a gang of men mending a road, or hoeing potatoes, the poor fellow not only asks for work immediately but, being told there is none for him, stands spellbound, without power to leave that sight of industry; while real beggars pass indifferently to and fro, laughing into their sleeves at all labouring men.

This man is now so interested in work of every kind that he even addresses little children. 'Hallo!' says he, 'what does father work at?' On being told he asks a second question, 'Is he working?' After receiving information he goes his way, feeling better satisfied than before. These questions are asked out of real respect for work and not, as some people would think, for the sake of giving a child pleasure in answering them. It is far different with the real tramp, for he is not interested in work and seldom speaks to children. Again, there is something about his manner that is not so open as the other's, and children fear him, and he knows it well.

To this innocent man out of work there are no real tramps; for he

---

164. *The English Review* 1 (December 1908), pp. 168–71.

thinks that every man is looking anxiously for work; so it can be imagined how he amuses those real beggars, who have no other object in inquiring for work than to know what places to avoid.

This new tramp begins to feel distressed when several weeks go by and still there is no prospect of work. He sees his shoes wearing away and his clothes beginning to change colour, and he does not know whether to return home or not. It is well for him that he has that strange fortune which guides staggering drunkards safely past glass windows and looks after infants that tumble downstairs; for this man – to the astonishment of real beggars – is continually being assisted one way or another. Every day he has an experience to tell of how some gentleman drove him part of the way in a trap, how another gave him sixpence, and a woman gave him threepence and a parcel of food. How does all this come about? Even real beggars, who go systematically to work, cannot tell, for they seldom get more than a penny at a time. The reason is that the real beggar whines in such humble tones that people would feel no shame in giving him a farthing. But this new beggar, not yet having lost the dignity and pride of a respectable human being, addresses them in such an open, manly way that a penny seems small indeed to offer such a man – and this is one reason for his success.

Again, he does not miss good opportunities, as the real beggar often does. This new beginner, being a respectable man, unfortunate for the time in being out of work, seldom thinks of the police. Why should he? He does not beg straight; but his innocent roundabout way of inquiring for work – which he really wants – is more profitable than straight begging would be. In his innocence, he does not suspect all tall men are detectives or constables in private clothes, and pass them by, as real tramps often do. The consequence is that he gets assistance from them – even if they are detectives.

Of course this man soon begins to see that the life of a man out of work is not so terrible after all. He gets enough to eat, and is free to go his way, and he has no responsibilities. A fine healthy appetite compensates for the low quality of his food; for he will now relish plain bread and cheese as he never relished the beef-steak and onions of his former days. Day after day he passes before strange eyes, and therefore has no need to study appearances. He loses all fret, and settles himself to a wandering life. He cannot fail to see how happy are the real beggars he meets on the road and in lodging-houses – and he soon becomes indifferent to work.

Although this man may become too indifferent to look for work, that is not to say that he will not take advantage of a good offer. A number of tramps do this, but if they have had a thorough taste of the road, they can never be relied on in after days. They hear the call of the road much the same as sailors working on land hear the call of the sea. Such a man is not to be trusted, even though he marries; for he is likely to welcome any slight provocation at home or at work, and take to the road again, deserting wife and little ones. I have often heard of men in a respectable position that boasted – to make their success in business look more important – that they had once been tramps on the road, but it is always to be found that the experiences of such men were limited to a week or two; and that they never properly filled their lungs with the air of freedom. It would be very difficult to find a man in a respectable position that had been for a whole summer a free wanderer.

I really cannot imagine any better life on earth than to be free of all tasks and duties; free, morning and night, to rise and retire at one's pleasure. Nothing amuses me more than to read of the activity of some of our leading men; how they are always trying with all their might to make up the time they wasted as babes in their mothers' arms, and in idle play in fields and streets.

The Career of Hurdy Gurdy Joe [165]

Although I do not countenance hard work, I still believe that a beggar should maintain his self-respect and try to get on in his profession. It is certainly better to be a slave than to be a beggar without ambition, without a bed at night and picking up bread in the gutter. The career of Hurdy Gurdy Joe, which I will here relate, is a good instance of how a poor, homeless wretch could rise in the world.

Some years ago, when I had a night out on the Embankment, I sat on a seat that happened to be shared by another man, houseless also. As usual in these cases, our greetings were short. 'Hallo mate', said he. 'Hallo!' I answered. The next instant, he, judging by his heavy breathing, was enjoying a short, violent sleep, and I was thinking of many things. Of course, we were not allowed this much inactivity for long, for we were soon ordered to move on. Without a word of complaint we did so and, although we were strangers to each other, kept walking side by side for a considerable time. All we seemed to be aware of was that we were companions in misery; and whether he followed me or I followed him, was a matter of no account. I don't know which had the most trust in the other as a guide; all I know is that we came to another seat and, like one body, fell upon it. On this occasion we were not quite so fortunate, for in less than five minutes we were again ordered to move on. Still without a word we got up and dragged ourselves from the Embankment into the back streets. In a little while I happened to turn my head and saw a cart in a dark alley. Touching my companion on the shoulder, I made towards it, got on the shaft, fell inside, and was asleep almost immediately. In fact, sleep came so soon that I could not keep awake long enough to see whether my companion followed or not, neither did I care.

The next morning, when I awoke through the cold, I was surprised to find myself alone. What had become of my companion of the preceding night? Had he followed me into the cart and risen

---

165. This is Davies ostensibly writing fiction, though the raconteur's tone, subject matter, and first-person narration contrive to make it hard to distinguish from much of his writing as a memoirist. Published in *The Tramp* (June 1910), pp. 337–40, with an ink illustration of a tramp by Joseph Simpson.

early? Had he some plans for the day, which he did not want me to know, and so thought it best to escape my presence? Asking myself these questions, I descended from the cart, and then saw, to my astonishment, my new friend fast asleep *under* the cart. Whether he had been too tired and sleepy to climb into the cart, or was not ambitious enough to sleep in that state of elevation, I cannot say: all I know is that he slept under instead of inside the cart. Of course I knew that the carter would soon arrive, for even now I began to see people pass, at the end of the alley, so I lost no time in rousing him. And when I had succeeded, and he stood before me, I was almost sorry that I had not left him to himself, for I knew that I must now leave him at once, for he was the most ragged and dirtiest man that I had ever seen. One look at him was quite enough, for I knew that I could not summon courage to walk by day at the side of a companion like that. 'Where are you going to get breakfast?' I asked. 'There is a school, not far from here, and I can pick up, after nine o'clock, a few crusts thrown away by the children, which will make me a good breakfast', he answered. With these words we parted, not to my regret.

Some time after this, when I was on the country road, I met him again, but he looked much cleaner, appeared more active, and his face had a more cheerful look. 'How long have you left London?' I asked. 'Ah', said he, with a shake of the head, 'ah, those were the days of misery indeed; don't you think so? But, thank God, they are passed, and I am doing better now'. On inquiring I learnt that he now walked from town to town, had a clean bed in a workhouse every night, and begged his food like a man, instead of picking it up in the gutter. 'What a difference', said he, 'in my past life and this!'

Three months after this meeting, I happened to be in Luton, and, having had good luck, was soon back and settled in the lodging-house kitchen. It must have been about five o'clock in the evening, when I had my attention drawn to the arrival of a stranger. The man was dressed very respectably in a suit of black, but the fit was outrageously bad. I at once recognised him as the man who had slept under the cart. 'Hallo!' he cried, on seeing me, 'I am very glad to meet some one I know, for this is my first experience in a lodging-house'. Hearing this, I began to give him points, relating to the simple rules of a lodging-house, which would save him the trouble of making inquiries of strangers, some of whom were not very polite.

That evening, after we had finished tea and sat smoking our pipes, and a dozen beggars were making merry at the expense of respectable workers – my companion began to talk. 'What a difference', said he, 'in this life and life in the workhouse! This day is a turning-point in my career, for I am determined never to enter a workhouse again. When I begged at a house this morning, the man not only gave me a good meal and these clothes, but a two-shilling piece as well. So I determined to pay for my bed like a man, instead of going into a workhouse. To-morrow I am going to earn my living as a street singer, and have done with workhouses for ever'.

And so he did, for the next morning, when I was passing a street corner, I heard a man singing a hymn and looking saw my old friend standing in the middle of the road. It was his voice, but he had had not yet learnt the beggar's tremolo, which, however, would soon come to him. He had not yet learnt the way to sing a song in two different keys, so as to attract notice, or to grind the notes, or give them a peculiar rasping noise, so that people in their houses would not mistake him for a man singing for his own pleasure. I stood long enough to see him receive money in two instances, and then made my way to a different part of the town, so as to give him plenty of room to earn his living.

Now it was not long after this when I happened to meet my old friend again. But he was no longer a common street singer – he was a proud pedlar, with a five-shilling licence in his pocket. He hinted to me that he was never without a shilling in his pocket for a rainy day, and the police had no power over him now. 'Since I received that suit of clothes and a two-shilling piece, and was advised to be a man – I have been one, and have made every effort to rise in the social scale. I am a far different man now from what I was when we first met in London and from what I was when I went in to workhouses. And I have not yet reached the height of my ambition', said he, smiling and winking his eye. I could hardly believe that this man was my companion of that wretched night in London; who was then so ragged and dirty that he would have soiled a coal cart and had crept under one to sleep.

The next morning we parted, and I did not see him again for twelve months; when I had been off the road for a winter and forced to take to it again in the following spring. I was then in the town of Swindon and it was market-day.

As I was passing down the main street, I heard an organ and, knowing well that most organ-grinders live in common lodging-houses with pedlars, beggars and navvies, I turned my head, curious to see if I knew the player. To my surprise I recognised in him my old friend that had slept like a dog under the cart; who had recovered his self-respect sufficiently to aspire to a bed in a workhouse; and who had become a man at last and paid for his bed in a lodging-house. However, this was no time for any more than a smile and nod of recognition, so I passed on to my own bit of business. I knew a lodging-house, kept by an Italian, where I would most likely meet him that same night.

That evening, when I arrived at the Italian's, my old friend was seated at a table, drinking tea and eating a mutton chop with two fried eggs. He no sooner saw me enter than he made a motion connecting me with his teapot. This is always a sign of goodwill among lodgers, to offer each other a drink of tea — much the same as the Red Indians offer the pipe of tobacco. So I went over to him and sat down at his side.

Now, I knew well that organ-grinders made good money, and I was not surprised to hear him say, after a time, that he had made more than six shillings on that particular day. It must he admitted that the town was a good one, and also that it was market-day, which would be the best day in the week. But when I thought of this man's career, how I had seen him sleeping under a cart, and how he was now rich enough to hire an organ — when I thought of these things, I was filled with astonishment. I hinted at this and, to my further amazement, he said, 'What! Me hire an organ? It is paid for, and every penny I make is clear profit, it is my own!' Hearing this, I was thunderstruck. For here was a man that had risen from the very lowest state to be a player of his own organ. He had risen from a picker-up of castaway bread, and a dog-like sleeper under carts, to be the most prosperous man — except the landlord — in a lodging-house. From common beggar and a frequenter of workhouses, to a street singer that paid four pence for his bed every night; from street singer to licensed pedlar that was never without a shilling in his pocket; and at last not only to become an organ-grinder, but to be the owner of it and average his three shillings a day. If anyone had told me these things would happen, on that wretched night of our first acquaintance, I would have laughed the idea to scorn.

We often hear of strange happenings in new countries, how men suddenly become rich or poor; how servants sometimes rise to such a position that they can, and do employ their old masters who have fallen with the same ease as their servants have risen. Even so, this man, who had slept on the bare ground under me, when I proudly slept over him in a cart — this man, I say, had now risen to such a position that he offered to hire me as his assistant!

My Memory of Edward Thomas [166]

Of all my literary friends, Edward Thomas was the kindest and the most sincere.[167] Just after the publication of my first book,[168] when my work made more noise than money, he placed at my disposal a small cottage in the country to give me all opportunity to write.[169] He himself rented a farmhouse, three fields away, and I saw him every day for about nine months. After that the farm changed hands, and the new tenant required the house for himself. He was quite happy in those days, for plenty of work came his way without having to beg for it. The fact of the matter was that Thomas was too gentle, and not blustering enough to compete with others who were less able to do the work. We find it the same when a big, saucy, able-bodied beggar can make more money than even a man that is blind. I remember that Thomas told me one day of how a certain literary giant, whom he had approached for work, kept him following at his heels for half an hour while he was doing other business; and when he looked into Thomas's face and saw its weariness and disgust, said – 'You don't look happy, but you must follow me if you want a bone to pick'. When I heard this story I made little of it, hoping that Thomas would do the same, but it made me furious to think a quiet, unassuming fellow like Thomas should be beholden to a pig like that.

It has not been mentioned what made Thomas suddenly take to writing poetry, after so many years of prose.[170] This was due to the

---

166. Published in *Voices in Poetry and Prose* 4.4 (October 1920), pp. 119–22.

167. Edward Thomas (1878–1917), Anglo-Welsh poet and critic. Enlisted to fight in the Great War in 1915 and killed in action during the Battle of Arras. Davies's elegy for Thomas, 'Killed in Action', is included in this book.

168. *The Soul's Destroyer* (1905).

169. Davies appears to be simplifying the facts a little. In the autumn of 1905, according to Lawrence Normand, Davies had returned to Newport to live with his mother and her family, and to start work on his autobiography. However, he could not find a productive living and working environment. Thomas had access to a cottage near his family home of Elses Farm, Sevenoaks, Kent, and invited Davies to share it rent free until the lease ran out in January 1906. Then Thomas paid the rent for Davies to live at Stidulph's Cottage, also close by, and with the pleasing address of Egg Pie Lane, The Weald, Kent. See Lawrence Normand, *W. H. Davies* (Bridgend: Seren, 2003), pp. 50–51.

170. Thomas was an extremely prolific reviewer of poetry, but only started writing it himself in 1914.

influence of Robert Frost, the American poet, to whom Thomas paid several long visits, down in Gloucestershire.[171] Robert Frost was a great talker and, judging by the little I saw of him, a thoroughly good chap in every way. I may say here that Thomas was always influenced by good talkers, in spite of the few things they say that can be remembered. I have only met two, in my experience, that were really very brilliant talkers; one was Edward Garnett,[172] Thomas' friend – and mine, as often proved – and the other Walter Sickert.[173]

After meeting Frost two or three times, poetry filled Thomas to such an extent that he kept on writing day after day, with all the eagerness and enthusiasm of a poet in his teens. Several of his poems were shown to me, when I was there on a week-end visit, but the surprise that he had written poems interfered with my power to give an opinion. However, I made Thomas chuckle for a long time, by warning him of the consequence. I reminded him that the poets he had been slating for years were also reviewers, and that no sooner would his book of poems be announced, than one would ask this journal for it, another would ask that journal, another a third, and so on; they would even offer to review it for nothing – and then they would all skin him alive. Thomas, whose sense of humour was strong, was so delighted at this picture that it prepared him for the worst.

Speaking of Thomas' sense of humour, I would like to suggest that, if he had known more men of a plain, simple humour and fewer men of sharp wit, it would have been better for him. In his soldier's life he was meeting such men, and I am certain he would have come out of the war, had he lived, a different man.

After Thomas had left Kent, where I remained for three more years, I used to meet him at lunch every Tuesday, with Edward Garnett, W. H. Hudson,[174] and others. Then we had tea at another place, with different people, Walter de la Mare[175] and Ralph Hodgson

171. The American poet Robert Frost (1874–1963) lived in England from 1912 to 1915, most notably in Dymock. He was one of the more prominent 'Dymock poets', and became friends with Thomas in England. Frost published his first two poetry books in London: *A Boy's Will* (1913) and *North of Boston* (1914). As noted in the 'Introduction' to the present volume, Frost's opinion of Davies appears to have been less enthusiastic than that of his friend.

172. Edward Garnett (1868–1937), English writer, critic and editor, helped Davies to edit *The Autobiography of a Super-Tramp* (1908), and provided other financial and practical assistance to Davies early in his literary career. He was also central to the London literary life of which Davies later became a part.

173. Walter Sickert (1860–1942), influential early modernist painter of German descent. Davies and Sickert were friends, and Sickert sketched Davies on several occasions.

174. William Henry Hudson (1841–1922), novelist.

175. Walter de la Mare (1873–1956) and Ralph Hodgson (1871–1962), both poets.

among them. By the way, in Mr de la Mare's Foreword to his friend's *Collected Poems,* he mentioned his first meeting with Thomas, saying that the waitress piled the chairs, as a hint to be going. I have an idea that I was present on that occasion, as the same thing happened when Thomas introduced me to a poet he was meeting for the first time.[176] I hardly think my body escaped notice altogether, although I am only five feet four inches. However, it was a very interesting time. We talked and talked until the disgusted waitresses, who wanted to close the shop, surrounded us with chairs to such an extent that we could hardly get out of the place. The success of the meeting was due to Thomas' humour, and my own poor experiences enriched by a little of Mr de la Mare's 'elfin music'.[177]

My only regret, in thinking of Edward Thomas, is in the early part of our friendship. I had been held back so long that, when the chance came for writing, I could think of nothing but my own work, and never once did I express a desire to see his. It will go far to explain his character when I say that he did not mention his own books at all.

The last time I met him was on the night when he was going to the Front. He had asked several friends to meet him, but for one reason or another only two came – Roger Ingpen and myself.[178] I was suffering from great nervous fatigue on that occasion, for I had been sitting all day to Epstein for a portrait bust. But I was glad to be there, especially as his other friends had such important engagements. After Roger Ingpen had gone, we walked up Charing Cross Road together, silent, and neither of us feeling comfortable. Probably I was the last, of his old friends, to wish him good-bye.

It is strange that Edward Thomas, in spite of keeping his poems going continually from editor to editor, did not succeed in getting one accepted – not even one! How quickly these editors have changed their minds! And he was so modest that I am certain he did not have the satisfaction of other poets who, looking into the future with a complacent smile, think they exchange winks with posterity.

---

176. Davies is apparently affecting not to remember whether this poet was de la Mare. Davies's relationship with de la Mare appears to have been complicated by a mixture of respect and jealousy on the part of Davies.

177. A perhaps slightly disparaging allusion to something that would go into Walter de la Mare's *Down-Adown-Derry: A Book of Fairy Poems* (1922), which includes five occurrences of the word 'elf', four of the word 'elfin' and one of the phrase 'elfin music'.

178. Roger Ingpen (1868–1936), biographer and editor.

A Foreword, *Shorter Lyrics of the Twentieth Century: 1900–1922*[179]

This is an anthology of poems, and not an anthology of poets. It is not made out of friendship to certain poets, but from the pure love of poetry. That speaks for its honesty.

In reading a great number of anthologies, I have come to the conclusion that most of the compilers work in this way: first, they think of a poet – let us say W. B. Yeats or John Masefield. Then, thinking that 'Innisfree' or 'Cargoes' must be their best lyrics, because they are their most popular, make those poems their first choice. But my first cry, on thinking of W. B. Yeats, was 'A Faery Song'; which I think is his most perfect poem, although it is not held in much esteem by anthologists.

I am not a fastidious bookworm, for there is probably not another author living who knows less about books. But when I have once read a beautiful poem, it clings to my memory. I have always criticised my own work severely, especially of late years. Several friends have advised me to use a poem of my own, 'A Great Time', because it has been called perfect, and been a favourite with anthologists. But my opinion is that the poem has a facile run in the middle, where four lines are made to do the work of three; and that's where its imperfection lies.[180] When I am in doubt about a poem, I consult my friends. But, unfortunately, an artist's friends are his enemies, as far as his work is concerned, and his real enemies are his best friends.

Patriotic poetry has been purposely avoided, as it is seldom enjoyed by lovers of real poetry, and I am determined to run no risk of being offered a knighthood. Anthologies of the patriotic kind, made for schools, are mostly bad. Their idea is to foster a love of patriotism, and not of poetry. As if both these things could not be done at one and the same time by such lines as these:

---

179. W. H. Davies (ed.), *Shorter Lyrics of the Twentieth Century: 1900–1922* (London: Poetry Bookshop, 1922).

180. 'A Great Time', from *The Bird of Paradise* (1914), is included in the present volume.

Oh, to be in England
Now that April's there[181]

instead of the rhetorical jingle we so often read. However, these anthologies are in the hands of Professors, and the life of a Professor is
usually a series of mistakes. What will our children think when they
grow up and find that the poets whose lines they were forced to
commit to memory were not the best poets of their day!

Although I have used very little war poetry, I have not made this
anthology a bowl of goldfish that have no dark companions, as will
be seen by a number of strong poems on other subjects.

My object in making this selection is to produce a book on every
page of which is a thing of beauty or interest. In reading modern
anthologies, it has seldom been my delight to find something new to
surprise me. Mrs Meynell's *Flower of the Mind* was worth doing if only
to make known that wildly beautiful lyric called 'Tom o' Bedlam',
which makes me think that, had Shakespeare known it, it would not
have remained anonymous.[182] The same pleasure came to me on
reading A. M.'s *Anthology of Modern Verse*, in which I read for the first
time T. E. Brown's 'Dora'.

There, are quite a number of poets at the present time who are
writing descriptive verse of a high order, which is to be seen in most
of our anthologies. But their work begins and ends in description,
and neither casts any light on their own minds nor on humanity
in general. These poets seem to lead easy and placid lives, without
having any burning sympathies to make themselves great as men.
A man can be a great man without being a great poet, but I doubt
whether there was ever a great poet who was not a great man. Most
of these poets are teetotallers, I believe, and lack the sympathy and
generosity of men that drink. Christ, to perform a miracle worthy of
our greatest wonder, did not turn water into tea, coffee or cocoa, but
into wine!

There can be no serious argument about free verse. The only thing
that can be said is that a number of people are using it who are not
poets at all. But the same thing can be said of a far greater number
who use the traditional form of verse. Whitman proves himself, in
quotation, a great poet, no matter what form he adopted. Lovers of
the traditional form must not be blind to the beauty of 'Out of the

---

181. The opening lines of Robert Browning, 'Home-Thoughts, from Abroad',
written in 1845.

182. Alice Meynell (ed.), *The Flower of Mind: A Choice Among the Best Poems* (1897).

Miscellaneous Prose

cradle endlessly rocking', or 'Laved in the flood of thy bliss O Death'. Nor must the lovers of free verse forget Whitman's greatness when he used rhyme in the old traditional form, like this:

> But O heart! heart! heart!
>   O the bleeding drops of red,
> Where on the deck my Captain lies,
>   Fallen cold and dead.[183]

As I am acting as a critic in doing this anthology, my own contribution is one poem. I would like to draw all the attention possible to the good poems I have discovered by other people. I am not cunning enough to leave my work out altogether, to have a chorus of voices complain of the omission.

I would like to say that although this book may be a guide to the best short poems, it is not meant to be a guide to the best poets. I have missed quite a number of good things owing to length. For that reason, this book does not do justice to the work of Lascelles Abercrombie, Gordon Bottomley, and some others.[184]

It is agreed that an anthology, to be good, must hold surprises. Some of the poems in this book have been discovered for the first time. Perhaps the reader will be interested in another surprise – the worst poets have charged the highest fees for the use of their work.

---

183. From Walt Whitman, 'O Captain! My Captain!', written in 1865. The two poems mentioned earlier in the paragraph are also both by Whitman. The former is known by the line Davies gives; the latter is from Part XIV of 'When Lilacs Last in the Dooryard Bloom'd'.

184. 'Some others' to be omitted from the anthology include the rather more enduring poets W. H. Auden, Wilfred Owen, and T. S. Eliot.

Poets and Critics

Rome was not built in a day, and it takes a hundred years and more to make a poet. First, we have to discover one quality in the poet, and then decide whether it is genuine or not. It may take years to do this. Then comes another critic who discovers a second quality, which goes through the same process. Then comes the third critic, with his discovery of a third quality, and so on. Finally, we have the last critic, who, with the reins of several good qualities already in his hand, finds a little more fresh matter; and it is then decided that the poet is out as a full team to take the road of time, without any more question as to his fitness. But this sometimes takes so long that even now we are not sure that Shakespeare is given credit for all his qualities.

When we consider this matter we must look with some suspicion on the question of living poets, and the position assigned to them by their critics. What has this tin hat, which we place on the head of a living poet, to do with the deathless laurel? This tin hat casts such a halo around the poet's head that even the wisest are for the time being deceived by the false light. All this comes from mentioning a poet's name so many times – often when there is no necessity to mention his name at all – that we come to think at last that his name is as necessary to our soul as bread is to our body. When we see his name time after time, and again and again, we lose all power of criticism, and his most feeble utterance leaves us breathless, with only one word on our lips, the word "magic". And so it goes on for a year or two, like a silly tune that we cannot escape, because of its repetition, which haunts us until it dies. And as that tune has its day and can never be revived, so does that poet's work pass away in the same manner. Who is to blame for this? Not the poet, but his friends the critics. One of our well-known critics – an excellent one too – thinks that a certain living poet is greater than Coleridge; and it would be easier to turn a donkey against his oats than to make that man alter his opinion. Yet Coleridge, if he had written a few more pages on the same level as his *Ancient Mariner* and *Christabel* would have been, I believe, our third English poet.

That there are a great number of bad poets, we admit; but that

185. From *New Statesman*, 21 (8 September 1923), p. 619.

there are a greater number of bad critics is not so well known. Where these bad critics show their failure is in quotation; but some of us are too wise to be taken in when critics quote indifferent verse with approbation; and when they say timidly, after quoting, 'but this is by no means the poet at his best," we recognise at once the friendly puff.

As I have had so little cause to complain of reviewers, perhaps I ought not to have written an article on this subject. My work has been attacked three times, I believe. The first attack was from a well-known literary editor who said, on reading my first book, that he had wasted half a crown on it, and he could not find one line good enough to quote. But since then he has said that he buys and saves all my first editions, as he is certain that each little book will some day be worth its weight in gold. But what makes the other two attacks amusing is that my two critics are in direct opposition on the same point. One man has for years, as my different volumes appear, attacked me with the same thought on each occasion. It is this: that my lyrics are perfect, such as they are; but the matter in them is so small that they are not of much account. The second critic claims that I write good lines occasionally, but none of my lyrics are perfect. Now, I would never think of answering critic number one, for, as I have said seeing that it takes a hundred years or more to make a poet – he may be right, But I would dearly like to get these two men together:

> As fierce as twenty angry cats,
> Rolled up and fighting in one ball.

In this case I can imagine myself, although the pitiful bone of their contention, acting like Charles Lamb, when in the excitement he stood up and booed furiously, with the audience, forgetting that he was booing the failure of his own play.

Critics as a rule try to say something original, and in a good many cases the truth does not matter. It seems curious that no reviewer has called Thomas Hardy a poet of joy. No doubt this will come, for a critic can prove anything by quotation. If he does not like a poet he quotes him at his worst; and if he is inclined to be friendly, he quotes the poet at his best.

It is quite certain that my fame will last. If I am not immortal as a poet, I shall be immortal as the greatest literary fraud of the twentieth century. As I believe that we have some kind of life beyond the grave, I have often imagined myself as a literary fraud in the regions of the dead and surrounded by questioning spirits. One will ask: 'How did you manage to deceive the public for so many years that you were thought to be a good poet? 'Another spirit, who had been an artist in his day, will say: 'How did you manage to persuade the master artists of your day that you were the one poet worthy of their brush?' Another, a politician this time, will want an answer to this: 'How did you manage to persuade the Government to give you a Civil List Pension?' And when I have all these spirits seated comfortably around me, I will recite my verses – the verses that fooled the greatest people of my day.

And what laughter there will be. Perhaps at that very moment we will be joined by another spirit, who has lately visited the earth, who will say to me: 'By the way, the *Westminster Bladder* has just mentioned your name. One of the critics has been warning a certain popular poet that he must not take himself too seriously, but 'remember the fate of W. H. Davies, whose work is now forgotten and whose only title to fame is that he deceived for a number of years the greatest people of his day'. None of the spirits will laugh more heartily than myself at this. When I recite the following lines, how amused they will be:

Oh for my greater days to come,
When I shall travel far from home:
On seas, that have no shade in sight,
Into the woods that have no light;
Over the mountains' heads so tall:
Cut by the clouds to pieces small;
Across wide plains that give my eye
No house or tree to measure them by;
And all the wonders I shall see
In some old city new to me.

But when I come to these other lines:

What sweet, what happy days had I,
When dreams made time eternity.[186]

When I come to this the hilarity will be so great that I shall not be heard when I say: 'This is the rubbish that fooled the twentieth century'.

---

186. From 'The Time of Dreams', originally published in W. H. Davies, *A Poet's Calendar* (1927). Included in *The Complete Poems of W. H. Davies* (London: Cape, 1963), p. 391.

Miscellaneous Prose

When we come across a thing of plain simple beauty, why should we try to analyse it? Is it not better to leave it to the imagination? Its richness lies in being undiscovered, like the riches of Eldorado. It is no more possible to give the full reasons of the curious fascination in the work of Defoe than it is to explain the magic in this simple line from Wordsworth: 'Will no one tell me what she sings?' All we know is that we are caught in a charmed circle, with only one fear – the fear of being released. The uneducated schoolboy and the literary professor are both sincere in their admiration, yet they each give a different reason for their enthusiasm.

The language of Defoe is so simple and direct that we do not regard him so much as a novelist as an historian; and even were his plots and stories the most unlikely and extravagant, we would never doubt their truth, because of their simple words. The story of Moll Flanders moves on in such a natural way that no reader can doubt its being a true history. If any man expressed such a doubt in our hearing, we would call him an ass turned loose in a bed of lilies; or a leprous reader to be shunned by all true lovers of literature.

Probably Defoe is the only one, among the Masters, who can write a story without digressions, and in a natural way. He does not moralise, like Fielding and Richardson; nor does he give us long passages of description like Sir Walter Scott. The story is always before us, and there is nothing to skip over, or read in a hurry. He moves with so much ease that we never get the impression that he has an overtrained mind, like the body of a prize-fighter when he is muscle-bound, and fails to extend himself. It is this ease, and this close attention to the narrative, that makes his work so real and true. He is so rich in the action of his story that he never requires help in the matter of describing locality, or unnecessary description of how his various characters are dressed. He does not require this help, neither do we; it is sufficient to feel ourselves on a strong current that runs straight on to the end, and never threatens to stop. We feel the beat

---

187. From Daniel Defoe, *Moll Flanders* (1722), introduced by W. H. Davies (London: Simpkin, Marshall, Hamilton, Kent and Co., 1924).

of a human heart all the time, and nothing else matters. We doubt if there was ever a reader who did not finish *Moll Flanders,* after once beginning it – unless prevented by some serious cause.

One of the sweetest songs in Nature is sung by the Robin Redbreast; and his song is all the sweeter for being heard when the other birds are silent. *But* the most effective notes of the Robin are not heard in his song; but at that time in autumn when he sits on a branch, alone, and does nothing but sob a few quiet notes. And in reading *Moll Flanders* we get something of the same effect. The sentences do not sing, but sob, and we feel them all the more for that; especially because of their restraint, and the strong guard against anything that approaches hysteria.

My own acquaintance with the work of Defoe did not begin until late in life, after the publication of my first book of prose,[188] when the critics were positive that I had founded my style on his. Seeing that I had never studied Style at all, and had no more knowledge of it than a man has of his own looks, I had a great curiosity to read this Master, if only to know what my own style was like. It was as a man that I read *Robinson Crusoe,* and not as a boy; and it was *Moll Flanders* that I read first. Needless to say, when I had read *Moll Flanders, Robinson Crusoe,* and *The Plague of London,* I thought myself a fine fellow indeed, that I had written a book in the manner of Daniel Defoe, without knowing anything about him or his work.

I shall never forget when, some years ago, on looking into the window of a bookshop, I happened to see one book opened, so as to show its title-page. But when I had read, without much emotion, *The Fortunes and Misfortunes of the Famous Moll Flanders,* etc., the reader can judge of my surprise when I began to read that she was 'Twelve Year a Whore, Five Times a Wife (whereof once to her own brother), Twelve Year a Thief, Eight Year a Transported Felon in Virginia', etc. Never before had I seen so much candour in print, with the exception of the Bible. So I judged *Moll Flanders* to be a second Bible that all true believers should study with profit and reverence. How much more to be preferred was this simple candour in *Moll Flanders* to the suggestive hints in some of our modern novels; works that have all the appearance of being pure wells, until we come to drink, and then find a loathsome reptile comes up from the bottom to join its lips to ours.

Although I had already written and published my Autobiography at that time, I imagined myself writing it again, with this more

---

188. *The Autobiography of a Super-Tramp* (1908).

attractive title: *The Life and Adventures of a Poet, Tramp, Cattleman, Thief, and Orphan.*[189] But if I did, some dishonest rival, with the help of a rascally publisher, would certainly bring out a book with the title: *The Life and Adventures of a Poet, Tramp, Shepherd, Thief, and Bastard.* And, in the eyes of a book-buying public, what chance would I, a poor orphan, have against a proud, ambitious bastard? I would stand no more chance than a young hedge-sparrow, when his nest is shared by a young cuckoo that grows twice as fast and twice as big.

Defoe, outside his political works, deals with human character, and little else. In *Robinson Crusoe* he makes one man his central figure, and keeps him before our eyes continually; and in this other book, *Moll Flanders,* he does the same thing with a woman. He never, to my knowledge, deviates from the telling of his story, like so many authors; and whatever happens to Moll Flanders inside a house is told without any description of its architecture, or its furniture, or whether it is new or old. And whatever happens to her in the open air is told without any setting of wind, sun, rain, or snow. It is this close attention to a human story that makes Defoe so attractive to the general reader, who, unlike literary people, has no question to ask about style. The reader is satisfied with the continual action of the story, told in a language he can easily understand. Surely we can expect no more from an author than this extraordinary gift – that he has power to please men of brawn as well as men of brain, and also includes the young. It is not often that Brawn does not admire Brain, but Brain seldom has much admiration for Brawn. But in reading this great Master, Daniel Defoe, they all stand on the same footing, without a difference.

I have always thought, and still believe, that the greatest writers can be quoted from the most, even when they write nothing but short poems and short stories; for there can be lyrics within lyrics, and short stories within short stories.

No great writer moves at the same pace all the time, no more than the waves of the sea. In both cases there comes a bigger wave of ecstasy to take our breath away. But I find Defoe to be the one exception, for there is scarcely a purple passage in all his work. It is one steady march of monosyllables, without a cry of surprise or the least attempt to become eloquent. But what strength there is in these little words of his, and how they reach the heart time after time; whether he describes how the people, in the Plague of London, sat on their

---

189. The 'super-tramp' label was something Davies had come to resent. See 'Introduction'.

doorsteps and died,[190] or relates this strange and Human life of Moll Flanders. Surely it is impossible to believe that Defoe's bare and quiet style is due to a lack of strong feeling – we would rather think it due to an intensity of feeling.

There is not one page in *Moll Flanders* that does not contain one or more passages that could be quoted as an example of clear and simple beauty. We are reminded again and again how much these monosyllables are like small ants that carry great loads of matter out of proportion to their size. They get their effect as they accumulate, like the little drops of water in Chinese torture, that drop on the head, and grow at last from feather- to hammer-weight. There is one passage, when Moll Flanders is a little girl, and innocent, with the ambition to be a gentlewoman, without knowing the exact meaning of the word. Here it is:

> As for my money, I gave it all to my mistress-nurse, as I called her, and told her she should have all I got for myself when I was a gentlewoman, as well as now. By this and some other of my talk, my old tutoress began to understand me about what I meant by being a gentlewoman, and that I understood by it no more than to be able to get my bread by my own work; and at last she asked me whether it was not so. I told her, yes, and insisted on it, that to do so was to be a gentlewoman; 'for', says I, 'there is such a one', naming a woman that mended lace and washed the ladies' laced-heads; 'she', says I, 'is a gentlewoman, and they call her madam'. 'Poor child', says my good old nurse, you may soon be such a gentlewoman as that, for she is a person of ill fame, and has had two or three bastards'.[191]

This passage is almost taken at random, for there are scores of others that could have served my purpose just as well. So this work of genius goes on and on, and never once loses its simple beauty. No doubt there were mountebanks in his day, as there are in ours, to leap and turn somersaults over the heads of the great; yet, surely, though slowly, the great man overtakes them, and leaves them lying behind him, dead and forgotten. There never was a generation yet, in literature or

---

190. A reference to Defoe's *A Journal of the Plague Year* (1922): an account of one man's experiences of the London plague of 1665. Defoe was only five in 1665, and the narrative is probably based on the memoirs of Defoe's uncle, Henry Foe. It was published anonymously, the original title page purporting it to be written by 'a citizen who continued all the while in London'.

191. This is taken from the first chapter of *Moll Flanders*.

art, that did not turn aside from its great men for a while, to worship some freak.

I suppose there are still people on earth, even literary people too, who, blind to the simple beauty of the above passage, would still prefer to read something of this kind:

> Oh, my sweet darling, if you only knew how much I love you, you would at once fly in to the arms of your devoted lover, who must for ever pine for your most angelic form!

This is the best example of an artificial style that I know of, and it is work like this that makes Smollett so much inferior to Defoe and Fielding; that makes him a humourist at all times, even in his most serious moments.[192]

It was only by allowing Moll Flanders to tell her own story that Defoe was able to avoid confusion of plot, and to appeal more to the heart than the brain. If he had neglected her in chapters here and there, to follow the fortunes and misfortunes of her associates, and sacrificed that curious fascination we find in the personal I – if he had done this, his work would not have had this plain face of truth, to rescue it from works of pure imagination. The personal I, still followed by the verb of action, is in every sentence, and we are never allowed to see the author himself behind his creation. This leads me to a confession – strange to say, I know nothing at all about Defoe himself, and admiration for his work has never made me curious about his person. When or where he was born; whether he was of the common people, the middle classes, or an aristocrat; whether he was self-taught or a scholar by education; whether he was a City or a Country gentleman, or led the wandering life of a vagabond – of these things I know nothing. Probably I could find a book on one of my shelves that would tell me all these particulars in a few moments, but, for some strange reason, I am in no hurry to know any of these things – perhaps I fear some kind of disappointment.

---

192. Tobias Smollett (1721–1771), Scottish author of picaresque novels, including *The Adventures of Roderick Random* (1748), *The Adventures of Peregrine Pickle* (1751), and *The Expedition of Humphry Clinker* (1771). I cannot find in Smollett the words Davies 'quotes', and suspect he simply made them up to serve his point.

Poets in these days have little to complain of in the matter of fair play – most of them are ruined by favour. If Robert Burns had only received fair play – without a question of favour – what a difference it might have made to his life! His life is now so well known that we will say no more here than that he was born of the people, made a name as a poet, was taken up by society, neglected: and died an unhappy man at the early age of thirty-eight.

What a pity it is that these society people do not know the full tragedy, when a poet, especially one belonging to the common people, is served like this! They do not know that he is left hanging in the air, that his old and his best friends, to whom he must return, are never the same to him again, and, spiritually, he becomes a homeless man. And seeing that Burns was not a Nature poet, like Wordsworth, or a poet of strange dreams, like Coleridge, but derived his main inspiration from brotherly love – this made his particular case all the more cruel.

If it is true that each time we see a shooting star a baby is born – if this is true, whoever saw the star that brought Robert Burns into the world must have been astonished at its radiance and beauty, to distinguish it from our more common mortals. It was as different from our other shooting stars as the great forked lightning is from the common sheeted flash, and must have taken the whole heavens in its course. The remembrance of that star – which was the birth of a great poet – would have been enough for one lifetime, and we could never hope to see the like of it again, though we sat up night after night.

Whenever we apply the word inspiration to a man's work, we are at once reminded of two men in particular – one is John Bunyan, and the other is Robert Burns. One was a tinker and the other was a ploughman; and it is because of their low origin and lack of education that we can find no other explanation for their wonderful work than to call them inspired men.[194] Such work cannot be done

---

193. Robert Burns, *Poetical Works* (London: Collins, 1928), pp. vii to xiii.

194. John Bunyan (1628–1688), author of *The Pilgrim's Progress* (1978), had worked as a tinker during his youth.

by others, who think that severe study and concentration will bring the same result. We know one man, a great critic, who could have given Burns during his lifetime the reputation he has now, after more than a hundred and fifty years; and yet this great critic, in spite of his almost uncanny knowledge of poetry, fails with all his efforts to do the thing himself. In fact, nearly all our best critics of poetry, at the present day, write poetry themselves; but their poems lack freshness and spontaneity, and all that can be said for them is that they are correct in form, and, morally, quite respectable. Judging by my own experience, as a poet of the people, our ploughman would not have received much encouragement from these scholars, were he a living poet. They would have been shocked by the same strong gusto which they are now forced to admire. There are some people, I believe, who are too delicate to enjoy the strong passions in a poet like Burns, who is certainly an Elizabethan in this matter. I remember on one occasion, when I was praising Burns, being cautioned in these words, by a Scotchman, too, 'He is not read and admired so much as you think by the better classes in Scotland.' But as my friend was a solid business man, without imagination, I did not think it worthwhile to defend Burns by quotation, so I simply said, 'So much the worse for Scotland.' It was a hard matter to deal with a man of that kind, for if I quoted passages of beauty he would not be able to see their beauty, and an argument might have led to bad feeling. So the best thing to do was either to change the subject, or to remain silent like the husband in the epigram who, though he knew the answer to his wife's retort, would never dare to utter it.

'I saved your life, when you were ill',
Retorted his forgetful wife:
For had she not half killed him first,
There'd been no need to save his life.

It is as a poet of love and humanity that Burns is so great, and not as a Nature poet, which, according to his life, we would have expected. His schools, where he acquired his fine knowledge, were the country tavern and the small cottage, much more valuable places for the student of life than either Oxford or Cambridge. For it is in those places where we find the elemental passions, the open heart and the bold tongue, and no mask. Let us be thankful that Burns did not spend more time in fashionable drawing-rooms, where life has a surface value, and nothing else. Even as it was, he had enough of that kind of life to make him dissatisfied with the simple life he had left, and to which he had to return. But he had already done enough good work to make his name immortal, and the pests of society, fortunately for the world, had to deal with a full-grown poet, and not a poet of promise. Whether he would have still done good work, if he had lived on as an unhappy and dissatisfied man, we cannot say. A little security, in the way of a Government pension, might have helped him considerably. But the Prime Minister of those days probably thought that a ploughman poet was a sensational oddity, like 'the smallest man in the world' or 'the fattest lady on earth.'

It is very seldom that Burns allows a Nature or descriptive passage to rely on its own beauty, without nailing it down with a fine bit of wisdom, or, what is often the case, a fine touch of personal emotion. In the matter of expressing emotion, Burns is supreme. It would be hard to find, outside the works of Shakespeare and Chaucer, any finer touches of true pathos. No poet who was accustomed to meeting society people would have written these four lines, that almost frighten us by their plain feeling and simplicity.

Had we never loved sae kindly,
Had we never loved sae blindly,
Never met – or never parted,
We had ne'er been broken-hearted.[195]

And then we read:

The wan moon is setting behind the white wave,
And time is setting with me, oh![196]

When we read this, we no longer cry for the moon, for all its beauty is shattered and dismissed in that fine second line of personal emotion. These are the things that matter. No lines of description on inanimate things, however beautiful, can equal these, where the poet throws the light on his own heart, or on human life in general.

In reading modern poets, we are often confounded as to what kind of men they are. There is no personality in their work, and no personal confession; and though they live in London, they prefer to mention Babylon. Thinking certain subjects are hackneyed, such as love and the moon, they write obscurely on other things, forgetting that every poet who is really great makes his own moon, and gives it

---

195. From 'Ae Fond Kiss', one of Burns's most popular love songs.
196. From Burns's song 'Open the door to me oh'.

an entirely new beauty. They are only English in language – God only knows what nationality they are in their vision! But no man needs to be told that Burns was a Scotchman; and there is many a thought such as 'Man was made to mourn', and 'A man's a man for a' that' – to prove that he belonged to the common people.

How unlike Burns our modern poets are, with his candour and sincerity. He was not ashamed to mention anything that gave him pleasure, whether it was love or ale; and he was too truthful and sincere to hide anything that made him grieve. Of all my poet friends, I do not know of one who would ever dream of writing like this:

> Thou'lt break my heart, thou bonny bird,
>   That sings upon the bough;
> Thou minds me o' the happy days
>   When my fause luve was true.

> Thou'lt break my heart, thou bonny bird,
>   That sings beside thy mate;
> For sae I sat, and sae I sang,
>   And wist na o' my fate.[197]

I do not know one modern poet who would write like this, with such a naked simplicity, and yet I have known more than one who had cause to do so. This seems to prove that modern poets are not great, and are only waiting for time to tell the truth. For the great poet is a man that speaks his mind, as children do. In fact, he is an overgrown child, and that is the difference between a poet and an ordinary man. Unless that serpent, society, enters into his garden, he is no more ashamed of showing his naked heart than Eve was of showing her naked flesh.

It is not often that we can hear the human heart beating in the work of a poet, as we do in the work of Robert Burns. Not even now, after all these years, can we look up to Burns as the great master – he was too intimate and friendly for that. It is not possible to forget the man and worship the poet, when we think of 'A man's a man for a' that', or that humorous but terrible satire against cant and hypocrisy, 'Holy Willie's Prayer'. I have often wondered how Wordsworth and Burns would have acted if placed in a similar position. For instance, if a beggar had approached Burns while he was following the plough

---

197. From Burns's song 'The Banks o' Doon'. In most printed versions, 'thou'll' replaces 'thou'lt'.

and composing one of his immortal songs, we know well that both song and plough would have to wait until the beggar had told his story and received help, if possible. But if this same beggar had approached Wordsworth, while he was striding down a lane and mumbling his own verses, what would have happened then? Wordsworth would have passed on – a solemn, serious man bent on a divine mission. This is not to say that Wordsworth was unkind and had no sympathy for the poor – although his stern lines to gipsies did not prove his heart to be very generous to those whose lives he did not understand.[198] If a beggar or a gipsy did not interfere with Wordsworth's inspiration, he might have been kind enough; for inspiration came first and charity second. But with Burns it was inspiration that came second, and charity that was first. Burns was a man before he was a poet, and Wordsworth was a poet before he became the man. In judging these two great poets, the following few words may be suggestive: Wordsworth solemnly called himself a poet; Burns laughed and called himself a rhymer. However, in drawing this comparison between two great poets, it must not be thought that I am doing an injustice to one to give an advantage to the other. It is as men I have been judging them, and not as poets. They are both great poets, and although Burns excelled in tenderness and brotherly love, it must not be forgotten that Wordsworth had certain different qualities that will stand longer than those hardy and long-living rivals – churches and inns.

Burns, I think, reached his very highest note in tenderness, such as we see in 'To a Mountain Daisy', and 'To a Mouse'. This is the great test of his greatness, for only a master can be tender without losing strength and becoming sentimental. Any poet who can write tenderly on the death of a sweetheart, wife or child, with the exact amount of restraint, is a master.

Like all great poets, Burns is rich in quotations, and is a splendid subject for the prentice hand of journalism. But we will leave our readers to find these things for themselves, and only say – they will not pass through many leaves before they come to fruit.

---

198. In Wordsworth's poem 'Gipsies' (1809), the speaker compares the apparent torpor of his subjects with his own activity, and the poem culminates in the claim that 'they are what their birth / And breeding suffer them to be; / Wild outcasts of society!'

Introduction, *Jewels of Song* (1930) 199

When daisies first appear in the spring, we look on them as angels of innocence and beauty; but as soon as they threaten to outnumber the leaves of grass, we mow them down as sinners. As the same thing can be said of anthologies, which have now become something of a pest, it is obvious that the editor must say a word to excuse himself. My excuse for this one is that I have attempted what no one has yet succeeded in doing. It is to bring together a number of little masterpieces within the limit of twenty-four lines; so that the reader can open the book at any page and find a thing of beauty, and be free of doubt. Alice Meynell, in her anthology called *The Flower of the Mind*,[200] has already succeeded in doing this; but although her inclusions are perfect on every page, her omissions are very serious. They are so serious that it would be possible to make another anthology that would be as rich in poetry as hers without actually using one poem that she has selected! However, her task has been much easier than mine, for I have had the courage to include living poets, and that is likely to be a debatable matter. In doing this I have adopted an unusual course, which will look very much like conceit. For instead of judging the work of my contemporaries according to the standard set by the old established poets – instead of doing this, I have judged them by no other than my own work; for as the *Times Literary Supplement* once said, I am 'something of a poet' myself. In fact, the only poems I have included by living authors are those that I am jealous of, and would be glad of the chance of stealing. But, to my misfortune, they are already written, signed, and published by others; and I could no more steal one of them than I could extract the stone from a cherry without breaking its skin.

And now for a little more conceit. On one occasion, when an old-time actor was asked what he would do if he suddenly forgot his part in a play by Shakespeare, he answered, without hesitation: 'That

---

199. W. H. Davies (ed.), *Jewels of Song* (London: Cape, 1930). This is a not dissimilar anthology to *Shorter Lyrics*, with perhaps an even more self-conscious introduction, part modest and part immodest.

200. Another reference to Alice Meynell (ed.), *The Flower of Mind: A Choice Among the Best Poems* (1897).

would not trouble me in the least, for I could easily say something equivalent!' The same answer is mine. If any of my critics will only mention and quote the choice lyrics I have left out of this anthology, I will endeavour, by your kind leave, ladies and gentlemen, to produce something equivalent, unknown, and unsigned. This challenge only applies, of course, to living poets. As I have already said, some of these poems by my contemporaries have caused me jealous pangs, and they are here for one reason only – that I could not do anything myself to take their place. In conclusion, I would like to say that my great ambition is to add more poems by living poets; and if any short lyrics come my way, whose beauty haunts me, and which persist in making me jealous, they will have to go into a future edition.

W. H. DAVIES, Shenstone, Nailsworth, Glos. *October 26th, 1929.*

Selected Poems

Davies saw himself primarily as a poet, and a prolific one. As he put it in Later Days, *'If I had said as many prayers as I have written poems, I would have probably been the Pope of Rome today, or at least a Bishop or Cardinal'.*[201] *However, though he published twenty-five books of verse in the second half of his life, between 1905 and 1939, some of these volumes are very short, and the posthumous* Complete Poems of W. H. Davies *includes a substantial but not overwhelming haul of 749 poems, most of which are short lyrics.*[202] *The title of his fourth collection,* Farewell to Poesy (1910), *implies that Davies thought his muse would depart almost thirty years before it did. However, it is fair to say that his poetry deals with a narrow range of subjects – typically nature, social injustice, sex, love, and the lives of vagrants and prostitutes, sometimes in combination – and much of his later verse suffers from a dearth of fresh subject matter or a fresh means of conveying it. Intriguingly, his physical disability is essentially absent from his poetry, and his time in America is only mentioned a few times. What is more, as Brian Waters put it, 'the scenery of the United States [did not] later find any reflection in the verse of the poet of nature'.*[203] *The life of the tramp and vagabond remains a touchstone, though as he gets older the poems about such lives are often tinged with the guilt of the comfortable man palpably aware both that he is fortunate, and that his life is missing something.*

At first, the success of Davies's poetry was very much on the back of the Autobiography, *and the novelty of a tramp publishing a book of poems undoubtedly appealed to the romantic impulses of contemporary readers. He also had the good fortune to come to prominence in time for Edward Marsh's five* Georgian Poetry *anthologies, published between 1912 and 1922. These books were initially very successful, and Davies shared that success; when they became less fashionable after the Great War, his poems shared that fate too, and his later poetry continued to be distinctly Georgian. Davies always had supporters, though, and the diverse array of twentieth-century writers who admired his verse included Dylan Thomas, Ezra Pound, Joseph Conrad, Edith Sitwell, and Robert Frost, who seems to have disliked Davies's 'asinine' behaviour but nevertheless referred to him as 'a very considerable poet, in spite of several faults and flaws everywhere'.*[204] *It is only in recent decades that his poems have ceased regularly to appear in anthologies.*

The following selection is intended to show a broad range of Davies's strengths as a poet. The poems have been chosen from across his career, though more are included from the earlier books.

---

201. W. H. Davies, *Later Days* (London: Cape, 1925), p. 25 – from the book's first chapter, 'The Camp'.

202. W. H. Davies, *Complete Poems of W. H. Davies* (London: Cape, 1963).

203. Brian Waters, 'Introduction', *The Essential W. H. Davies*, ed. Brian Waters (London: Cape, 1951), pp. 9–20, at p. 11.

204. From a letter, dated May 1914. Quoted in Barbara Hooper, *Time to Stand and Stare: A Life of W. H. Davies* (London: Peter Owen, 2004), p. 94.

The Lodging House Fire [205]

My birthday – yesterday,
Its hours were twenty-four;
Four hours I lived lukewarm,
And killed a score.

I woke eight times and rose,
Came to our fire below,
Then sat four hours and watched
Its sullen glow.

Then out four hours I walked,
The lukewarm four I live,
And felt no other joy
Than air can give.

My mind durst know no thought,
It knew my life too well:
'Twas hell before, behind,
And round me hell.

Back to that fire again,
Ten hours I watch it now,
And take to bed dim eyes,
And fever's brow.

Ten hours I give to sleep,
More than my need, I know;
But I escape my mind
And that fire's glow.

For listen: it is death
To watch that fire's glow;
For, as it burns more red
Men paler grow.

---

205. From *The Soul's Destroyer* (1905) – Davies's first collection, written before he found any literary fame and when he was living in accommodation like that described in this poem. As Hooper notes, this poem 'is the outburst of a depressed and desperate man […] when his life had reached its lowest ebb'. See Barbara Hooper, *Time to Stand and Stare: A Life of W. H. Davies* (London: Peter Owen, 2004), pp. 79–80.

O better in foul room
That's warm, make life away,
Than homeless out of doors,
Cold night and day.

Pile on the coke, make fire,
Rouse its death-dealing glow;
Men are borne dead away
Ere they can know.

I lie; I cannot watch
Its glare from hour to hour;
It makes one sleep, to wake
Out of my power.

I close my eyes and swear
It shall not wield its power;
No use, I wake to find
A murdered hour

Lying between us there!
That fire drowsed me deep,
And I wrought murder's deed –
Did it in sleep.

I count us, thirty men,
Huddled from Winter's blow,
Helpless to move away
From that fire's glow.

So goes my life each day –
Its hours are twenty-four –
Four hours I live lukewarm,
And kill a score.

No man lives life so wise
But unto Time he throws
Morsels to hunger for
At his life's close.

Were all such morsels heaped –
Time greedily devours,
When man sits still – he'd mourn
So few wise hours.

But all my day is waste,
I live a lukewarm four
And make a red coke fire
Poison the score.

Angry [206]

My love sits angry; see!
   Her foot shakes in the light;
Her timid, little foot,
   That else would hide from sight

Her left hand props her cheek;
   Its little finger plays
Upon her under-lip,
   And makes a harp-like noise.

Her lip's red manuscript
   She has unrolled and spread;
So I may read ill news,
   And hang my guilty head.

My love sits angry; see!
   She's red up to her eyes;
And was her face flogged by
   The wings of butterflies?

Her right hand's in her lap,
   So small, so soft, so white;
She in her anger makes
   Five fingers hide from sight.

Two golden curls have now
   Dropped out of their silk net;
There they must stop, for she
   Will not restore them yet.

My love, she is so fair
   When in this angry way,
That did she guess my thoughts,
   She'd quarrel every day.

---

206. From *Farewell to Poesy* (1910).

This life is sweetest; in this wood
I hear no children cry for food;
I see no woman, white with care;
No man, with muscles wasting here.

No doubt it is a selfish thing
To fly from human suffering;
No doubt he is a selfish man,
Who shuns poor creatures sad and wan.

But 'tis a wretched life to face
Hunger in almost every place;
Cursed with a hand that's empty, when
The heart is full to help all men.

Can I admire the statue great,
When living men starve at its feet?
Can I admire the park's green tree,
A roof for homeless misery?

When I can see few men in need,
I then have power to help by deed,
Nor lose my cheerfulness in pity –
Which I must do in every city.

For when I am in those great places,
I see ten thousand suffering faces;
Before me stares a wolfish eye,
Behind me creeps a groan or sigh.

207. From *Farewell to Poesy* (1910).

The Kingfisher [208]

It was the Rainbow gave thee birth,
  And left thee all her lovely hues;
And, as her mother's name was Tears,
  So runs it in my blood to choose
For haunts the lonely pools, and keep
In company with trees that weep.

Go you and, with such glorious hues,
  Live with proud Peacocks in green parks;
On lawns as smooth as shining glass,
  Let every feather show its marks;
Get thee on boughs and clap thy wings
Before the windows of proud kings.

Nay, lovely Bird, thou art not vain;
  Thou hast no proud, ambitious mind;
I also love a quiet place
  That's green, away from all mankind;
A lonely pool, and let a tree
Sigh with her bosom over me.

208. From *Farewell to Poesy* (1910). Though distinctly sub-Keatsean in some of its poeticisms, this poem appealed to many contemporary readers and was included by Edward Marsh in *Georgian Poetry 1911–12*, at Davies's specific request. See Robert Ross, *The Georgian Revolt: The Rise and Fall of a Poetic Ideal 1910–1922* (London: Faber, 1967), p. 122. Davies thought so highly of this poem that he included it as his sole contribution to *Shorter Lyrics of the Twentieth Century: 1900–1922*, ed. W. H. Davies (London: Poetry Bookshop, 1922).

The Philosophical Beggar 209

When I went into the woods this morn to sleep,
I saw an old man looking on the ground.
Said he: 'Here, where a beggar ate his crust,
We see ten thousand little ants at work,
And they are earning now their winter's ease.
As for myself, I cannot rest from work,
I have no patience with those idle fools
That waste their day in mourning wasted time –
My brain must ever be at work. They say
Much work, and just a little pleasure mixed,
Is best for life; as flowers that live in shade
For twenty hours and sunlight four keep fresh
The longest and enjoy the longest life;
They do say this – but all my pleasure's work.
I work on small, when great themes fail my mind –
As cats, when they can catch no mice, content
Themselves with flies. If once I take a rest,
Then sudden famine takes my mind for days,
Which seeks but cannot find the barest feast.
How it doth fret my active Heart to see
The sloven Mind recovering from a day
Of idleness – letting Thoughts peep and none come out.
Ah, wretched hours that follow rest! When men
Have no desire for pleasure, and would work,
But still their Minds do sulk from past neglect.
This world, this mystery of Time, of Life
And Death, where every riddle men explain
Does make another one, or many more –
Can always keep the human mind employed;
Old men that do persuade themselves life's work
Is but half done, must all die happy men.
E'en though we think the world and all things vain,
There lives a noble impulse in our minds
To strive and help to reach the perfect state.
Work, work, and thou hast joy; it matters not
If thou dost start upon a quest as vain
As children, when they seek a cuckoo's nest –
The joy is on the way, not at the end.

209. From *Farewell to Poesy* (1910).

When I am in this world's society,
Then do I feel like some poor bird that would
Attend its young when people loiter near;
I see my thoughts like blossoms fade, and know
That they will die and never turn to fruit.
What juicy joints I threw away when young!
To think of those rich joints makes this meat sweet,
Near to the bone, which Time doth offer now.
Work, work, I say; sleep is sufficient rest;
It is the wage that Nature pays to all,
And when we spend our days in idleness,
She gives short time; and they that earn the least
Do grumble most, when she keeps back full pay.
Now, woodman, do thy work, and I'll do mine –
An active man can almost break Death's heart.'
Then with a pencil and a book he went
Mumbling and writing, into the deep woods.

    Now, what an old, mad fool is that, methought;
He tries to make one hour do work for two,
To keep away the ghosts of murdered ones
He foully did to death when a small boy.
He'll work his brains, and then the world will rob
His hive of its pure honey; in its place
Put for his food cheap syrup of weak praise.
His mind's a garden, all the flowers are his;
But when he markets his sweet honey goods,
Then scoundrel bees, that have their hives elsewhere,
Will make themselves rich on his flowers' sweets.
I count the tramp as noble as that man
Who lives in idleness on wealth bequeathed,
And far more wise than yon old thinking fool.
Show me one happier than the tramp who has
His belly full, and good boots not too tight.
His careless heart has buried kin that live,
Those that have died he resurrects no more.
He does not know the farmer's spiteful joy,
Who, envying his near neighbour, laughs to see
The wild birds knock that man's fruit blossoms down;
He does not laugh to spite a bachelor,
As mothers do, that hear their babies scream.
We scorn the men that toil, as deep sea men
Scorn those that sail on shallow lakes and streams –

Yet by our civil tongues we live and thrive.
Our tongues may be a venomous as those
Small flies that make the lazy oxen leap;
Like a ship's parrot I maybe could swear;
Like a ship's monkey for my cunning tricks –
But I have found a gently uttered lie
And civil tongue sufficient for my ends;
For we can find excuse for our escape –
As rats and mice pursued can find dark holes.
Is there a sound more cheerful than the tramp's
'Good morning, sir'? For in that sound he puts
His whole heart's gratitude that you do work
And sweat, and then make sacrifice for him.
His lips do whine, but how his heart does laugh!
To think that he is free to roam at will,
While others toil to keep that thing 'Respect',
Which makes them starve – if they become like him.
If I hear not my belly's voice, nor feel
The cold; if I toil not for other men –
I ask no more; contented with my bread
Ten times outweighing meat, and water fresh.
When I this morn did beg a rich man's house,
'Go to the bees, thou sluggard' – he replied.
'And to the devil, you' – I answered him.
Then stood and cursed him, worse than farmer when
He sees the Crows turn his green meadow black.
Go to the bees, thou sluggard! Me! From *him*!
And must I be a slave, like thousands more,
To rise before the Sun, and go – in spite
Of fog, rain, wind or hail – to serve his like?
And if perchance I'm hungry at my work,
I still must fast until a certain hour;
If I am sleepy still, when I should rise,
I must not sleep, but up and work for him!
Nature gave me no extra bone for this;
The rich man cannot know the poor man's life –
No more than hands, that are unwiped and wet,
Can feel if clothes are dry. Go, sluggard, work!
It makes me laugh; Care has them soon her slaves
Who dream of duty to their fellow-men
And set a value on each passing hour.
If rich men are the winter's kings, the kings

Of summer are true beggars – that be sure.
Then, happy beggars can recline on stones
With more content than lords sit cushioned chairs;
Their pleasant houses are the leafy trees,
Whose floors are carpeted with grass or moss;
They sleep upon the new-mown hay at night,
And in the daytime to their liking mix
The sun and shade. Oft in forsaken house –
Where spirits drove the living out – they sleep;
Ghosts cannot deal with beggars bold, who have
Less reverence than the spiders that weave webs
Inside the sacred nostrils of a joss.
And see our health; we live on sun and air,
Plain food and water, and outlive rich men,
With all their physic, wines and cleanliness.
Ah, cleanliness! That strikes a woeful note
To those poor tramps that seek the workhouse oft,
That fear to beg, and should be working men;
For, after they have ta'en a workhouse bath,
And their clothes cleaned, how lonely they must feel
When all the fleas that tickled them are dead.
Of Death – who still surprises foolish men,
As though he came but yesterday – the tramp
Thinks not; or takes a little laugh at Death
Ere Death grins everlastingly at him.
The happy tramp cares not if he doth lie
At last between white sheets or on cows' dung.
He has no squeamish taste: he could almost
Eat things alive, in little bits, like birds –
Or lick the streets like Turkey's sacred dogs.
Ah, dogs! that strikes another woeful note.
Many a village have I left through them,
When one had cause – or thought he had – to bark,
And in a while a score of others joined,
Barking because he barked, and nothing more,
And hungry I have had to leave that place.
Some dogs will bite; those small dogs with big heads –
It is the size of these dogs' *heads* we fear,
And not so much how big their bodies are.
If one thing spoils our life it is the dog.
    Now, wherefore should I work my flesh or mind?
I knew Will Davies well; a beggar once,

Till he went mad and started writing books.
Nature, I swear, did ne'er commit worse crime
Than when she gives out genius to the poor;
He is a leper every man would shun;
A lighthouse fast upon the rocks of Want,
To warn men, with his light, to keep away;
And so they do – as far as body goes –
So that they may not witness his distress,
But still they pester him from distant parts.
A beggar's body has far better friends
In nibbling fleas that will not let him sleep,
Than any people's poet whose soul has
More friends than wanted, but scarce one
Real friend to question how his body fares.
Fame's like a nightingale, so sweet at first,
Whose voice soon like a common frog doth croak,
Until we wonder if we hear the same sweet bird.
I cannot see at all why I should work
My mind or body for this cruel world –
I'm no mad poet, like the one I name.
'Tis work, work, work – in every place; it haunts
Me like a painted lady whose sad eyes
Can watch us still, whichever way we look.
Now, let me eat; here's cake, and bread and jam –
I wonder if there's butter in between.
And here's a Christian journal a kind dame
Wrapped round the food to help my happy soul.
What! Here's a poem by the poet-tramp.

> Out, life of care!
>   Man lives to fret
> For some vain thing
>   He cannot get.

> The Cities crave
>   Green solitude;
> The Country craves
>   A multitude.

> Man lives to want;
>   The rich man's lot
> Is to want things
>   The poor know not.

And no man dies
　　But must look back
With sorrow on
　　His own past track.

If beggar has
　　No child or wife,
He, of all men,
　　Enjoys most life.

When rich men loathe
　　Their meat and wine,
He thinks dry bread
　　And water fine.

When Fame's as sick
　　As Failure is,
He snores on straw,
　　In quiet bliss.

　A truthful song, but 'twill not pay his rent.
An English poet! Where's the milk? Me-aw!
If he would thrive, let him be false as hell,
And bow-wow fierce at France or Germany.
　What makes us tramps the happiest of all men?
Our hearts are free of envy, care and greed.
The miser thinks the Sun has not one flower
As fair as his gold heap the dark has grown;
He trembles if the Moon at night comes through
His lattice, with her silver of no worth;
True beggars laugh at him, and do not shake
With greed, like rats that hear a glutton eat,
When they behold a man more richly clad.
Nay, let plain food but keep their bellies tight,
And they will envy none their cloth or land.

A Dream [210]

I met her in the leafy woods,
    Early a summer's night;
I saw her white teeth in the dark,
    There was no better light.

Had she not come up close and made
    Those lilies their light spread,
I had not proved her mouth a rose,
    So round, so fresh, so red.

Her voice was gentle, soft and sweet,
    In words she was not strong;
Yet her low twitter had more charm
    Than any full-mouthed song.

We walked in silence to her cave,
    With but few words to say;
But ever and anon she stopped
    For kisses on the way.

And after every burning kiss
    She laughed and danced around;
Back-bending, with her breasts straight up,
    Her hair it touched the ground.

When we lay down, she held me fast,
    She held me like a leech;
Ho, ho! I know what her red tongue
    Is made for, if not speech.

And what is this, how strange, how sweet!
    Her teeth are made to bite
The man she gives her passion to,
    And not to boast their white.

O night of joy! O morning's grief!
    For when, with passion done,
Rocked on her breast I fell asleep,
    I woke, and lay alone.

---

210. From *Songs of Joy* (1911).

Selected Poems

Christ, the Man [211]

Lord, I say nothing; I profess
    No faith in thee nor Christ the Son:
Yet no man ever heard me mock
    A true believing one.

If knowledge is not great enough
    To give a man believing power,
Lord, he must wait in thy great hand
    Till revelation's hour.

Meanwhile he'll follow Christ, the Man
    In that humanity he taught,
Which to the poor and the oppressed
    Gives its best time and thought.

211. From *Songs of Joy* (1911).

Days that have Been [212]

Can I forget the sweet days that have been,
    When poetry first began to warm my blood;
When from the hills of Gwent I saw the earth
    Burned into two by Severn's silver flood:

When I would go alone at night to see
    The moonlight, like a big white butterfly,
Dreaming on that old castle near Caerleon,
    While at its side the Usk went softly by:

When I would stare at lovely clouds in Heaven,
    Or watch them when reported by deep streams;
When feeling pressed like thunder, but would not
    Break into that grand music of my dreams?

Can I forget the sweet days that have been,
    The villages so green I have been in;
Llantarnam, Magor, Malpas, and Llanwern,
    Liswery, old Caerleon, and Alteryn?

Can I forget the banks of Malpas Brook,
    Or Ebbw's voice in such a wild delight,
As on he dashed with pebbles in his throat,
    Gurgling towards the sea with all his might?

Ah, when I see a leafy village now,
    I sigh and ask it for Llantarnam's green;
I ask each river where is Ebbw's voice –
    In memory of the sweet days that have been.

212. From *Songs of Joy* (1911).

What is this life if, full of care,
We have no time to stand and stare.

No time to stand beneath the boughs
And stare as long as sheep or cows.

No time to see, when woods we pass,
Where squirrels hide their nuts in grass.

No time to see, in broad daylight,
Streams full of stars like skies at night.

No time to turn at Beauty's glance,
And watch her feet, how they can dance.

No time to wait till her mouth can
Enrich that smile her eyes began.

A poor life this if, full of care,
We have no time to stand and stare.

---

213. From *Songs of Joy* (1911). Initially overlooked, this slight poem has become Davies's most famous contribution to English literature. The first two lines have been engraved on a memorial stone on the front of Davies's last home, a cottage called Glendower, in Nailsworth, Gloucestershire.

Sheep [214]

When I was once in Baltimore,
  A man came up to me and cried,
'Come, I have eighteen hundred sheep,
  And we will sail on Tuesday's tide.

'If you will sail with me, young man,
  I'll pay you fifty shillings down;
These eighteen hundred sheep I take
  From Baltimore to Glasgow town.'

He paid me fifty shillings down,
  I sailed with eighteen hundred sheep;
We soon had cleared the harbour's mouth,
  We soon were in the salt sea deep.

The first night we were out at sea
  Those sheep were quiet in their mind;
The second night they cried with fear –
  They smelt no pastures in the wind.

They sniffed, poor things, for their green fields,
  They cried so loud I could not sleep:
For fifty thousand shillings down
  I would not sail again with sheep.

---

214. From *Songs of Joy* (1911). Davies worked on several such ships during his time living in America.

A dear old couple my grandparents were,
And kind to all dumb things; they saw in Heaven
The lamb that Jesus petted when a child:
Their faith was never draped by Doubt: to them
Death was a rainbow in Eternity,
That promised everlasting brightness soon.
An old seafaring man was he; a rough
Old man, but kind; and hairy, like the nut
Full of sweet milk. All day on shore he watched
The winds for sailors' wives, and told what ships
Enjoyed fair weather, and what ships had storms;
He watched the sky, and he could tell for sure
What afternoons would follow stormy morns,
If quiet nights would end wild afternoons.
He leapt away from scandal with a roar,
And if a whisper still possessed his mind,
He walked about and cursed it for a plague.
He took offence at Heaven when beggars passed,
And sternly called them back to give them help.
In this old captain's house I lived, and things
That house contained were in ships' cabins once:
Sea-shells and charts and pebbles, model ships;
Green weeds, dried fishes stuffed, and coral stalks;
Old wooden trunks with handles of spliced rope,
With copper saucers full of monies strange,
That seemed the savings of dead men, not touched
To keep them warm since their real owners died;
Strings of red beads, methought were dipped in blood,
And swinging lamps, as though the house might move;
An ivory lighthouse built on ivory rocks,
The bones of fishes and three bottled ships.
And many a thing was there which sailors make
In idle hours, when on long voyages,
Of marvellous patience, to no lovely end.
And on those charts I saw the small black dots
That were called islands, and I knew they had
Turtles and palms, and pirates' buried gold.

---

215. From *Songs of Joy* (1911). This poem was also included in the first Georgian anthology, *Georgian Poetry 1911–12*.

There came a stranger to my granddad's house,
The old man's nephew, a seafarer too;
A big, strong able man who could have walked
Twm Barlum's hill all clad in iron mail;
So strong he could have made one man his club
To knock down others – Henry was his name,
No other name was uttered by his kin.
And here he was, in sooth ill-clad, but oh,
Thought I, what secrets of the sea are his!
This man knows coral islands in the sea,
And dusky girls heart-broken for white men;
This sailor knows of wondrous lands afar,
More rich than Spain, when the Phoenicians shipped
Silver for common ballast, and they saw
Horses at silver mangers eating grain;
This man has seen the wind blow up a mermaid's hair
Which, like a golden serpent, reared and stretched
To feel the air away beyond her head.
He begged my pennies, which I gave with joy –
He will most certainly return some time
A self-made king of some new land, and rich.
Alas that he, the hero of my dreams,
Should be his people's scorn; for they had rose
To proud command of ships, whilst he had toiled
Before the mast for years, and well content;
Him they despised, and only Death could bring
A likeness in his face to show like them.
For he drank all his pay, nor went to sea
As long as ale was easy got on shore.
Now, in his last long voyage he had sailed
From Plymouth Sound to where sweet odours fan
The Cingalese at work, and then back home –
But came not near his kin till pay was spent.
He was not old, yet seemed so; for his face
Looked like the drowned man's in the morgue, when it
Has struck the wooden wharves and keels of ships.
And all his flesh was pricked with Indian ink,
His body marked as rare and delicate
As dead men struck by lightning under trees,
And pictured with fine twigs and curlèd ferns;
Chains on his neck and anchors on his arms;
Rings on his fingers, bracelets on his wrist;

And on his breast the *Jane* of Appledore
Was schooner rigged, and in full sail at sea.
He could not whisper with his strong hoarse voice,
No more than could a horse creep quietly;
He laughed to scorn the men that muffled close
For fear of wind, till all their neck was hid,
Like Indian corn wrapped up in long green leaves;
He knew no flowers but seaweeds brown and green,
He knew no birds but those that followed ships.
Full well he knew the water-world; he heard
A grander music there than we on land,
When organ shakes a church; swore he would make
The sea his home, though it was always roused
By such wild storms as never leave Cape Horn,
Happy to hear the tempest grunt and squeal
Like pigs heard dying in a slaughter-house.
A true-born mariner, and this his hope –
His coffin would be what his cradle was,
A boat to drown in and be sunk at sea;
Salted and iced in Neptune's larder deep.
This man despised small coasters, fishing-smacks,
He scorned those sailors who at night and morn
Can see the coast, when in their little boats
They go a six days' voyage and are back
Home with their wives for every Sabbath day.
Much did he talk of tankards of old beer,
And bottled stuff he drank in other lands,
Which was a liquid fire like Hell to gulp,
But Paradise to sip.
         And so he talked;
Nor did those people listen with more awe
To Lazurus – whom they had seen stone dead –
Than did we urchins to that seaman's voice.
He many a tale of wonder told: of where,
At Argostoli, Cephalonia's sea
Ran over the earth's lip in heavy floods;
And then again of how the strange Chinese
Conversed much as our homely Blackbirds sing.
He told us how he sailed in one old ship
Near that volcano Martinique, whose power
Shook like dry leaves the whole Caribbean seas;
And made the sun set in a sea of fire

Which only half was his; and dust was thick
On deck, and stones were pelted at the mast.
So, as we walked along, that seaman dropped
Into my greedy ears such words that sleep
Stood at my pillow half the night perplexed.
He told how isles sprang up and sank again,
Between short voyages, to his amaze;
How they did come and go, and cheated charts;
Told how a crew was cursed when one man killed
A bird that perched upon a moving barque;
And how the sea's sharp needles, firm and strong,
Ripped open the bellies of big, iron ships;
Of mighty icebergs in the Northern seas,
That haunt the far horizon like white ghosts.
He told of waves that lift a ship so high
That birds could pass from starboard unto port
Under her dripping keel.

                Oh, it was sweet
To hear that seaman tell such wondrous tales:
How deep the sea in parts, that drowned men
Must go a long way to their graves and sink
Day after day, and wander with the tides.
He spake of his own deeds; of how he sailed
One summer's night along the Bosphorus,
And he – who knew no music like the wash
Of waves against a ship, or wind in shrouds –
Heard then the music on that woody shore
Of nightingales, and feared to leave the deck,
He thought 'twas sailing into Paradise.
To hear these stories all we urchins placed
Our pennies in that seaman's ready hand;
Until one morn he signed for a long cruise,
And sailed away – we never saw him more.
Could such a man sink in the sea unknown?
Nay, he had found a land with something rich,
That kept his eyes turned inland for his life.
'A damn bad sailor and a landshark too,
No good in port or out' – my granddad said.

One night when I went down
Thames' side, in London Town,
A heap of rags saw I,
And sat me down close by.
That thing could shout and bawl,
But showed no face at all;
When any steamer passed
And blew a loud shrill blast,
That heap of rags would sit
And make a sound like it;
When struck the clock's deep bell,
It made those peals as well.
When winds did moan around,
It mocked them with that sound;
When all was quiet, it
Fell into a strange fit;
Would sigh, and moan, and roar,
It laughed, and blessed, and swore.
Yet that poor thing, I know,
Had neither friend nor foe;
Its blessing or its curse
Made no one better or worse.
I left it in that place –
The thing that showed no face.
Was it a man that had
Suffered till he went mad?
So many showers and not
One rainbow in the lot;
Too many bitter fears
To make a pearl from tears?

216. From *Songs of Joy* (1911). This poem was also included in the first Georgian anthology, *Georgian Poetry 1911–12*.

The Sleepers 217

As I walked down the waterside
　This silent morning, wet and dark;
Before the cocks in farmyards crowed,
　Before the dogs began to bark;
Before the hour of five was struck
By old Westminster's mighty clock:

As I walked down the waterside
　This morning, in the cold damp air,
I saw a hundred women and men
　Huddled in rags and sleeping there:
These people have no work, thought I,
And long before their time they die.

That moment, on the waterside,
　A lighted car came at a bound;
I looked inside, and saw a score
　Of pale and weary men that frowned;
Each man sat in a huddled heap,
Carried to work while fast asleep.

Ten cars rushed down the waterside
　Like lighted coffins in the dark;
With twenty dead men in each car,
　That must be brought alive by work:
These people work too hard, thought I,
And long before their time they die.

217. From *Songs of Joy* (1911).

To a Rich Lady 218

Though thou hast silk to wear, and though
Thou'rt clad in it from head to toe –
Still in your hair, that soft warm nest,
My mind would hatch its thoughts and rest.

Though thou hast gems as well, and though
They brighter than the dewdrops glow –
Still would I take my full supplies
Of warmth and light from those two eyes.

Though thou hast cars to drive, and though
Thou'rt driven as the winds that blow –
Still would I find a greater pleasure
To see thee walk an easy measure.

Though thou hast rooms to spare, and though
More than friends need, that come and go –
Still would I ask for no more space
Than where two bodies could embrace.

218. From *Songs of Joy* (1911).

Thou hadst no home, and thou couldst see
   In every street the windows' light:
   Dragging thy limbs about all night,
No window kept a light for thee.

However much thou wert distressed,
   Or tired of moving, and felt sick,
   Thy life was on the open deck –
Thou hadst no cabin for thy rest.

Thy barque was helpless 'neath the sky,
   No pilot thought thee worth his pains
   To guide for love or money gains –
Like phantom ships the rich sailed by.

Thy shadow mocked thee night and day,
   Thy life's companion, it alone;
   It did not sigh, it did not moan,
But mocked thy moves in every way.

In spite of all, the mind had force,
   And, like a stream whose surface flows
   The wrong way when a strong wind blows,
It underneath maintained its course.

Oft didst thou think thy mind would flower
   Too late for good, as some bruised tree
   That blooms in Autumn, and we see
Fruit not worth picking, hard and sour.

---

219. From *Foliage* (1913). Having moved to London in 1885, hoping to make headway as a writer, Francis Thompson (1859–1907) instead became an opium addict and homeless vagrant who slept by the Thames – perhaps not dissimilar to the human subject of 'The Heap of Rags'. In 1888, Wilfrid and Alice Meynell, prominent figures in literary London, discovered his poetry, gave him a home, and helped with the publication of his first book *Poems* (1893). His destitution soon returned, however. Thompson was saved from suicidal depression by a vision of the Romantic poet Thomas Chatterton, who had killed himself, and then by meeting his 'saviour', a prostitute whom Thompson never named but who assisted him both financially and emotionally. He died of tuberculosis. Davies met Thompson shortly before his death, and realised they had once been staying at the same lodging-house at the same time. See Richard J. Stonesifer, *W. H. Davies: A Critical Biography* (London: Jonathan Cape, 1963), p. 55.

Some poets *feign* their wounds and scars:
    If they had known real suffering hours,
    They'd show, in place of Fancy's flowers,
More of imagination's stars.

So, if thy fruits of Poesy
    Are rich, it is at this dear cost –
    That they were nipt by Sorrow's frost,
In nights of homeless misery.

A Great Time [220]

Sweet chance, that led my steps abroad,
    Beyond the town, where wild flowers grow –
A rainbow and a cuckoo, Lord,
    How rich and great the times are now!
      Know, all ye sheep
      And cows, that keep

On staring that I stand so long
    In grass that's wet from heavy rain –
A rainbow and a cuckoo's song
    May never come together again;
      May never come
      This side the tomb.

---

220. From *The Bird of Paradise* (1914).

Nell Barnes [221]

They lived apart for three long years
    Bill Barnes and Nell, his wife;
He took his joy from other girls,
    She led a wicked life.

Yet oft times she would pass his shop,
    With some strange man awhile;
And, looking, meet her husband's frown
    With her malicious smile.

Until one day, when passing there,
    She saw her man had gone;
And when she saw the empty shop,
    She fell down with a moan.

And when she heard that he had gone
    Five thousand miles away,
And that she'd see his face no more,
    She sickened from that day.

To see his face was health and life,
    And when it was denied,
She could not eat, and broke her heart –
    It was for love she died.

---

221. From *The Bird of Paradise* (1914).

Here comes Kate Summers who, for gold,
　　Takes any man to bed:
'You knew my friend, Nell Barnes', said she;
　　'You knew Nell Barnes – she's dead.

'Nell Barnes was bad on all you men,
　　Unclean, a thief as well;
Yet all my life I have not found
　　A better friend than Nell.

'So I sat at her side at last,
　　For hours, till she was dead;
And yet she had no sense at all
　　Of any word I said.

'For all her cry but came to this –
　　"Not for the world! Take care:
Don't touch that bird of paradise,
　　Perched on the bedpost there!"

'I asked her would she like some grapes,
　　Some damsons ripe and sweet;
A custard made with new-laid eggs,
　　Or tender foul to eat.

'I promised I would follow her,
　　To see her in her grave;
And buy a wreath with borrowed pence,
　　If nothing I could save.

'Yet still her cry but came to this –
　　"Not for the world! Take care:
Don't touch that bird of paradise
　　Perched on the bedpost there!"'

---

222. From *The Bird of Paradise* (1914). This poem was also included in the second
Georgian anthology, *Georgian Poetry 1913–15*.

Friends [223]

They're creeping on the stairs outside,
    They're whispering soft and low;
Now up, now down, I hear his friends,
    And still they come and go.

The sweat that runs my side, from that
    Hot pit beneath my shoulder,
Is not so cold as he will be,
    Before the night's much older.

My fire I feed with naked hands,
    No sound shall reach their ears;
I'm moving like the careful cat,
    That stalks a rat it fears.

And as his friends still come and go,
    A thoughtful head is mine:
Had Life as many friends as Death,
    Lord, how this world would shine.

And since I'll have so many friends,
    When on my death-bed lying –
I wish my life had more love now,
    And less when I am dying.

223. From *Child Lovers* (1916).

Killed in Action [224]
(Edward Thomas)

Happy the man whose home is still
   In Nature's green and peaceful ways;
To wake and hear the birds so loud,
   That scream for joy to see the sun
Is shouldering past a sullen cloud.

And we have known those days, when we
   Would wait to hear the cuckoo first;
When you and I, with thoughtful mind,
   Would help a bird to hide her nest,
For fear of other hands less kind.

But thou, my friend, art lying dead:
   War, with its hell-born childishness,
Has claimed thy life, with many more:
   The man that loved this England well,
And never left it once before.

---

224. From *Forty New Poems* (1918). Edward Thomas was killed at Arras in 1917.
The poem appears to recall the early part of their friendship, when Davies had lived
(at Thomas's expense) in a cottage in Kent, and the two men had spent a lot of time
walking the countryside together.

My youth is gone – my youth that laughed and yawned
In one sweet breath, and will not come again;
And crumbs of wonder are my scanty fare,
Snatched from the beauty on a hill or plain.
So, as I look, I wonder if the land
Has *breathed* those shadows in the waters blue!
From all first sounds I half expect to hear,
Not only echoes, but *their* echoes too.
But when I see – the first time in my life –
Our Sussex Downs, so mighty, strong and bare
That many a wood of fifteen hundred trees
Seems but a handful scattered lightly there –
'What a great hour', think I, 'half-way 'twixt Death
And Youth that laughs and yawns in one short breath.'

225. From *The Hour of Magic* (1922).

Wild Oats ²²⁶

How slowly moves the snail, that builds
A silver street so fine and long:
I move as slowly, but I leave
Behind me not one breath of song.
Dumb as a moulting bird am I,
I go to bed when children do,
My ale but two half-pints a day,
And to one woman I am true.
Oh! what a life, how flat and stale –
How dull, monotonous and slow!
Can I sing songs in times so dead –
Are there no more wild oats to sow?

226. From *The Hour of Magic* (1922).

The Rabbit [227]

Not even when the early birds
Danced on my roof with showery feet
Such music as will come from rain –
Not even then could I forget
The rabbit in his hours of pain;
Where, lying in an iron trap,
He cries all through the deafened night –
Until his smiling murderer comes,
To kill him in the morning light.

227. From *Secrets* (1924).

When, with my window opened wide at night,
To look at yonder stars with their round light,
In motion shining beautiful and clear –
As I look up, there comes this sudden fear:
That, down on earth, too dark for me to see,
Some homeless wretch looks up in misery;
And, like a man that's guilty of a sin,
I close my blinds and draw my body in.
Still thinking of that heaven, I dare not take
Another look, because of that man's sake;
Who in the darkness, with his mournful eyes
Has made *my* lighted home his paradise.

228. From *Secrets* (1924).

E is for Eyes [229]

I need no glass to help my eyes,
   My naked sight shows no decline;
A rich blind man would give his all
   For one of these two jewels of mine.

But I'd give any poor blind man
   One of these precious jewels free –
Could he restore the inward sight
   That Time is taking away from me.

---

229. From *A Poet's Alphabet* (1925). This collection has a poem for every letter of
the alphabet.

Sport [230]

Hunters, hunters,
Follow the Chase.
I saw the Fox's eyes,
Not in his face
But on it, big with fright –
Haste, hunters, haste!

Say, hunters, say,
Is it a noble sport?
As rats that bite
Babies in cradles, so,
Such rats and men
Take their delight.

230. From *A Poet's Calendar* (1927).

The White Horse ²³¹

What do I stare at – not the colt
   That frisks in yon green field; so strong
That he can leap about and run,
   Yet is too weak to stand up straight
When his mother licks him with her tongue.

No, no, my eyes go far beyond,
   Across that field to yon far hill,
Where one white horse stands there alone;
   And nothing else is white to see,
Outside a house all dark and still.

'Death, are you in that house?' think I –
   'Is that horse there on your account?
Can I expect a shadow soon,
   Seen in that horse's ghostly ribs –
When you come up behind, to mount?'

---

231. From *A Poet's Calendar* (1927). The image at the end of the first stanza is rather close to Robert Frost's 'The Pasture', from *North of Boston* (1915) – though Davies's poem ultimately goes its own way.

Song of the Miners [232]

When starving cattle see
　　Their blades of grass
Locked up in ice that cuts
　　Their mouths, like glass –
What can they do but lie in heaps and die?

And shall our people starve,
　　Like these wild herds?
We, with our power to think,
　　Our gift of words –
Shall we lie down like these dumb brutes and die?

---

232. From *The Birth of Song* (1936).

Select Bibliography

The following editions of Davies's books have been especially useful in the editing of this volume:

The Adventures of Johnny Walker, Tramp (London: Cape, 1926)

The Autobiography of a Super-Tramp (London: Fifield, 1908)

Beggars (London: Duckworth, 1909)

The Complete Poems of W. H. Davies (London: Cape, 1963)

Later Days (1925) (London: Cape, 1927)

My Garden and My Birds (London: Cape, 1939)

A Poet's Pilgrimage (1918) (London: Cape, 1927)

The True Traveller (London: Duckworth, 1912)

True Travellers: A Tramp's Opera (London: Cape, 1923)

Young Emma (London: Cape, 1980)

Selected criticism and context:

Cullup, Michael, *W. H. Davies: Man and Poet, a Reassessment* (London: Greenwich Exchange, 2014)

Davies, W. H., *The Essential W. H. Davies*, ed. and introd. by Brian Waters (London: Cape, 1951)

Hockley, Lawrence, *W. H. Davies* (Cardiff: University of Wales Press, 1971)

Hooper, Barbara, *Time to Stand and Stare: A Life of W. H. Davies* (London: Peter Owen, 2004)

Normand, Lawrence, *W. H. Davies* (Bridgend: Seren, 2003)

Pound, Ezra, 'William H. Davies, Poet', in *Poetry* 11.1 (1918), pp. 99–102.

Ross, Robert, *The Georgian Revolt: Rise and Fall of a Poetic Ideal, 1910–1922* (London: Faber, 1967)

Thomas, Helen, *Time and Again: Memoirs and Letters*, ed. Myfanwy Thomas (Manchester: Carcanet, 1978)

Sitwell, Osbert, 'W. H. Davies', in *Noble Essences: Being a Book of Characters* (London: Macmillan, 1950), pp. 207–44.

Stonesifer, Richard J., *W. H. Davies: A Critical Biography* (London: Cape, 1963)

Is life on earth a viler thing
　　Than ever was known before?
Who shall we ask – the wise old man
　　Whose years have reached five score?

When we have questioned Church and State,
　　Is there anyone else to ask?
Is it the Baby, three weeks old,
　　That wears a gas-proof mask?

Is it the Infant armed to meet
　　A poisoned earth and sky –
A thing too weak to lift its hand
　　To rub a sleepy eye?

---

233. From *The Loneliest Mountain* (1939).